JavaBeans™ For Dummies®

Cheat Sheet

"So You Want to Be a Bean" Checklist

Considering whether or not to implement a piece of software as a JavaBeans component? Answering "yes" to the following questions suggests that you have a prime bean candidate on your hands:

- ❑ Does the potential bean represent one conceptual task? In other words, can you describe in a simple sentence what the potential bean will do?

- ❑ Can you imagine using the potential bean in many different application scenarios?

- ❑ Does the potential bean lend itself to customization — that is, does it have at least a few characteristics that can be modified?

Indispensable Online Resources

Resource	Description
http://splash.javasoft.com/beans/	JavaBeans home page
http://www.javasoft.com:80/products/jdk/1.1/	JDK and hands-on Java tutorial
comp.lang.java.programmer	Technically oriented Java newsgroup
beans-users*	JavaBeans LISTSERV list

* To subscribe, send a message to listserv@javasoft.com that contains the following line: SUBSCRIBE BEANS-USERS Your name

Java APIs Classified by Bean-Related Function

Bean-Related Function	Java API Packages
Introspection (interface publishing/discovery)	java.lang.reflect, java.beans
Customization (application builder support)	java.beans
Event handling	java.util
Persistence	java.io
Miscellaneous	java.awt

Properties

Property names should be short, descriptive nouns — and the first character of the name should be lowercase. Example: name, address, phoneNumber.

...For Dummies: #1 Computer Book Series for Beginners

JavaBeans™ For Dummies®

Cheat Sheet

Events

In the context of JavaBeans, an *event* is any significant occurrence. (For example, a user clicking a mouse, pressing a key, or attempting to change a property value are all perfectly reasonable events.) When you create your own events, make sure that you observe the following naming conventions:

Broadcast	Type of Listener*	Adding a Listener	Removing a Listener
multicast	EventListener	addEventListener()	removeEventListener()
unicast	(Same as multicast but also throws java.util.TooManyListenersException)		

* EventListener must extend the java.util.eventListener interface.

Creating Bean Classes

If You Want to Do This	Follow This Example

Define a new bean class	```public class MyBean extends MyParent {```
	``` // variable declarations```
	``` // constructors```
	``` // methods```
	```}```

Define a constructor	```MyBean (type param1, type param2…) {```
	``` // some setup statements```
	```}```

Define a property	```type propertyName;```

Define a getter accessor method	```public type getPropertyName() {```
	``` // code to retrieve the property name```
	```}```

Define a setter accessor method	```public setPropertyName(type param) {```
	``` // code to set the property value```
	```}```

Accessor methods

You must provide two accessor methods for each property you define: one to get the value of the property (a getter method) and one to set the value (a setter method).

Type	Name	Getter Method	Setter Method
Simple	propertyName	getPropertyName()	setPropertyName(type)
Boolean	propertyName	isPropertyName()	setPropertyName(type)
Indexed	propertyName	getPropertyName()	setPropertyName(index, type)

...For Dummies: #1 Computer Book Series for Beginners

JAVABEANS™ FOR DUMMIES®

by Emily A. Vander Veer

Foreword by Joseph H. McIntyre,
Director of Engineering
Component Integration Laboratories (CILabs)

IDG Books Worldwide, Inc.
An International Data Group Company

Foster City, CA ♦ Chicago, IL ♦ Indianapolis, IN ♦ Southlake, TX

JavaBeans™ For Dummies®

Published by
IDG Books Worldwide, Inc.
An International Data Group Company
919 E. Hillsdale Blvd.
Suite 400
Foster City, CA 94404
http://www.idgbooks.com (IDG Books Worldwide Web Site)
http://www.dummies.com (Dummies Press Web Site)

Library of Congress Catalog Card No.: 97-70729

ISBN: 0-7645-0153-4

Printed in the United States of America

10 9 8 7 6 5 4 3 2 1

1B/RX/QU/ZX/IN

Distributed in the United States by IDG Books Worldwide, Inc.

Distributed by Macmillan Canada for Canada; by Transworld Publishers Limited in the United Kingdom and Europe; by WoodsLane Pty. Ltd. for Australia; by WoodsLane Enterprises Ltd. for New Zealand; by Longman Singapore Publishers Ltd. for Singapore, Malaysia, Thailand, and Indonesia; by Simron Pty. Ltd. for South Africa; by Toppan Company Ltd. for Japan; by Distribuidora Cuspide for Argentina; by Livraria Cultura for Brazil; by Ediciencia S.A. for Ecuador; by Addison-Wesley Publishing Company for Korea; by Ediciones ZETA S.C.R. Ltda. for Peru; by WS Computer Publishing Company, Inc., for the Philippines; by Unalis Corporation for Taiwan; by Contemporanea de Ediciones for Venezuela. Authorized Sales Agent: Anthony Rudkin Associates for the Middle East and North Africa.

For general information on IDG Books Worldwide's books in the U.S., please call our Consumer Customer Service department at 800-762-2974. For reseller information, including discounts and premium sales, please call our Reseller Customer Service department at 800-434-3422.

For information on where to purchase IDG Books Worldwide's books outside the U.S., please contact our International Sales department at 415-655-3023 or fax 415-655-3299.

For information on foreign language translations, please contact our Foreign & Subsidiary Rights department at 415-655-3021 or fax 415-655-3281.

For sales inquiries and special prices for bulk quantities, please contact our Sales department at 415-655-3200 or write to the address above.

For information on using IDG Books Worldwide's books in the classroom or for ordering examination copies, please contact our Educational Sales department at 800-434-2086 or fax 817-251-8174.

For press review copies, author interviews, or other publicity information, please contact our Public Relations department at 415-655-3000 or fax 415-655-3299.

For authorization to photocopy items for corporate, personal, or educational use, please contact Copyright Clearance Center, 222 Rosewood Drive, Danvers, MA 01923, or fax 508-750-4470.

is a trademark under exclusive license to IDG Books Worldwide, Inc., from International Data Group, Inc.

About the Author

Emily A. Vander Veer is the author of numerous computer-related magazine articles and books, including IDG Books' *JavaScript For Dummies* and *JavaScript For Dummies Quick Reference*. She is currently employed by IBM in Austin, Texas, where she spends her time writing about all things Internet-related.

Contact Emily at emilyv@vnet.ibm.com.

ABOUT IDG BOOKS WORLDWIDE

Welcome to the world of IDG Books Worldwide.

IDG Books Worldwide, Inc., is a subsidiary of International Data Group, the world's largest publisher of computer-related information and the leading global provider of information services on information technology. IDG was founded more than 25 years ago and now employs more than 8,500 people worldwide. IDG publishes more than 275 computer publications in over 75 countries (see listing below). More than 60 million people read one or more IDG publications each month.

Launched in 1990, IDG Books Worldwide is today the #1 publisher of best-selling computer books in the United States. We are proud to have received eight awards from the Computer Press Association in recognition of editorial excellence and three from *Computer Currents'* First Annual Readers' Choice Awards. Our best-selling ...For Dummies® series has more than 30 million copies in print with translations in 30 languages. IDG Books Worldwide, through a joint venture with IDG's Hi-Tech Beijing, became the first U.S. publisher to publish a computer book in the People's Republic of China. In record time, IDG Books Worldwide has become the first choice for millions of readers around the world who want to learn how to better manage their businesses.

Our mission is simple: Every one of our books is designed to bring extra value and skill-building instructions to the reader. Our books are written by experts who understand and care about our readers. The knowledge base of our editorial staff comes from years of experience in publishing, education, and journalism — experience we use to produce books for the '90s. In short, we care about books, so we attract the best people. We devote special attention to details such as audience, interior design, use of icons, and illustrations. And because we use an efficient process of authoring, editing, and desktop publishing our books electronically, we can spend more time ensuring superior content and spend less time on the technicalities of making books.

You can count on our commitment to deliver high-quality books at competitive prices on topics you want to read about. At IDG Books Worldwide, we continue in the IDG tradition of delivering quality for more than 25 years. You'll find no better book on a subject than one from IDG Books Worldwide.

John Kilcullen
CEO
IDG Books Worldwide, Inc.

Steven Berkowitz
President and Publisher
IDG Books Worldwide, Inc.

*Eighth Annual
Computer Press
Awards ≫1992*

*Ninth Annual
Computer Press
Awards ≫1993*

*Tenth Annual
Computer Press
Awards ≫1994*

*Eleventh Annual
Computer Press
Awards ≫1995*

IDG Books Worldwide, Inc., is a subsidiary of International Data Group, the world's largest publisher of computer-related information and the leading global provider of information services on information technology. International Data Group publishes over 275 computer publications in over 75 countries. Sixty million people read one or more International Data Group publications each month. International Data Group's publications include: **ARGENTINA:** Buyer's Guide, Computerworld Argentina, PC World Argentina; **AUSTRALIA:** Australian Macworld, Australian PC World, Australian Reseller News, Computerworld, IT Casebook, Network World, Publish, Webmaster; **AUSTRIA:** Computerwelt Osterreich, Networks Austria, PC Tip Austria; **BANGLADESH:** PC World Bangladesh; **BELARUS:** PC World Belarus; **BELGIUM:** Data News; **BRAZIL:** Annuário de Informática, Computerworld, Connections, Macworld, PC Player, PC World, Publish, Reseller News, Supergamepower; **BULGARIA:** Computerworld Bulgaria, Network World Bulgaria, PC & MacWorld Bulgaria; **CANADA:** CIO Canada, Client/Server World, ComputerWorld Canada, InfoWorld Canada, NetworkWorld Canada, WebWorld; **CHILE:** Computerworld Chile, PC World Chile; **COLOMBIA:** Computerworld Colombia, PC World Colombia; **COSTA RICA:** PC World Centro America; **THE CZECH AND SLOVAK REPUBLICS:** Computerworld Czechoslovakia, Macworld Czech Republic, PC World Czechoslovakia; **DENMARK:** Communications World Danmark, Computerworld Danmark, Macworld Danmark, PC World Danmark, Techworld Denmark; **DOMINICAN REPUBLIC:** PC World Republica Dominicana; **ECUADOR:** PC World Ecuador; **EGYPT:** Computerworld Middle East, PC World Middle East; **EL SALVADOR:** PC World Centro America; **FINLAND:** MikroPC, Tietoverkko, Tietoviikko; **FRANCE:** Distributique, Hebdo, Info PC, Le Monde Informatique, Macworld, Reseaux & Telecoms, WebMaster France; **GERMANY:** Computer Partner, Computerwoche, Computerwoche Extra, Computerwoche FOCUS, Global Online, Macwelt, PC Welt; **GREECE:** Amiga Computing, GamePro Greece, Multimedia World; **GUATEMALA:** PC World Centro America; **HONDURAS:** PC World Centro America; **HONG KONG:** Computerworld Hong Kong, PC World Hong Kong, Publish in Asia; **HUNGARY:** ABCD CD-ROM, Computerworld Szamitastechnika, Internetto online Magazine, PC World Hungary, PC-X Magazin Hungary; **ICELAND:** Tolvuheimur PC World Island; **INDIA:** Information Communications World, Information Systems Computerworld, PC World India, Publish in Asia; **INDONESIA:** InfoKomputer PC World, Komputek Computerworld, Publish in Asia; **IRELAND:** ComputerScope, PC Live!; **ISRAEL:** Macworld Israel, People & Computers/Computerworld; **ITALY:** Computerworld Italia, Macworld Italia, Networking Italia, PC World Italia; **JAPAN:** DTP World, Macworld Japan, Nikkei Personal Computing, OS/2 World Japan, SunWorld Japan, Windows NT World, Windows World Japan; **KENYA:** PC World East African; **KOREA:** Hi-Tech Information, Macworld Korea, PC World Korea; **MACEDONIA:** PC World Macedonia; **MALAYSIA:** Computerworld Malaysia, PC World Malaysia, Publish in Asia; **MALTA:** PC World Malta; **MEXICO:** Computerworld Mexico, PC World Mexico; **MYANMAR:** PC World Myanmar; **NETHERLANDS:** Computer! Totaal, LAN Internetworking Magazine, LAN World Buyers Guide, Macworld Netherlands, Net, WebWereld; **NEW ZEALAND:** Absolute Beginners Guide and Plain & Simple Series, Computer Buyer, Computer Industry Directory, Computerworld New Zealand, MTB, Network World, PC World New Zealand; **NICARAGUA:** PC World Centro America; **NORWAY:** Computerworld Norge, CW Rapport, Datamagasinet, Financial Rapport, Kursguide Norge, Macworld Norge, Multimediaworld Norge, PC World Ekspress Norge, PC World Nettverk, PC World Norge, PC World ProduktGuide Norge; **PAKISTAN:** Computerworld Pakistan; **PANAMA:** PC World Panama; **PEOPLE'S REPUBLIC OF CHINA:** China Computer Users, China Computerworld, China InfoWorld, China Telecom World Weekly, Computer & Communication, Electronic Design China, Electronics Today, Electronics Weekly, Game Software, PC World China, Popular Computer Week, Software Weekly, Software World, Telecom World; **PERU:** Computerworld Peru, PC World Profesional Peru, PC World SoHo Peru; **PHILIPPINES:** Click!, Computerworld Philippines, PC World Philippines, Publish in Asia; **POLAND:** Computerworld Poland, Computerworld Special Report Poland, Cyber, Macworld Poland, Networld Poland, PC World Komputer; **PORTUGAL:** Cerebro/PC World, Computerworld/Correio Informático, Dealer World Portugal, Mac*In/PC*In Portugal, Multimedia World; **PUERTO RICO:** PC World Puerto Rico; **ROMANIA:** Computerworld Romania, PC World Romania, Telecom Romania; **RUSSIA:** Computerworld Russia, Mir PK, Publish, Seti; **SINGAPORE:** Computerworld Singapore, PC World Singapore, Publish in Asia; **SLOVENIA:** Monitor; **SOUTH AFRICA:** Computing SA, Network World SA, Software World SA; **SPAIN:** Communicaciones World España, Computerworld España, Dealer World España, Macworld España, PC World España; **SRI LANKA:** Infolink PC World; **SWEDEN:** CAP&Design, Computer Sweden, Corporate Computing Sweden, Internetworld Sweden, it.branschen, Macworld Sweden, MaxiData Sweden, MikroDatorn, Nätverk & Kommunikation, PC World Sweden, PCaktiv, Windows World Sweden; **SWITZERLAND:** Computerworld Schweiz, Macworld Schweiz, PCtip; **TAIWAN:** Computerworld Taiwan, Macworld Taiwan, NEW ViSiON/Publish, PC World Taiwan, Windows World Taiwan; **THAILAND:** Publish in Asia, Thai Computerworld; **TURKEY:** Computerworld Turkiye, Macworld Turkiye, Network World Turkiye, PC World Turkiye; **UKRAINE:** Computerworld Kiev, Multimedia World Ukraine, PC World Ukraine; **UNITED KINGDOM:** Acorn User UK, Amiga Action UK, Amiga Computing UK, Apple Talk UK, Computing, Macworld, Parents and Computers UK, PC Advisor, PC Home, PSX Pro, The WEB; **UNITED STATES:** Cable in the Classroom, CIO Magazine, Computerworld, DOS World, Federal Computer Week, GamePro Magazine, InfoWorld, I-Way, Macworld, Network World, PC Games, PC World, Publish, Video Event, THE WEB Magazine, and WebMaster; online webzines: JavaWorld, NetscapeWorld, and SunWorld Online; **URUGUAY:** InfoWorld Uruguay; **VENEZUELA:** Computerworld Venezuela, PC World Venezuela; and **VIETNAM:** PC World Vietnam.   3/24/97

Dedication

To my husband, Clay, and especially to Anita and Bill (sorry it took me so long to say "thanks").

Author's Acknowledgments

Many thanks to Gareth Hancock for giving me the opportunity to write this book, as well as to the other members of IDG Books' outstanding staff who contributed so much to this effort: Colleen Rainsberger, Bill Barton, and Kathy Simpson. Thanks also to the IDG Books Production folks, including Regina Snyder, Maridee Ennis, Rachel Garvey, and Brent Savage, who created the line drawings that appear in this book. Special thanks to technical editor Garrett Pease of Discovery Computing.

I'd also like to thank my colleagues at IBM, for whose generosity and support during the writing of this book I remain humbly grateful.

Publisher's Acknowledgments

We're proud of this book; please send us your comments about it by using the IDG Books Worldwide Registration Card at the back of the book or by e-mailing us at feedback/dummies@idgbooks.com. Some of the people who helped bring this book to market include the following:

Acquisitions, Development, and Editorial

Senior Project Editor: Colleen Rainsberger

Acquisitions Editor: Gareth Hancock

Product Development Director: Mary Bednarek

Media Development Manager: Joyce Pepple

Associate Permissions Editor: Heather H. Dismore

Copy Editors: William A. Barton, Patricia Yuu Pan, Kathy Simpson

Technical Editor: Garrett Pease

Editorial Assistant: Chris H. Collins

Editorial Manager: Seta K. Frantz

Production

Project Coordinator: Regina Snyder

Layout and Graphics: Linda M. Boyer, Elizabeth Cárdenas-Nelson, J. Tyler Connor, Dominique DeFelice, Maridee V. Ennis, Angela F. Hunckler, Drew R. Moore, Brent Savage

Proofreaders: Henry Lazarek, Joel K. Draper, Rachel Garvey, Nancy Price, Dwight Ramsey, Robert Springer, Karen York

Indexer: David Heiret

Special Help
Tamara S. Castleman, Copy Editor; Steven H. Hayes, Editorial Assistant; Stephanie Koutek, Proof Editor; Kevin Spencer, Associate Technical Editor; Access Technology, CD developer

---

General and Administrative

IDG Books Worldwide, Inc.: John Kilcullen, CEO; Steven Berkowitz, President and Publisher

IDG Books Technology Publishing: Brenda McLaughlin, Senior Vice President and Group Publisher

Dummies Technology Press and Dummies Editorial: Diane Graves Steele, Vice President and Associate Publisher; Judith A. Taylor, Brand Manager; Kristin A. Cocks, Editorial Director

Dummies Trade Press: Kathleen A. Welton, Vice President and Publisher; Stacy S. Collins, Brand Manager

IDG Books Production for Dummies Press: Beth Jenkins, Production Director; Cindy L. Phipps, Supervisor of Project Coordination, Production Proofreading, and Indexing; Kathie S. Schutte, Supervisor of Page Layout; Shelley Lea, Supervisor of Graphics and Design; Debbie J. Gates, Production Systems Specialist; Tony Augsburger, Supervisor of Reprints and Bluelines; Leslie Popplewell, Media Archive Coordinator

Dummies Packaging and Book Design: Patti Sandez, Packaging Specialist; Lance Kayser, Packaging Assistant; Kavish + Kavish, Cover Design

◆

The publisher would like to give special thanks to Patrick J. McGovern, without whom this book would not have been possible.

◆

Contents at a Glance

Cartoons at a Glance

By Rich Tennant • Fax: 508-546-7747 • E-mail: the5wave@tiac.net

page 7

page 313

page 53

page 285

page 167

page 95

Table of Contents

· ·

Part IV: The Nitty Gritty: The JavaBeans API (java.beans) 167

Chapter 11: Introspection Makes for Happy, Well-Adjusted Beans 169

Foreword

· ·

*A*s the software industry has evolved, component software has moved from being the "light at the end of the tunnel" to being on the tip of every developer's tongue. However, while we have begun taking advantage of components in application development, we have still to leverage the component resources that are available.

JavaBeans provides us with another way of implementing the principles of component software, with some distinct advantages over the technologies that preceded it, including VBX, OCX, and OpenDoc. First, JavaBeans is part of, and a natural extension of, the base toolset for Java. Second, creating a bean is easy — though beans lack the end user function of OpenDoc, the learning curve (especially after reading this book) is almost trivial compared to the others. Third, every vendor selling beans will have an instant market since all Java tools that support beans will support them in the same way. Lastly, "write once, run anywhere."

Beans may not replace the other technologies, but may well be the technology with the most components. With the availability of bridges between Beans and ActiveX/OpenDoc, developers have a basic development plan laid out in front of them: to use JavaBeans to develop the building block components and the other technologies as the higher function containers that allow users to manipulate those components. This complementary relationship is what component technology is all about — selecting the best technology for each component and combining the best components into deliverable applications.

Typical development environments of the near future will consist of component developers and application assemblers. Component developers receive work-to-order specifications from the application assembly teams, create a new component or customize an existing one, validate the component, and deliver it. The application assembly team binds the components together, validates the application function, and deploys the component application. In many cases, the application assembly team will be IS departments or system integrators and the component developers will be external vendors.

We are now seeing the evolution of beans to incorporate the elements of cooperative components, the continuing work to standardize component interoperability and the availability of innovative new tools to support the creation of applications from high level components. These elements combine to provide the basis for moving application development forward by moving the assembly of applications closer to the users' domain.

As we improve our standards, components, and tools, the quality of software improves — and the ability to deliver the correct function the first time around becomes a reality. As the building blocks for component applications, JavaBeans components will play an important role as their platform independence, open specifications, wide availability, and industry-wide support ensure their place in the standard development toolset.

Joseph H. McIntyre, Director of Engineering
Component Integration Laboratories (CILabs)

Introduction

· ·

*W*elcome to a new and exciting world: the world of programming with JavaBeans! Whether you're a seasoned Java programmer or don't know beans about Java, you can use the advice and examples in this book to create and use Java components, called *beans,* to build really cool (and useful) Internet applications.

These days, few topics are hotter among software and marketing types than component software in general — and JavaBeans in particular. Why? Because once you create a component, you can use it over and over again in lots of different applications: Web pages, intranet applications, Internet-based ordering systems — any software application you can think of, really. And reuse, as you learn in this book, leads straight to The American Dream: more reliable goods (software applications, in this case) that you can build cheaper and faster than ever before.

So component software is a Good Thing; but with all the other component models available, why JavaBeans? In a word, "Internet." JavaBeans is implemented in Java, the first widely adopted programming language optimized for developing Internet applications. Because JavaBeans is implemented in Java, when you develop with JavaBeans you get not only a first-class component model, but all of Java's Internet-exploitive features, too — no extra charge!

If you're not familiar with the way component software works, though, you might find your first attempt at developing beans a little confusing. That's where *JavaBeans For Dummies* comes in. In *JavaBeans For Dummies,* I introduce you to the JavaBeans component model and show you how it works by using non-geek explanations, real-world examples, and even a judiciously placed diagram or two. Sometimes I use formal notation, but only when I have to; and if I do, I always accompany it with a recap in plain English. Most important, I've included lots of working sample code to help you understand the concepts as you read along. And even better, you can use this code as the basis of your very own Java applications.

But wait! There's more. At the back of this book is a companion CD-ROM. This CD-ROM contains all of the example code covered in the text, along with some pointers to other cool beans on the World Wide Web. I also threw in some Java (and other Web-based) development tools that I'm sure you'll find helpful as you begin your adventure in bean-town.

About This Book

This book is your one-stop shop for beginning development with JavaBeans. You don't have to know anything about Java to understand the examples and concepts you'll find in *JavaBeans For Dummies* (although if you *are* comfortable with Java, you'll find that you can apply the techniques in this book just that much easier). Here's an example of the topics you can find in this book:

- ✔ Understanding the JavaBeans component model and the role components play in Web-based application development
- ✔ Determining what kinds of functions would make a good bean (and what kinds wouldn't)
- ✔ Coding and testing simple beans
- ✔ Combining beans with other software components to create complex Web-based applications
- ✔ Investigating the latest JavaBeans-enabled development tools

Building Java applications with JavaBeans components might seem a little daunting at first, but the basics really aren't so hard. This book helps by boring through the marketing hype and paring off the techno-babble to expose the simple, elegant concepts at the heart of creating reusable software components. (As I was writing, I kept the motto from my favorite bumper sticker firmly in mind: *"Eschew obfuscation!"* I hope you agree I've succeeded.)

System Requirements

To get the most out of this book and the enclosed CD-ROM, check to make sure that you have the following:

- ✔ A computer with a CD-ROM drive and a modem
- ✔ SPARC/Solaris (version 2.4 or later) or one of the following: Microsoft Windows 95, Windows NT 3.5.1, or Windows NT 4.0
- ✔ A copy of a Java-enabled Web browser, such as Microsoft's Internet Explorer or Netscape Navigator
- ✔ A copy of the Java Developers Kit version 1.1 or higher (included on the companion CD)
- ✔ A copy of the JavaBeans Development Kit version 1.0 or higher (also included on the companion CD)

How to Use This Book

The rules are pretty simple. All code appears in a special font, like this:

```
import java.applet.Applet
```

Be sure to follow the examples' syntax exactly. Sometimes your code will compile and run if you add or delete spaces or type your keywords in a different case, but sometimes it won't — and I guarantee you'll have more than enough bugs to track down without spending your time on those caused by spacing errors!

Type anything you see in **bold** print letter for letter. These are generally Java keywords, and they need to be exact. *Italicized* directives are placeholders, and other values can be substituted for them. For example, in the following line of code you could replace `myMethod()` and `parameterOne`, but you need to leave the rest of the statement the way it's shown.

```
public void myMethod(int parameterOne) {
```

About code listings: Due to the margins of this book, sometimes lines of code are wrapped. Also, ellipses in code listings (ellipses are three dots, like this:) mean that some code that was non-essential to the example at hand was left out of the listing.

Everything You Are

Okay, everybody put on your assumption caps! *You* assume I know what I'm talking about, and *I'll* start out with the following assumptions about you, the reader:

- ✔ You have a working connection to the Internet and have done a fair amount of surfing.
- ✔ You've heard about Java (maybe even about JavaBeans) and are itching to know what all the fuss is about.
- ✔ You have access to, and know how to use, a basic text editor.
- ✔ You've got an inkling of what object-oriented development is all about (or can at least fake it).
- ✔ You may even have written some computer programs in an object-oriented language like C++ or Java.

How This Book Is Organized

This book contains five major segments, or *parts*. Each part contains several chapters, and each chapter contains several sections. You can read the book start-to-finish if you like, or you can dive in whenever you need help on a particular topic. The sections that follow provide a breakdown of what you'll find in each of the five parts.

Part I: Getting to Know Beans about JavaBeans

This part begins with an introduction to Java and then moves on to an overview of the Java component model called JavaBeans. You'll find answers to all your basic beans questions here, like:

- ✔ What's Java?
- ✔ Are Java and JavaBeans related?
- ✔ What's a component model, and why do I care?
- ✔ What do I need on the machine in front of me to create and use JavaBeans components?
- ✔ What *exactly* is a bean?

Part II: Beans 101: Creating and Using Beans

Take off your shoes, grab a cup of coffee, and get comfortable. This part takes you step-by-step through the process of creating and using simple beans. A sampling of the topics covered in this part includes:

- ✔ Installing the Java Developers Kit and the JavaBeans Development Kit
- ✔ Using a text editor to create a bean file
- ✔ Compiling and testing your bean
- ✔ Exploring the bean-related utilities available in the toolkits

Part III: Advanced Bean Recipes

After reading this part, you'll be intimately familiar with the subset of the (non-bean-specific) Java language that's most useful to bean developers. You explore the Java APIs (*application programming interfaces*) — and find out which ones to pay the closest attention to (and why) in your quest to produce real, usable beans. You also see how JavaBeans components can be incorporated with other component models like ActiveX and OpenDoc, which effectively extend bean portability beyond the Internet to include stand-alone desktop applications.

Part IV: The Nitty-Gritty: The JavaBeans API (`java.beans`)

Here's where the rubber meets the road, as it were: the JavaBeans API reference. In this part are descriptions of the JavaBeans API broken out by function — introspection, event handling, persistence, and application builder support.

Part V: The Part of Tens

Part V pulls together bits and pieces from the rest of the book and organizes them into lists of ten (or so). The categories include ten characteristics all top-notch beans should possess, the ten most common misconceptions developers have about beans, and ten essential bean-related online resources.

Part VI: Appendixes

In this final part, you find two appendixes. The first appendix spells out all the nitty-gritty details you need to successfully install the toolkits and IDEs provided on the companion CD-ROM. The second appendix contains an in-depth look at a handful of real-life beans and bean utilities culled from the Web.

Icons Used in This Book

This icon flags really cool stuff (sample code, development tools, that kind of thing) that you can find on the CD-ROM included in the back of this book.

This icon is followed by some arbitrary amount of nerdy technical information. You can skip these paragraphs if you want; reading through all of these isn't absolutely necessary in order to understand *how* to do something (but it sure helps if you're interested in *why*).

This icon flags practical suggestions you can apply directly to your bean development effort.

You might want to make a habit of reading the text next to these puppies: They clue you in to potential bugs, mistakes, and other nasties that may be coming your way.

When you see this icon, you can be sure that some really nifty bean-related Web site URL is coming up.

Now What?

So, what are you waiting for? Dust off that mouse. Grab this book by the covers and bend it back real hard so it'll lay flat (that way you can continue reading as you try out the examples for yourself). Break open the seal on the CD, if you like, and load it up in your CD-ROM drive so that it'll be all set to go when you're ready to explore the goodies it contains. (Turn to Appendix A for detailed installation instructions.) Then roll up your sleeves and dive right on in!

Note: No animals were harmed during the writing of this book.

Part I
Getting to Know Beans about JavaBeans

The 5th Wave   By Rich Tennant

"The WordPro and Worms ain't selling so good, but the JavaBeans 'n Grubs are moving like hotcakes."

In this part . . .

*J*avaBeans is one of the coolest new Web-related technologies going. An extension to Java, the popular Internet-exploitive programming language that's taken the software world by storm, the JavaBeans component model makes it easy for developers to create Java components — and then to combine those components (like building blocks) to create a variety of different software applications.

Part I starts out with an introduction to Java and then continues with a description of component models in general — and JavaBeans in particular. You learn exactly what JavaBeans components are, what they look like, and what you need to get hold of in the way of software tools to create and use them.

Chapter 1

JavaBeans Basics

*I*f you're serious about developing and using JavaBeans, a little background is in order before you plunge directly into the how-to part of this book. (That's Part II.)

This chapter explains how and why JavaBeans sprouted from the Java programming language. The chapter also provides a quick overview of Java and the unique role this language plays in the worldwide phenomenon known as the Internet. After you finish this chapter, you should have a solid understanding of why and when you may want to use the JavaBeans model to develop special Java components called *beans*.

In the Beginning There Was Java — and It Was Cool

Unless you've been hiding out under a rock for the last year or so (and maybe even if you have), you've heard about *Java,* the object-oriented programming language designed especially for writing World Wide Web applications. Java has taken the Internet world by storm and is touted by some as the most revolutionary innovation to come along since prewashed salad-in-a-bag. Because the JavaBeans model is an extension to the Java language that enables you to create a special kind of Java program called a Java component, or *bean,* this chapter provides a quick overview of Java proper before diving straight into bean specifics.

This is not your father's programming language

Why another programming language, you may ask? After all, at last count, quite a few already existed. Truly, how many does the world need? Well, programming languages, like human vocabularies, come into existence if someone either has something new to communicate or some new way to communicate the same old stuff. The Internet, as things turn out, is a prime example of both reasons.

First off, the recent explosion of Internet accessibility — infrastructure, software, increasingly reasonable hardware prices — represents a relatively new way for average folks to communicate. Sure, computer networks existed before the Internet came into being, but nothing that was available had the worldwide scope and easy access of the Internet. Not only that, but the Internet has made a completely new medium, the World Wide Web, possible which enables users to present information (called *content*) in new ways — ways we've only begun to explore.

Second, the Internet makes the dissemination of new kinds of information possible. The Net gives voice to previously disenfranchised groups: the young, the poor, the small business owners, the radical — people with such tightly focused or unpopular interests that traditional media are either editorially inaccessible to these groups or prohibitively expensive (or both).

A new medium *and* new information calls for a new language — and Java is it!

Java's raison d'être

Sure, you can program for the Internet without using Java. (You can herd sheep with a pig, too, but doing so isn't exactly the most efficient way to accomplish the job.) Because it was designed specifically for Internet application development, however, the Java language offers some mighty unique and compelling benefits — as described in the following list:

  ✔ **Cross-platform performance.** Thanks to something called a *virtual machine* (a virtual machine is special software that runs compiled Java programs and comes bundled with Java-enabled Web browsers), you can develop Java programs on any of the many Java-supportive plat-forms (Windows, Macintosh, UNIX, and so on) and then execute those programs without change on any of the other platforms. Cross-platform capability is indispensable if you develop Internet applications, be-cause all kinds of computers connect to the Internet — not just whatever kind you happen to use for your development. (Flip to Chapter 7 for everything you ever wanted to know about cross-platform capability and the Java virtual machine.)

✔ **Object-oriented development.** Although object-oriented development is nothing new (having been around for about a quarter of a century), this type of development is getting a lot of attention lately. Object-oriented languages are so much more natural for programmers to use than are traditional programming languages that using object-oriented languages makes writing complex, distributed applications (such as Internet applications) much easier. Object-oriented languages such as Java also promote reusability, which means that developers don't need to write as much code from scratch.

✔ **Streamlined language features.** Many programming languages are complex and support features that only the most savvy code jockeys can understand (much less use effectively). Java's designers decided to simplify the language as much as possible while still providing enough goodies to make Java programming feasible for real-world applications. Less complexity means less potential for coding buggy programs! (*Question:* What's the easiest way to annoy people all around the world simultaneously? *Answer:* Create a Java applet with a handful of memory leaks and have all those people download and run the applet on the same day.)

✔ **Optimized execution.** *Bandwidth* refers to the speed and capacity of the hardware connections that make up the physical infrastructure of the Internet. Bandwidth is a significant limiting factor in Internet communications — in fact, a limited bandwidth can cause quite the bottleneck at times (as anyone who's logged on to a favorite news server at 10 a.m. on a Monday morning can attest). Recognizing this limitation — and keeping in mind that servers all across the planet routinely distribute Internet programs to devices ranging from main-frames to (soon) personal digital assistants, or PDAs — Java's creators designed Java to produce the smallest, most compact executables possible.

✔ **Secure transmission.** Because Internet application development poses unique security threats, the Java environment has three different levels of security built right in. (Chapter 7 explains each individual layer of security in more detail.)

How many platforms was that again?

At the time of this writing, about a dozen platforms support Java and several more have Java support under consideration, as the following table lists. (Of course, by the time you read this, chances are even more platforms will have jumped on the Java bandwagon!)

Current Java-Supported Platforms		Proposed Java-Supported Platforms
AIX	NCR SysV	Amiga
Digital UNIX	OS/400	BeOS
HP-UX	Sony NEWS	JVOS
Linux	Intel x86 Solaris	NeXT
Macintosh 7.5	SPARC Solaris (2.3 or later)	OS/2
MVS (OS/390)	Windows 3.1, 95, NT	

Light meat or dark? The two kinds of Java programs

Before the advent of JavaBeans, Java programmers had two choices: They could create stand-alone Java applications, or they could create special Java programs, called *applets,* designed for integration into HTML-based Web pages. (HTML stands for *HyperText Markup Language.*)

All alone: Java applications

A *stand-alone Java application* is like any other normal software application: After you start it (typically either from a command line or by clicking an icon), the application does whatever its creator programmed it to do. Java applications don't depend on any other applications (on a Java-enabled Web browser, for example, as do Java applets), but Java applications do need *the Java runtime environment* installed on the same machine you want to run them on. (See Chapter 4 for an overview of the Java runtime.) An example of a stand-alone Java application is *HotJava,* the World Wide Web browser from Sun Microsystems.

If you're interested in Sun's HotJava, check out the following URL: http://java.sun.com/HotJava/index.html.

Application or applet: Which is which?

As you may know, you need to call up applets from (or *integrate* them *into*) another application, such as an HTML Web page (or the Java **appletviewer** utility, which you find out more about in Chapter 5); applets can't run all by themselves, as can Java applications. But how does a browser tell which is which?

The answer is familiar to the C and C++ programmers among you: Stand-alone applications contain a special function, called `main()`, and applets don't. The Java runtime environment automatically looks for the declaration of a block of code named `main()` in any program you try to run, just as the C/C++ runtime environments do. If the runtime environment finds one, it runs the program; if not, it produces an error message that looks something like the following:

```
In class MyVeryFirstClass:
void main(String argv[]) is
undefined
```

In contrast, Java-enabled Web browsers don't expect applets to contain a `main()` function at all. (In fact, they ignore `main()` if they see it.) Instead, browsers expect applets to define the following routines: `init()`, `start()`, `paint()`, `stop()`, and `destroy()`.

(Don't worry if you find some of the terms in the preceding explanation a little confusing; Chapter 7 contains a list of all of the object-oriented and programming terms used here, and you see these same concepts repeated throughout the book. Besides, the Java runtime figures out whether or not a Java program is an applet or an application all by itself; this information falls into the nice-to-know-but-don't-worry-you-won't-be-tested category.)

In the company of pages: Java applets

A Java *applet* is an application designed so that you can incorporate it into an HTML-based Web page. Because the Java runtime environment is bundled inside Java-enabled Web browsers, such as Netscape Navigator and Microsoft's Internet Explorer, users don't need to download the Java runtime (or even have the vaguest idea of what the Java runtime environment is, for that matter) to run Java applets. All they need do is load a Web page that embeds a Java applet into their Java-enabled browsers and — presto! Change-o! The browser takes care of everything; the Java applet runs; and the world is good again.

Okay, So What Are Beans?

Now that you're comfortable with Java applications and Java applets, you're ready for the next step: *JavaBeans* (affectionately known as *beans* from here on in). A bean is a special kind of Java program, called a *component,* that you design specifically for use with other beans (and other component-based technologies, as you see in Chapter 9) to create useful, even complex, distributed applications. (A *distributed application* is an application that consists of at least two chunks that run on different computers; for example, some pieces may be downloaded from one remote machine, other pieces from another, and so on.)

Works well with others: A+

You can sum up the big difference between beans on the one hand and Java applets and applications on the other in one word (okay, two words): *component model.* Chapter 2 contains a nice, thorough discussion of component models (which is a pretty important concept, so I devoted an entire chapter to the subject). For now, all you need to understand is that the Java component model (JavaBeans, that is) extends the Java programming language so that it includes the following highly attractive bean-related features:

- **Beans are discrete.** Think of beans as building blocks. Generally they're small and do one thing really well; that way, you can build lots of different applications with different bean combinations. (Of course, "small" is in the eye of the beholder. To one developer, "small" may mean a nifty-looking push button; to another, the same term may mean a configurable search utility.)

- **Beans are reusable.** Once a bean, always a bean. You can use the same bean in one application or a thousand. Heck, why not license the really neat beans you create (for a fee, of course!) to others so that *they* can use them?

- **Beans are visually configurable.** Henry Ford is famous for once saying of his cars that customers could get the vehicles in any color they wanted — as long as they wanted black. A similar anecdote is attributed to Ray Kroc, founder of a certain ultrafamous hamburger chain, whom some repute to have forbidden his employees to customize burgers, maintaining that everybody likes the same condiments, and besides — it *just plain took too long!* Both companies later went on to change their approaches; ordering a lemon-yellow car from Ford Motors or a cheeseburger with no pickles from that hamburger chain is now perfectly acceptable. So what can you pick up from these stories? First, bosses tend to be cranky, and second, most items become more useful to more people if they can be customized — beans included.

Magic beans

What makes beans capable of working together to form complex, Internet-exploitive applications? Magic? No, something just slightly less elusive: industry cooperation. When Sun decided to extend the Java language to include the JavaBeans component model, the company actively sought help from other companies and individuals. Sun published something called a *specification*, which is a document outlining the first design attempt, and distributed the document on the Web. Folks experienced with component models contributed to the design, made suggestions, and offered advice, all of which was incorporated into the very first JavaBeans implementation. This kind of cooperation between potential competitors, usually restricted to academic (read: not-for-profit) pursuits, is still fairly rare, but it's beginning to become more and more common as participants realize that, in the post-Internet environment, standards benefit everyone involved.

✔ **Beans know how to work together.** By definition, beans can interact with other beans. As you see in Chapter 2, the beauty of a component model is that all the hard stuff associated with software component integration — things such as consistent ways to figure out what a particular bean does, to customize the bean, and how to add the bean to your application — have been simplified for you by the component model.

✔ **You can snap beans together to form complex applications.** Not only can beans interact with each other, but they can also communicate with other software components (even non-Java components). Check out Chapter 9 for an in-depth look at how you can combine beans with ActiveX components, Netscape plug-ins, and more.

If you're familiar with *ActiveX*, Microsoft's platform-dependent component model, you're no doubt aware of the large (and growing) market of ActiveX components built and marketed by so-called third-party vendors. (*Third party* means "someone other than Microsoft or the company purchasing and using the components.") People whose job is to know such things expect a similar third-party market of JavaBeans components to become available before the snow melts.

Of course, because beans are really just souped-up Java programs (bean soup, of course!), beans automatically inherit all the characteristics of any other Java program, including the capability to run on any Java-supported platform, regardless of the bean's development platform; built-in security; and the ease of a streamlined, optimized, object-oriented development environment.

Great! Where do I sign?

Now that you know what beans are, you're probably jumping up and down with excitement. You've got the theory — now all you need to pull everything together is a description of how to start developing and using beans. Read on.

What you need to create JavaBeans components

If you want to create, or *construct,* JavaBeans components (and I assume that you do, because you're reading this book), you need to get hold of a few things, as the following list notes:

- The latest version of the Java developer's kit (JDK 1.1)
- The latest version of the bean developer's kit (BDK 1.0)
- A text editor
- A Java-enabled Web browser
- A bean construction tool (this one's optional)

Chapter 3 tells you exactly how to obtain, install, and use each of these items, and the Introduction spells out the prerequisites for running them on your machine (what kind of operating system and hardware configuration you need — that kind of thing). What's more, all the items in the preceding list that you don't find on the companion CD you can downloaded from the Web at absolutely no charge to you! (No salesman will call; no one will visit.) Hey, whoever said "The best things in life are free" was right!

What you need to use JavaBeans

You have two options when it comes to using, or *consuming,* beans: You can run applications that someone built with beans (in which case you're actually not doing any development whatsoever, just using the bean-based application), or you can use "presoaked" beans to construct larger applications. The software requirements vary depending on the scenario, as you see in the following list:

- **Using beans.** If all you want to do is use applications that someone has already built with beans, your life is simple indeed. All you need is a Java-enabled Web browser.

- **Developing with beans.** If you want to develop applications that include beans, you need all of the tools listed in the preceding section, "What you need to create JavaBeans components," including a bean-based application development tool. (This last item is still technically optional, but I highly recommend trying at least one or two — see Chapter 6 for some suggestions.)

Enough with the Theory Already!

If you're having trouble visualizing what kind of function would make a good bean, here are some examples to get your imagination going.

Say that you're in the business of selling legal forms over the Internet. You may want to create a Web site that enables people to browse through a catalog, make selections, place orders, purchase, and download the legal forms of their choosing. Wouldn't it be cool if you could build the application from a collection of prebuilt, configurable beans such as those described in the following list, instead of coding it from scratch? Think how the following beans may fit into such an application:

- ✔ A **database bean** could enable you to connect your Web page to the database of your choice and fill your page with a list of the forms you have for sale by using customized database queries.

- ✔ A **credit bean** could enable you to accept a person's credit card information, transmit the information safely to the correct banking institution, and process or deny the order.

- ✔ A **download bean** could automatically validate a customer's request to download a purchase based on information obtained from the credit bean so that the customer could download his purchase safely and quickly.

Only your imagination limits the kinds of things you can create by using JavaBeans. Anything that you want to do as part of a Web application is a possible candidate. Think, for example, how you could use the following types of beans:

- ✔ A **speech bean** to translate data from text to speech

- ✔ A **mainframe communications bean** to enable easy transfer of information between Java clients and mainframe applications

- ✔ A **fax bean** so that developers can add fax capabilities to their Java-based applications quickly and easily

- ✔ A **handwriting-recognition bean** so that developers can add to their Web applications the capability to recognize a user's handwritten signature

The preceding examples are Internet-specific applications; that is, they all involve communicating information from one point on the Web (from a server) to somewhere else (to a client who's loaded your Web page, for example). Beans needn't be limited to communications work to be useful, however. Consider the potential utility of the following types of beans:

✔ A **spell-checker bean** to check text for accuracy

✔ A **font bean** to add font capabilities to text-based display elements

✔ A **3-D button bean** that developers can use to build really fancy custom Web pages

All in all, a good rule of thumb to follow when you're considering whether a program (or piece of a program) might best be implemented as a bean is to ask yourself the following questions. If you can answer "yes" to all of them, congratulations! You've got a prime bean candidate on your hands.

✔ **Can you describe what the potential bean will do in a simple sentence?**

For example, "the bean will check text for spelling errors" or "the bean will allow users to change the font of any displayed text."

✔ **Can you imagine the potential bean being useful in more than one scenario?**

A spell-checker bean, for example, would be valuable in all different kinds of applications, from business-oriented to educational (all applications that deal with text, to be exact).

✔ **Can you think of any ways to make the potential bean customizable?**

Still using the spell-checker bean as an example, you could increase the bean's value greatly by allowing users to configure the bean to operate in different languages (English, Spanish, French) or to make use of different specialized dictionaries (medical, legal, or what have you).

Chapter 2

What's a Component Model?

· ·

In This Chapter

▶ Getting familiar with the JavaBeans component software model

▶ Understanding component services

▶ Recognizing the difference between containers and "regular" (noncontaining) components

▶ Discovering other component models and how they relate to JavaBeans

· ·

*Y*ou may know that beans are Java components, but this knowledge isn't of much use unless you understand what a component is. This chapter explains what a software component model is, why it's useful, and how you can use it to create components and component-based software applications. Along with examples of other component models, this chapter also provides an overview of the specific component services that the JavaBeans architecture supports.

Standard Component Model Services

First off, it will be helpful for you to understand exactly what I mean by *component model*. It's simple, really. A component model is composed of two separate things:

> ✔ **A description (in the form of a specification) that explains how individual components should behave.**
>
> For example, the JavaBeans specification lists the minimum characteristics that every self-respecting bean should possess (beans should be configurable, savable, and so on). It also describes the particular APIs developers should use to implement these characteristics.
>
> ✔ **A software implementation of the specification.**
>
> The JavaBeans implementation consists of several API packages that you become intimately familiar with in Part IV.

The folks at Sun Microsystems weren't the first to come up with the idea of a software component model — although they were the first to extend the concept of a component model specifically to Internet development. (In fact, the last section in this chapter, "Some Other Component Models," describes a few of the more popular component architectures that had already hit the market by the time the very first JavaBeans specification was completed.)

Because they wanted to build on others' expertise instead of starting from scratch, and also because they wanted to make sure that JavaBeans would be a completely open — or *vendor-neutral* — standard, the bean architects invited other software vendors to participate in the creation of the first JavaBeans specification.

The result of all that input was the cataloguing of four main categories of function that, according to the best minds in the industry, any successful component model must implement. Put another way, these categories described the four standard *services* that a component model must provide each and every component:

- ✔ Customization (also called *interface publishing*)
- ✔ Introspection (also called *interface discovery*)
- ✔ Event handling
- ✔ Persistence

The following sections explain each of these services in detail.

Introspection

Okay, so beans are Java components, and the reason for creating JavaBeans (as opposed to plain vanilla Java programs) is that beans, unlike plain vanilla Java programs, are set up to work together. By *work together,* I mean that one bean can *call,* or invoke a method on, another bean — and also, of course, receive information back from the call. (A *method,* as you see in Chapter 7, is nothing more than a named series of programming statements that together perform some logical task.) For example, if one bean contains a method called `turnOrange()`, another bean can ask the first bean to turn orange by calling the first bean's `turnOrange()` method.

As you may guess, for this process to work, two things have to happen:

- ✔ **Customization (interface publishing)**

  The developer of the first bean must expose, or *publish,* all of the first bean's methods (also referred to as *interfaces*), which he or she can do by implementing special *customization* classes.

↙ **Introspection (interface discovery)**

Whoever's interested in interacting with the first bean must query the first bean to see what interfaces (methods) are available, what the names of the interfaces are, and so on. Typically "whoever" is an application-building tool developer; application-building tools are expected to make use of the introspection APIs to expose bean characteristics graphically to application developers. (Because introspection is generally assumed to be the job of developers creating application building tools, introspection APIs are sometimes referred to collectively as *application builder support.*)

Introspection can take one of two forms: *reflection* or *explicit bean specification*. (For a lowdown on exactly how you implement each kind of introspection in a real, live bean, take a gander at Chapter 11.)

Here are some low-budget definitions:

↙ **Customization:** You (most excellent bean developer) describe your bean's interfaces by using special customization classes.

Customization is also referred to as *interface publishing,* because the process can be compared (conceptually, at least!) to your writing and publishing a newsletter containing all of your bean's interfaces and then distributing the newsletter so that other developers can examine it later.

↙ **Introspection:** You (developer of an application development tool) try to figure out which interfaces define a bean by using special introspection classes. Introspection is also known as *interface discovery.*

Introspection can take one of two forms: *reflection* or *explicit specification.*

Size really does count

Why make a distinction between the two different kinds of methods (those useful during design time and those useful at runtime)? Simple: economics. Sun reasoned that some beans may have scores of design-time (configuration-related) methods but only a couple of runtime methods. By keeping the two different types of methods separate, the executable bean code need only contain the methods that are useful at runtime, which enables the executable file to stay as slim and trim as possible. After all, why keep overhead around that's going to make your executable file bigger and bulkier if you can't even use all that excess baggage at execution time?

Until the Internet boasts unlimited bandwidth, file size is going to remain an issue. Until then, the smaller you can keep your files, the better.

> ✔ **Reflection:** In this approach to introspection, the Java environment "guesses" what methods, properties, and events have been defined for a particular bean based on standard naming conventions. Reflection is the default approach and is used when no BeanInfo class was defined for a bean (that is, when interface details can't be derived from explicit specification).
>
> ✔ **Explicit specification:** In this approach to introspection, the Java environment queries a class called BeanInfo defined in advance by the bean programmer. BeanInfo comes right out and specifies what methods, properties, and events are defined for the bean.

On further reflection: implicit analysis of a bean's innards

Reflection is the bargain-basement brand of introspection. In this approach, an application-building tool developer can use a special Java class (called, appropriately enough, the Introspector class) to figure out what a given bean's properties, methods, and supported events look like. The Introspector class uses a set of rules, known in bean programming circles as *design patterns,* to make intelligent guesses based on source code syntax. Suppose that the Introspector finds a statement that looks something like the following example as it hunts through a bean's source code:

```
public void takeItToTheLimit()
```

Using its collection of design patterns, the Introspector concludes that the preceding statement represents a public method called takeItToTheLimit() that takes no parameters and returns no value. Why? Because the statement starts with the keyword public, followed by a recognized method return type (void), followed by a nonkeyword string (takeItToTheLimit), and a pair of parentheses.

Coming right out with it: explicit bean specification

Some bean developers (and you know who you are) don't feel comfortable leaving things to the Introspector's guesswork. Why leave things so that the Java environment must infer what properties, methods, and events a bean supports if you can come right out and tell the world in your very own words? Developers who want to specify any (or all) of their beans' characteristics or behaviors explicitly are more than welcome to do so: All they need to do is implement something called the BeanInfo interface, which I cover at length in Chapter 11.

Customization

A bean must play the following two very different roles in application development:

✓ Participating in the construction of a bean-based application (*design time*)

✓ Actually running in an application (*runtime*)

This section describes the role a bean plays at design time, because design time is when customization comes into play. Two different Java *interfaces* directly support the organization of methods that a bean developer wants to make available to other bean developers at design time: PropertyEditor and Customizer. I briefly describe both these interfaces in the following sections; for more in-depth information, check out Chapter 14.

One at a time, please! The PropertyEditor interface

Implementing the PropertyEditor interface for a simple property is the easiest way to enable other developers to customize that property. (By "simple," I mean a property that associates with a built-in data type, such as an int, long, or char.)

Each different property type that a bean contains should have its very own PropertyEditor associated with it.

A group of property editors associated with a given bean is known collectively as a *property sheet*.

Everything including the kitchen sink: the Customizer interface

In some cases, a bean may be so large and complex that a developer may want to develop a single custom editor for the bean (which you implement via the Customizer interface) rather than just a bunch of property editors. If a bean's customizable properties are tightly dependent on one another, for example, presenting the bean for customizing (or *editing*) as a whole may prove easier than presenting it in unrelated bits and pieces.

Here's an example: If a bean contains properties that represent a background color, a foreground color, and a border color, a developer may want to create a Customizer that incorporates the ColorPropertyEditor but also contains logic to warn developers that setting all the properties' values equal to frog-belly white results in an impossible-to-see bean.

Event handling

Event handing is a special case of ordinary bean-to-bean method calling. In addition to one bean calling a method on another bean, the Java runtime environment itself invokes certain methods automatically whenever particular events occur.

An *event* to the Java runtime environment is pretty much anything you define it to be. (I have a friend who thinks that spending the evening listening to live mariachi music is an event. I have *another* friend who wouldn't be caught dead listening to a mariachi band; she considers an out-of-town ski weekend a "real" event.)

The point is that user interaction itself defines several events, such as a mouse-clicking event, a keystroke event, and so on. You can even use one of the events defined and delivered as part of the BDK (JavaBeans Development kit) — for example, the "a-property-value-just-changed" event. Bean developers must themselves define any other events that they need. (For an in-depth examination of events and event handling, turn to Chapter 12.)

Persistence

Remember the old adage: "Genius is 1 percent intelligence and 99 percent persistence"? Well, the definition of *persistence* in computer-speak is pretty similar to its definition in plain English: in a word, *tenacity*. *Persistent data* is data that hangs around even after a given computer program finishes running so that, after the program resumes (say, after the weekend is over and you're back in the office), the data still exists on your computer somewhere.

If, for example, you use a word processing program to create a document, you typically save the document before you turn off your computer. The saved, or persisted, document is still there on your computer the next time you turn on your computer and start your word processing program.

The opposite of persistent data is *volatile data*. You keep volatile data only in memory, so if you terminate a program (for example, after you close down your Web browser), volatile data disappears into thin air.

Beans are typically configurable by a human developer, and you probably want to make most of (if not all) your beans' configurable information persistent. That way, if a developer configures your bean via an application-building tool, the changes aren't lost after the developer exits the tool.

In This Corner: Component versus Container

A *container* is a special kind of software component. As the name implies, containers can *contain* other components; and just as you can real-world containers (peanut butter jars, shoe boxes, and so on), you can contain most containers in still *other* containers. Some examples of software containers include a Web page, a browser window, and a word processing application.

Of course, developers design some containers only to contain, not to *be* contained. A real-life example of this type of "ultracontainer" is an oil tanker; a software example may be your desktop. You can't contain either of these examples in another container; their creators designed both only to incorporate other stuff — crude oil and icons, respectively. (Okay, technically, the Earth contains an oil tanker, but work with me here!)

Reuse: The Holy Grail of Software Development

Reuse is the pot of gold at the end of the software rainbow. The JavaBeans architecture certainly enables the creation of reusable components; some may even say that the JavaBeans architecture strongly encourages developers to create reusable components. But alas, reuse, like lunch, isn't free. If you want to create a bean that someone can reuse over and over again, whether that someone is you or someone else, you need to follow a few basic rules, as described in the following list:

✓ **Plan for reuse.**

Keep reuse in the back of your mind as you design your bean. Ask yourself what other applications someone may conceivably use your bean to create. If the answer is "Not in my wildest dreams can I imagine another application that could use this function," perhaps you may better implement your bean as a Java applet or (who knows?) something else altogether.

✓ **Abstract as much function as possible.**

Take advantage of the fact that you can customize beans and abstract as much of the behavior and characteristics of your bean as you can. The more generic you make your bean, the wider is its applicability.

✓ **Refine your design.**

No matter what those seductive application-building tool vendors tell you, building the perfect reusable beast is very much an iterative (repetitive) process. The best way to tell whether your bean is both generic and function-rich enough for reuse is to reuse it! If the bean is easy to reuse *and* provides a big programming bang for the buck, buy yourself a flavored latte and take the afternoon off. If not, rethink your design, tweak the thing a little, and try again. (Repeat as necessary.)

Some Other Component Models

As you may remember from the "Standard Component Model Services" section earlier in this chapter, JavaBeans wasn't the first component model to hit the streets (although it *was* the first widely publicized cross-platform, Internet-ready component model).

Because the JavaBeans designers were bound and determined to provide a completely open (read: *nonproprietary*) component architecture, they built support for each of the following popular models right into the beans specification. Chapter 9 describes the nitty-gritty details of exactly how the designers accomplished this model-to-model integration. For now, just be aware that any bean you create can (at some point in the near future and with only the slightest sleight of hand necessary) interact with a component or application created in any of the environments discussed in the following sections.

ActiveX: Microsoft Internet Explorer +

Microsoft's component solution is called *ActiveX*. (For you history buffs, ActiveX components were once known as *OLE controls*.) The good news about ActiveX components is that you can use these components to create both Web applications and desktop-based applications. The bad news is that if you want to create and use ActiveX components, your choice of platforms is currently limited to Windows and Macintosh.

If ActiveX developers want to take advantage of the JavaBeans capability to run on additional platforms, they will be able to do so without rewriting any of their code, thanks to something called a *bridge*. A bridge is a program that translates ActiveX API calls into corresponding JavaBeans API calls "under the covers." (That is, a developer will be able to call ActiveX APIs just like always; at runtime, the bridge will figure out which JavaBeans APIs provide similar functions and call them automatically.)

At the time of this writing, the JavaBeans-ActiveX bridge is available in early beta form. You can see the bridge in action in Chapter 9, "Making ActiveX Components and JavaBeans Work Together."

Visit the following URLs to find out more about the JavaBeans-ActiveX bridge and Microsoft's ActiveX technology, respectively:

```
http://splash.javasoft.com/beans/bridge/
http://www.microsoft.com/intdev/sdk/
```

LiveConnect (Netscape Navigator)

LiveConnect is the name of the technology built into the Netscape Navigator Web browser (beginning with Navigator Version 3.0) that enables developers to integrate plug-ins, JavaScript scripts, Java applets, and now, of course, JavaBeans.

To find out more about how you can use Netscape Navigator's LiveConnect technology with JavaBeans, go to this URL:

```
http://home.netscape.com/eng/mozilla/3.0/handbook/plugins/
                  index.html
```

OpenDoc

OpenDoc is a component software technology that Apple developed. Both Apple and IBM now implement this technology on several different hardware and software platforms. A not-for-profit consortium, called CILabs, currently promotes OpenDoc. The original design goal for OpenDoc was similar to that of JavaBeans: to be fully cross-platform and nonproprietary.

OpenDoc was one of the first such really ambitious, really comprehensive component models (much more comprehensive even than JavaBeans), and as such, its critics claim that it has initially fallen just a little short of industry expectations. OpenDoc is platform independent in theory, for example, but is platform *dependent* in reality (for any but the tiniest, or most *trivial*, components). Some good application development tools could fix this flaw right up, however, and because OpenDoc is still in its infancy, such tools may even be on the market by the time you read this book.

Macintosh developers have really taken a shine to OpenDoc; even though the program represents a fairly new technology, OpenDoc-enabled applications and components are already commercially available for the Mac. Developers who prefer to continue developing OpenDoc components can do so, and if they want to take advantage of JavaBeans, they should be able to without rewriting any of their code to be bean-specific — courtesy of a bridge for mapping OpenDoc API calls to JavaBean API calls that Sun Microsystems is currently designing (with some help from the good folks at IBM).

Visit `http://www.opendoc.apple.com/` to keep up on the latest happenings in the land of OpenDoc.

Chapter 3
Anatomy of a Bean

▶ Declaring bean properties

▶ Defining bean methods

▶ Understanding bean events

• •

*W*hat is this thing called *bean*? This chapter takes you up-close and personal with a typical bean. You get a complete picture of what every bean needs, including the syntax for specifying bean properties and defining bean methods and events.

A Bean by Any Other Name Is Still an Object

Java is an object-oriented language, and so each JavaBeans component is also an object. In software terms, an *object* is a self-contained piece of code that defines a real-world thing or concept. Some examples of an object are a Web page, a push button, and a graphic image.

By definition, an object must contain the following two items:

✔ Data

✔ Some operations that can be performed on that data

Constructs called *properties* are used to define JavaBeans data, as you can see in the following section. Operations, on the other hand, are defined by a combination of *methods* and *events*. I explain both methods and events later in this chapter, in (what else?) the sections titled "Methods" and "Events."

Boardwalk, Park Place, and Other Properties

A bean *property* (sometimes known as an *attribute*) represents a single piece of data that affects a bean's appearance or behavior. You must name properties, as demonstrated in the examples in the following table. Together, a descriptive name and a corresponding value constitute a property.

As you can see in the examples contained in the following table, a bean *property* comprises

- ✔ A descriptive name
- ✔ A corresponding value

Together, these elements represent a single piece of data that affects a bean's appearance or behavior.

Example Property Name	Corresponding Property Value
color	"red"
age	29
fileName	"aBigFile.txt"
city	"Cincinnati"
isComplete	yes

A bean can contain three different basic kinds of properties: *indexed*, *bound*, and *constrained*.

Just your (primitive data) type

Because the JavaBeans APIs are really just an extension of the Java language, the same data types that are available to you in the Java language proper are available for use in your beans. *Java Programming For Dummies*, by Donald J. Koosis and David Koosis (published by IDG Books Worldwide, Inc.), explains all the ins and outs of Java's built-in data types, as well as "special" data types that you can implement as classes. For the bare minimum, however, all you need to know is the information in Table 3-1, which shows the Java built-in data types (which are familiar to you if you have a C or C++ background) along with their corresponding Java wrapper classes.

Encapsulation: Accessing property values the *right* way

One of the hallmarks of an object-oriented development language such as Java is that it protects an object's data from unauthorized access, thanks to a concept known as *encapsulation. Encapsulation* means that the only way anyone can access an object's data is by "asking" the object (that is, calling one of the object's methods) to get or set the property's value. This restriction is a Good Thing, because encapsulation prevents programmers from setting properties to really weird, inappropriate values that the object has no clue how to handle. (Setter methods, which are described in the "Methods" section later in this chapter, typically contain code to filter out inappropriate values.)

To illustrate what I mean, here is the *right* way to set a property's value:

```
aBean.setIsComplete( Yes ) //
    using a method: correct!
```

And now, take a look at an example of the *wrong* way to set a property's value:

```
aBean.isComplete =  Who knows?
    // direct assignment: wrong!
```

(Actually, if the Java environment encounters a statement such as that of the preceding example, it's smart enough not to make the assignment point-blank. Instead, Java understands what the developer is trying to do and does the right thing: It calls `aBean.setIsComplete( Who knows? )` and has the `setIsComplete()` method decide whether `Who knows?` is a valid value for the `isComplete` property.)

You can find more on this subject in the section "Methods," later in this chapter.

A *wrapper class* is a class (as you see in Chapter 7, a *class* is a type of object) that holds the value of the built-in data type but adds some additional object characteristics. The `Integer` class, for example, holds the value of an integer and, as you may expect, provides a method (`intValue()`) that returns the integer value. Additionally, however, the `Integer` class also provides tons of other methods: You can get the integer value in the form of a byte (`byteValue()`), a long (`longValue()`), and much, much more.

Table 3-1	Basic Java Data Types	
Built-in Data Type	*Java Wrapper Class*	*Data Type Description*
byte	Byte	Whole number from −128 to 127
short	Short	Whole number from −32768 to 32767
int	Integer	Whole number from −2147483648 to 2147483647

(continued)

Table 3-1 *(continued)*

Built-in Data Type	Java Wrapper Class	Data Type Description
long	Long	Whole number even longer than int
float	Float	Fractional number
double	Double	Fractional number with more precision than float
boolean	Boolean	*True* or *false*
char	Character	A single character
char []	String	An array of characters (read-only)
char []	StringBuffer	An array of characters (read/write)

When should you use a built-in primitive type versus a wrapper class? Usually, your decision depends on what you're trying to do. In Java (unlike some other programming languages, like Smalltalk), primitive types aren't considered objects. Many Java methods, however, accept only object values — so if you need to pass a primitive value (for example, a char value) to a method that accepts only objects (for example, Character objects), you need to transform the primitive into an instance of the corresponding wrapper class. Fortunately, that's easy for a developer to do, as shown in the following example:

```
Character myCharacter = new Character( x );
```

The preceding line of code takes a primitive char value, 'x', and transforms it into an instance of Character called myCharacter.

Regarding numeric data types: Unless you're programming some kind of scientific application, you can probably stick with the float data type for money values and the int data type for all the rest of your numeric needs.

Indexed properties: A little array of sunshine

An *indexed property* is a property that you associate with an index. (An index can be any nonnegative integer.) A collection of indexed properties is known as An *array*. An array named dessertMenu, for example, may contain the following indexed properties:

Index	Property value
0	chocolate cake
1	lemon meringue pie
2	pecan shortbread
3	coconut pudding

Declaring indexed properties

Indexed properties can prove quite handy. If you define an array as containing, say, 10 properties, however, and you attempt to access the 15th property of that array, the Java runtime, not surprisingly, complains by throwing an *exception*. (See Chapter 7 forthe scoop on handling exceptions.)

Here is the generic syntax:

```
PropertyType[] arrayName = new type [index];
```

And here is a real-life example:

```
String[] listOfDesserts = new String[10];
```

Accessing indexed properties

To get or set the value of an indexed property, you need to define two separate methods in your Java source file: one to get a value (affectionately known as a *getter*) and one to set the value (a *setter*). Take a look at getter and setter definitions for an indexed array of properties, which you can find on the companion CD.

For a first-hand look at declaring and accessing indexed properties, take a look at the Java source file IndexedProperties.java, which contains source code that declares and accesses a bunch of indexed properties. Then, to see this code in action, load the HTML file IndexedProperties.html.

Here is the generic syntax for declaring *getter* and *setter* methods:

```
PropertyType getMethod(int index) // getter
void setMethod(int index, PropertyType value) // setter
```

And here is a real-life example:

```
String getDessert(int index) { // getter
    return listOfDesserts[index];
}

void setDessert(int index, String value) { // setter
    listOfDesserts[index] = value;
}
```

And here's how you may call the `getter` and `setter` methods declared in the preceding example:

```
// Create a new menu (RestaurantMenu is the class that
// defines the getDessert()and setDessert() methods above
RestaurantMenu myMenu = new RestaurantMenu();

// Set some desserts
myMenu.setDessert(0,  chocolate cake );
myMenu.setDessert(1,  lemon meringue pie );
myMenu.setDessert(2,  coconut pudding );

// Get some desserts
System.out.println( First dessert is   +
    myMenu.getDessert(0));
System.out.println( Second dessert:   +
    myMenu.getDessert(1));
System.out.println( Third dessert:   +
    myMenu.getDessert(2));
```

Don't worry if the bean code in this section strikes you as a little difficult. Parts III and IV of this book contain plenty of code examples, along with helpful step-by-step explanations. Understanding bean code gets easier the more times you see it — I promise!

Accessing arrays

With the following statements you can get or set an entire array's worth of values all at once. (An *array* is a group of indexed properties, as described previously in this chapter.)

Here is the generic syntax you use to declare accessor methods:

```
PropertyType[] getMethod() // getter
void setMethod(PropertyType[] values) // setter
```

And here is a real-life example:

```
String[] getListOfDesserts() { // getter
      return listOfDesserts;
}


void setListOfDesserts(String[] inputList) { //setter
    listOfDesserts = inputList;
}
```

And the following example shows how you can call the array accessor methods declared in the preceding example:

```
String[] temporaryList = new String[10];
temporaryList[0] = "marzipan torte";
temporaryList[1] = "chocolate-pecan pie";
temporaryList[2] = "babas au rum";
RestaurantMenu myMenu = new RestaurantMenu();

// setter
myMenu.setListOfDesserts(temporaryList);


...
// getter
String[] returnedList = myMenu.getListOfDesserts();
```

Bound (and determined) properties

You implement bound properties by using the beans event-handling model, which I describe in Chapter 12.

A *bound property* is a property that makes an announcement to the world at large whenever its value changes. Bound properties are a great way to implement logic between beans. Suppose that you hook up a savings-account bean to a bunch of other beans (a 401K bean, a checking-account bean, a stock-ticker bean, and so on) to manage your personal finances. If the stock-ticker bean contains the bound property AcmeStockPrice, that bean can broadcast a message if the price of Acme stock dips to your buying point. The savings-account bean can pick up the message immediately, check to see whether you have enough in savings to make a purchase, and complete the transaction.

You may wonder why programmers call bound properties *bound* instead of oh, say, *tattletale* properties. (After all, they squawk every time something changes.) Because techno-geeks view these properties as *bound* to a *change notification service*. Pretty fancy, huh?

In a nutshell, here's how bound properties work: Pretend that a bean called `chatterbox` contains a bound property called `gossip`. The `chatterbox` bean source needs to include the following two things:

- ✔ A strategically placed call to `firePropertyChange()` (for example, inside `setGossip()`) to fire off the alert that the `gossip` property has changed
- ✔ Declarations for a pair of methods, `addPropertyChangeListener()` and `removePropertyChangeListener()`, that other beans can call to get on (and off) the notification list

Now `chatterbox` is set up to tell other beans when the value for `gossip` changes. What's left? Well, because the bean architects didn't want beans to be bombarded with messages that the beans didn't care anything about, beans (like some people I know) hear only what they want to hear — that is, beans receive notifications only from other beans in which they've registered an active interest. To register interest in a property change event, a bean needs to include separate snippets of code: a call to a special method called `addPropertyChangeListener()`, and some logic to perform every time it receives notification of a property change event.

For example, here's what a bean (call it `busybody`) that wants to register interest in `chatterbox`'s `gossip` property should include:

- ✔ A call to `chatterbox`'s `addPropertyChangeListener()` method to register its interest (in other words, to "put itself on the list" to receive an event notification every time the `gossip` property value changes)
- ✔ The declaration of a method to do something when `busybody` receives an alert message from `chatterbox` bringing the news that `gossip` has changed

Generic syntax

I break up the syntax for bound properties into two sections. One section describes what the bean doing the broadcasting (supporting the bound property) needs to look like; the other describes what the interested party (the bean doing the listening) needs to include.

Here is the syntax for a broadcasting bean (a bean with support for a bound property). Note the `addPropertyChangeListener()` method, which lets other beans "sign up" to receive event notifications, and the `firePropertyChange()` method, which actually sends off the event notifications.

```
// Declare a method to let other beans register
// their interest
public void addPropertyChangeListener(PropertyChange
        Listener listener) {
    changes.addPropertyChangeListener(listener)
}


// Declare a method to let other beans de-register
// when they re no longer interested
public void removePropertyChangeListener(PropertyChange
        Listener listener) {
    changes.removePropertyChangeListener(listener)
}


// Fire off a message specifying exactly what
// changed
changeSupportObject.firePropertyChange( message , newValue,
        oldValue);


// You need to declare this so you can call the
// firePropertyChange() method
private PropertyChangeSupport changeSupportObject = new
        PropertyChangeSupport(broadcastObject);
```

And here is the syntax for the listening side of the equation (that is, a bean that's interested in receiving event notifications regarding a bound property). Two items are of special interest in the following syntax. The first is the fact that the listening bean implements the PropertyChangeListener interface. The second is that when the broadcasting bean sends an event notification by calling the listener bean's propertyChange() method, the propertyChange() method, in turn, calls the listener bean's reportChange() method.

```
// PropertyChangeListener is an interface, so you
// have to define a class that implements it
// concretely (the class must implement the
// propertyChange() method)
class PropertyChangeAdapter implements
        PropertyChangeListener {
    public void propertyChange(PropertyChangeEvent anEvent)
        {
```

(continued)

(continued)

```
            reportChange(anEvent);
    }
}



// Create an instance of the PropertyChangeAdapter
// defined above to set the automatic notification
// service in motion
PropertyChangeAdapter anAdapter = new
            PropertyChangeAdapter();



// reportChange() will be called automatically when
// the other bean s property changes; all you
// have to do is decide what you want to do with
// the notification information you receive
public void reportChange(PropertyChangeEvent theEvent) {
    // Some actions to perform when a message
    // is received notifying this object that
    // the bound property being monitored has changed
}
```

A real-life example

Again, I separate syntax for the broadcasting bean and the listening bean into two different sections.

Following is the code for the bean doing the broadcasting, which in this case is OurButton. (The OurButton bean is one of the example beans that ships with the BDK. Because the BDK is included on the companion CD, you can examine the OurButton.java source file in its entirety if you'd like.)

If you refer to the generic syntax shown in the preceding section, you notice that there are no surprises here; basically, all that's happening is that OurButton is providing

- ✔ An addPropertyChangeListener() method other beans can call to register their interest in receiving event notifications from OurButton
- ✔ A firePropertyChange() method that OurButton will call on every one of its registered listeners every time the value for OurButton's label changes

```
public void addPropertyChangeListener(PropertyChange
        Listener x) {
    changes.addPropertyChangeListener(x)
```

```
    }

    public void removePropertyChangeListener(PropertyChange
            Listener x) {
        changes.removePropertyChangeListener(x)
    }

    ...

    public void setLabel(String newLabel) {

        ...

        // fire off an event notification when the
        // value for the label is changed
        changes.firePropertyChange("label", oldLabel,
            newLabel);

        ...

    }

    private PropertyChangeSupport changes = new
            PropertyChangeSupport(this);
```

The following section gives you an inside look at the bean doing the listening, which in our case is the `ChangeReporter` bean. Before you take a look at the listening bean, though, check out the code inside the BeanBox.

This bit of code defines a class called `PropertyChangeAdapter`, which is a bona fide, card-carrying `PropertyChangeListener`. It translates the standard `propertyChange()` method into another method call — `reportChange()`.

Now, you may wonder why on Earth anyone would go to all the trouble of defining a separate class just to have one method turn around and call another method. Well, in this case, frankly, the adapter class isn't providing a lot of value-add (in fact, the only reason the adapter is included here is to demonstrate the overall mechanics). Adapters typically do a lot more than just one-to-one method mapping, though, as you can see in Chapter 12, "Adapting to Change." For now, just think of the adapter class as an intermediate go-between step between the broadcasting bean (`OurButton`) and all of the beans that are interested in receiving event notifications from `OurButton` (in our example, the only interested bean is `ChangeReporter`).

```
class PropertyChangeAdapter implements
    PropertyChangeListener {
    public void propertyChange(PropertyChangeEvent event) {
    aListener.reportChange(event);
    }
}

...

PropertyChangeAdapter adapter = new
    PropertyChangeAdapter();
```

And finally, here is what the `ChangeReporter` class (the listener bean) looks like. Because of the adapter in the preceding section, when `OurButton` (the broadcasting bean) calls `propertyChange()` to signify that a property change event has occurred, `OurButton.propertyChange()` in turn calls the `reportChange()` method of `ChangeReporter`.

```
public void reportChange(PropertyChangeEvent theEvent) {
    String propertyName = theEvent.getPropertyName();
    String newValue = theEvent.getNewValue();
    ...
}
```

You can find complete source code for the snippets listed in this section (`OurButton.java`, `ChangeReporter.java`, and `BeanBox.java`) on the companion CD (version 1.0 of the BDK).

Constrained properties

You implement constrained properties, as you do bound properties, by using the beans event-handling model (which I describe in detail in Chapter 12).

A *constrained property* is a property you associate with predefined limits. You may, for example, constrain a property named `age` to positive values, because generally the ages of people and things start at zero and go up. Constraining a property is an easy way of catching out-of-bounds values as soon as a developer (or user) attempts to enter such values.

The neat thing about constrained properties is that lots of beans can keep an eye on one bean's property's value. Constrained properties are similar to bound properties, except that the beans that register an interest in a constrained property not only receive notification that something is about to change, but they can also say, "Hey! I disapprove of that change, so *you* can't accept it!"

If you study the source code for both the bound and constrained properties, you notice that both are very similar event implementations. The only real difference, in fact (other than the actual events each detects), is that constrained property listeners get to throw *exceptions* — that is, they get to disapprove of what's going on and stop the process that's under way from continuing. (You can find out all about exceptions in Chapter 7.)

Generic syntax

I divide the syntax for constrained properties into two sections: what the bean doing the broadcasting (supporting the constrained property) needs to look like, and what the interested party (the bean doing the listening) needs to include.

Following is the syntax for a broadcasting bean (a bean with support for a constrained property). Following are the most important things to note about this syntax:

✔ **The** addVeotableChangeListener() **method.**

   Other beans can call this method to register an interest in listening for (and potentially vetoing) a property value change.

✔ **The** setMethod() **method.**

   This method will attempt to set a property value. Before this method actually makes the change to the property value, it notifies all registered listener beans (by calling the fireVetoableChange() method) — which give the listener beans the opportunity to veto the attempted change. (fireVetoableChange() is defined as part of the VetoableChangeSupport class.) If any listener bean vetoes the attempted change, that listener bean throws a property veto exception which prevents the change from occurring.

```
// Throw an exception if the value can t be set
// due to a veto
void setMethod(PropertyType value) throws
          PropertyVetoException {
    interestedList.fireVetoableChange( message ,
      SomeType oldValue, SomeType newValue);

    // If the compiler gets to here, that means no
    // one vetoed the change, so make the change
    // and tell all the interested beans
    changeSupportObject.firePropertyChange( message ,
      SomeType oldValue, SomeType newValue);
}


// Declare a method to let other beans register
// their interest
public void
          addVetoableChangeListener(VetoableChangeListener
    listener) {
  changeSupportObject.addVetoableChangeListener(listener)
}
```

(continued)

(continued)

```
// Declare a method to let other beans de-register
// when they re no longer interested
public void
          removeVetoableChangeListener(VetoableChangeListener
    listener) {
changeSupportObject.removeVetoableChangeListener(listener)
}


// You need to declare these so you can call the
// firePropertyChange() and fireVetoableChange()
// methods
private PropertyChangeSupport changeSupportObject =
    new PropertyChangeSupport(broadcastObject);

private VetoableChangeSupport interestedList =
    new VetoableChangeSupport(broadcastObject);
```

This is the code you'd expect to see in any controlling container application
(for example, the BeanBox, or any other application building tool.) Notice
that this syntax defines a new listener class called VetoableChangeAdapter
that contains just one method: vetoableChange(). (I discuss adapters in
detail in Chapter 12; for now, just be aware that the fireVetoableChange()
method that the broadcasting bean calls turns right around and calls
vetoableChange().)

```
// VetoableChangeListener is an interface, so you
// have to define a class that implements it
// concretely (the class must implement the
// vetoableChange() method)
class VetoableChangeAdapter implements
    VetoableChangeListener {
    public void vetoableChange(PropertyChangeEvent
        anEvent)throws PropertyVetoException{
        vetoableChange (anEvent);
    }
}



// Create an instance of the VetoableChangeAdapter
// defined above to set the automatic notification
```

```
// service in motion
VetoableChangeAdapter anAdapter =
    new VetoableChangeAdapter();
```

And here is the syntax for the listening side of the equation (that is, a bean interested in listening for any attempt to change a constrained property and potentially vetoing that change). All that's going on here is that the listener bean is defining one method (called vetoableChange() in this example).

```
// vetoableChange() will be called automatically when
// the broadcasting bean s property changes; all you
// have to do is decide what you want to do with
// the notification information you receive
public void vetoableChange(PropertyChangeEvent theEvent)
    throws propertyVetoException {
    // Some logic to figure out whether or not
    // the proposed change is acceptable; if not,
    // throw an exception
}
```

A real-life example

Again, I separate the syntax for the broadcasting bean and the listening bean into two different sections — the broadcasting section and the listening section.

Here is an example that shows methods and properties of a broadcasting bean you may be familiar with from the BDK: the JellyBean bean. In this example, the setPrice() method ensures that before the value of a JellyBean price is actually changed, all interested listener beans are notified of the pending change (that is, the fireVetoableChange() method is sent to every bean on the interestedList. If any listener bean objects to, or *vetoes*, the change, the change will not take place. (How's that for power?)

```
void setPrice(int newPrice) throws PropertyVetoException {
    int oldPrice = price;
    interestedList.fireVetoableChange( price ,
      new Integer(oldPrice), // convert values to
        new Integer(newPrice)); // integer objects

    // If the compiler gets to here, that means no
    // one vetoed the change, so make the change
    // and tell all the interested beans
```

(continued)

(continued)

```
     changes.firePropertyChange("price",
       new Integer(oldPrice), // convert values to
     new Integer(newPrice); // integer objects
}


...
public void addVetoableChangeListener(VetoableChange
          Listener x) {
    vetos.addVetoableChangeListener(x);
}


...
public void removeVetoableChangeListener(VetoableChange
          Listener x) {
    vetos.removeVetoableChangeListener(x)
}


...
private PropertyChangeSupport changes =
              new PropertyChangeSupport(this);

private VetoableChangeSupport interestedList =
    new VetoableChangeSupport(this);
```

This is the code you'd expect to see in any controlling container
application — for instance, the BeanBox, or any other application building
tool. Notice that this code first defines an adapter and then instantiates the
adapter. After the adapter (called `anAdapter` in this example) is in place,
the application is free to attempt to set the value of a `JellyBean`'s price.

```
class VetoableChangeAdapter implements
    VetoableChangeListener {
    public void vetoableChange(PropertyChangeEvent
        anEvent) throws PropertyVetoException{
                aListener.vetoableChange(anEvent);
    }
}


...
VetoableChangeAdapter anAdapter = new
    VetoableChangeAdapter(); ...
// Here's where the action takes place: an instance
```

```
// of JellyBean, called bean, is created
JellyBean bean = new JellyBean();

// And now the Voter registers interest in JellyBean s
// properties (check out VetoableChangeSupport.java
// if you find this confusing).
bean.addVetoableChangeListener(anAdapter);

// The following line of code will try to set the price
// of the JellyBean instance to 123.
bean.setPrice(123);
```

The following example shows you what the listener bean (in this case, the Voter class) looks like. The logic here is pretty simple: after the listener bean is informed that a property value has changed (that is, the broadcasting bean calls the listener bean's vetoableChange() method), all the listener bean has to do is figure out whether or not to throw a fuss.

In the public eye

Properties, methods, and even classes can have different levels of visibility: *public*, *private*, or *protected*. Following is a quick rundown of what each of these privacy-related keywords means:

Keyword	Visibility
public	Visible to everybody
private	Visible to nobody (except inside the declaring class)
protected	Visible to everybody in the same file or package
(no privacy keyword)	Visible to everyone in the same file or package for inheritance purposes only

If, for example, you declare a property (or method or class) as private, other programmers writing other classes and applications can't directly access that property. On the other hand, if you declare a property (or method or class) as public, other programmers *can* access the property. Case in point: Every Java applet needs to define at least a few methods so that you can integrate the applet into a Web page: init(), start(), stop(), and destroy(). You must declare these methods as public — otherwise, the Java-enabled browser can't call them, and the applet is about as responsive as a lump of wood!

Here are a couple general rules of thumb regarding privacy:

✔ Always declare properties (data) as *private*.

✔ Always declare accessor methods as *public*.

The following example shows the method of Voter class (inside the listening bean):

```
public void vetoableChange(PropertyChangeEvent theEvent)
    throws propertyVetoException {
        // Some logic to figure out whether or not
        // the proposed change is acceptable; if not,
        // throw an exception
    ...

        throw new PropertyVetoException("NO!", theEvent);
}
```

If you're interested, take a look at the source code for the snippets listed in this section (JellyBean.java and Voter.java) located on the companion CD.

Methods

A *method* is a function that's attached to a specific object (for example, a bean). A method's name is typically a verb that describes what that method can do — for example, toLowerCase(), trim(), and length() are methods on the built-in String object that enable you to set a string to lowercase text, trim the white space from a string, and figure out the length of a string, respectively.

The next section briefly describes the different kinds of methods you can define for your own classes. (Even if you don't define your own, though, you still want to be able to recognize these different types of methods so you can call, or *invoke*, them correctly if you encounter them in built-in Java classes).

Constructors

A *constructor* is a special kind of method that (if you use it in conjunction with the new keyword) enables you to create an example of a class. You always name a constructor the same as the name of the class; it can (but doesn't need to) accept parameters. You can have multiple constructors if you want — one that accepts no parameters, one that accepts one or two parameters, and so on.

Assume, for example, that the Invoice class contains the following constructor definitions:

```
public class Invoice {

    // null constructor (accepts no arguments)
    Invoice() {
        // do some initialization here
    }

    // constructor that accepts two arguments
    Invoice(float amount, String payee) {
        // do some initialization here
        invoiceAmount = amount;
        invoicePayee = payee;
    }
    ...
}
```

The following example shows how you call the constructors defined in the preceding example:

```
// calling the constructor with no arguments
Invoice myInvoice = new Invoice();

// calling the constructor with two arguments
Invoice myInvoice = new Invoice(98.35,
    "Sack O' Taters Produce Company")
```

You can skip defining a constructor for your class altogether, if you want; if you do skip this step, however, the Java compiler still calls a constructor — the constructor that your class's *parent* class defines. This result is all thanks to a little something called inheritance!

Suppose that you create a bean called PooBear that you extend, or derive from, the built-in class java.awt.Canvas — but you don't define a constructor in your PooBear class definition. When you attempt to create an instance of PooBear, the Java compiler first looks for a constructor in the PooBear class definition. When it doesn't find one there, it continues to look for a constructor in the Canvas class definition (and if it doesn't find one there, it looks for a constructor in Canvas's parent class, and so on, all the way up the ancestral chain).

This result is all thanks to a handy little something called *inheritance*, which you can learn more about in Chapter 7.

Accessor methods

Encapsulation is a powerful object-oriented principle that means, in a nutshell, "keeping the data hidden from prying programmers' eyes." The best way to create encapsulated beans is to declare all of a bean's properties as private and then, in the same class, declare two *accessor methods* for each property: one to access the value of the property by retrieving, or getting, it (a *getter*), and one to access the value of the property by setting it (a *setter*). That way, programmers can do what they need to do — access and change property values — and you get to "screen" the values they try to set for your properties. Following are examples of accessor methods for a private property called address that you declare as part of the Invoice class.

Getters

Defining a getter accessor method lets programmers get the value of properties safely and consistently. Here's an example definition of a getter named getStreetAddress():

```
public String getStreetAddress() {
    return theStreetAddress;
}
```

Notice that getAddress() returns a String value (a String representing the street address) and that you declare this method as public. Here's how another class may call getStreetAddress():

```
Invoice anInvoice = new Invoice();
...
String mailingAddress = anInvoice.getStreetAddress();
mailingAddress += anInvoice.getCity();
mailingAddress += anInvoice.getState();
```

Setters

Defining a setter accessor method lets programmers set property values safely. Here's an example definition of a setter named setStreetAddress():

```
public void setStreetAddress(String incomingAddress) {
    if incomingAddress != "" {
        theStreetAddress = incomingAddress;
    }
}
```

What's in a name?

Technically, you can call your accessor methods whatever you like; your best bet, however, is to follow these conventions: First, change the first character of the property name to uppercase. Then, for getter names, add **get** to the front; for setter names, add **set** to the front. The following examples illustrate these conventions:

Property Name	Getter Name	Setter Name
phoneNumber	getPhoneNumber()	setPhoneNumber()
displayWidth	getDisplayWidth()	setDisplayWidth()
priceInPounds	getPriceInPounds()	setPriceInPounds()

Following these conventions not only makes working with and understanding your classes easier for other people, but also enables something called *reflection*, which is an automatic process that developers can use to figure out the names of your beans' properties and methods. See Chapter 11 for details on the part that naming conventions play in bean reflection in particular and introspection in general.

In this example, the value for the streetAddress property is changed to the incoming address only if the incoming address isn't null (if incomingAddress !=). In real life, you can put any logic in your setters that you think is appropriate to make sure that programmers don't set assign a completely invalid value to a property.

Garden-variety methods

You're not limited to constructors and accessor methods if you create your own classes; they're just two special types of methods you can use. You can define as many additional methods as you need. Just keep in mind the following two points:

- Name your methods with verb phrases that describe the behavior each method is responsible for performing (for example, getPhoneNumber() and setDisplayWidth()).

- Declare methods as private if you want to hide them from other programmers (that is, if you mean to call them only from inside the class you're defining and you don't want anyone else to have access to them).

Events

Where programmers are concerned, few subjects seem as muddled and confusing as *event handling*. Heretic that I am, I suggest that you bypass the convoluted diagrams you run across from time to time that try to define events as some Big Deal that regular humans can never understand. Why? Because events *aren't* a big deal — at least not conceptually. Sure, events involve a few method calls, but working with events sure ain't rocket science, as you soon see!

To a bean, an *event* is any significant occurrence. The event may be a mouse movement; it may be a property value that suddenly changes. An event can be anything you want it to be! The following sections describe the mechanics of how events work.

Using existing events

The sections "Bound (and Determined) Properties" and "Constrained Properties," both located previously in this chapter, describe how to use two kinds of event that already exist — the property change event and the vetoable change event. Following is a brief generalization of what those two sections describe in detail. (Chapter 12 explores the subject of event handling in even greater detail.)

Any given event-handling situation involves at least the following two players:

- ✔ The bean that's the source of the event
- ✔ The bean or beans that care about that event and want to hear about it (These beans are the *event listeners*, or *target listeners*.)

First off, the source bean needs to provide the following two things:

- ✔ A method call to fire off an event notification as soon as the event occurs, which describes the event in detail
- ✔ Declarations for a pair of methods, `addWhateverEventListener()` and `removeWhateverEventListener()`, that other beans can call to get on (and off) the event notification list

Second, every bean that wants to listen needs to perform the following two actions:

- ✔ Call the source bean's `addWhateverEventListener()` method to register its interest.
- ✔ Declare a method to perform some action after receiving the event from the source bean.

An event to remember

Here's a real-life example of an event: The source bean, Sarah, was playing in the woods. Specifically, she climbed to the top of a fir tree and was busily engaged in popping pitch pockets (those irresistible bumps on fir tree bark that spurt a glorious-smelling, honey-colored sap after you pierce them with a pint-sized thumbnail).

Now, Sarah's Dad, the listener bean, had previously registered his interest in Sarah. (Technically, he was interested in anything dangerous that befell Sarah.) And he had also defined an action to perform if and when he received a "danger" event. So after a gigantic glob of pitch sailed into Sarah's eye, stinging furiously and causing her to shriek from the top of her lungs, he promptly received an event notification. (The notice sounded something like "Aiiyee!! Daddy!!!")

Sarah's Dad immediately performed his response method ("rush Sarah to the doctor"), and they all lived happily ever after. True story.

Creating new events

To understand how to create and handle your own unique events, all you need to do is take a look at how the folks at JavaSoft implemented the property change event. Specifically, you need to define the following items:

- ✔ A new event support class (much like `PropertyChangeSupport`)
- ✔ A new type of event object (à la `PropertyChangeEvent`)
- ✔ A new type of event listener (such as `PropertyChangeListener`)
- ✔ A pair of registration/cancellation methods (Remember `addPropertyChangeListener()` and `removePropertyChangeListener()` from earlier in this chapter?)

Chapter 12 explains event handling in far more detail than discussed here. That chapter contains listings of all the files mentioned in this chapter, as well as detailed descriptions of all the APIs related to event handling.

Part II
Beans 101: Creating and Using Beans

The 5th Wave   By Rich Tennant

"They're fruit flies, Rog. For gosh sake, how many applets have you written today?!"

In this part . . .

Get ready to grab the bull by the horns! This part takes you step-by-step through the process of creating and using simple beans. Here you see how to install the necessary toolkits, create and compile JavaBeans source code files, and test your newly created bean. By the time you finish this part, you have a solid understanding of bean development mechanics, from soup to nuts.

Chapter 4

Getting Started I: Creating a Bean

*I*n this chapter, you find instructions for finding and installing the tools you need to create JavaBeans — specifically, instructions on the Java Developers Kit and the JavaBeans Development Kit —, along with sensible descriptions of each of these kits, including how each fits into the overall bean-building process. You become acquainted with the bean-testing utility (and sample beans) that come as part of the JavaBeans Development Kit, and then — hold onto your hats! — you create your very first JavaBean from scratch. (Okay, not *exactly* from scratch; beans are objects, after all, so you also find out how to apply a marvelous thing called *inheritance* to keep the amount of actual code you must write to the barest of minimums.)

The Basics

If you're like me, you like getting the nuts and bolts of a new subject securely under your belt before going off to study the finer points. If so, look no farther than this chapter!

Installing the Java Developers Kit (JDK 1.1)

The first thing you want to do is download a copy of the *Java Developers Kit*, or *JDK*. At the time of this writing, the only version that supports bean development directly is the JDK 1.1, which you find either on this book's companion CD or at the following URL:

```
http://www.javasoft.com/products/JDK/1.1
```

Downloading the JDK from the Java Web site is fairly straightforward. All you need to do is choose the correct version for your platform (Windows 95/NT or Solaris/SPARC), click the Download button on the Web page, and wait for cybernature to take its course. A separate link, README, contains step-by-step instructions for unpacking the downloaded file and configuring your brand new Java development environment.

Make sure that you follow the configuration instructions regarding the *path* and *classpath* environment variables carefully. Your operating system looks at the directories listed in the *path* to find executable files; if you don't have the directory that contains the Java executables listed in your *path* statement, your computer can't find them. Likewise, Java utilities look in the directories listed in *classpath* to find all the .class files they need, so getting your *classpath* statement set correctly is important.

Getting hold of the Java runtime

The JDK comes complete with a Java interpreter (also known as the *Java runtime environment*) that you can use to run beans and bean applications. In addition, however, you probably want to get hold of a Java-enabled Web browser, such as Netscape Navigator or Microsoft's Internet Explorer. As you probably know, you need a Java-enabled Web browser if you want to integrate JavaBeans into Web pages. To get familiar with Netscape Navigator, load this page:

```
http://home.netscape.com/comprod/products/navigator/ver-
         sion_3.0/index.html
```

If Internet Explorer is more to your liking, scope out the following URL:

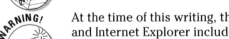

```
http://www.microsoft.com/ie/default.asp
```

At the time of this writing, the latest versions of both Netscape Navigator and Internet Explorer include support for the JDK 1.02, which doesn't (unfortunately) contain support for JavaBeans (the first version of the JDK that includes JavaBeans support is version 1.1). By the time you read this book, there's a good chance that both of these popular Web browsers will have upgraded to JDK 1.1 (and hence JavaBeans) support. If that's not the case, you can make do with the Java runtime that's bundled with the JDK itself to exercise your beans and bean-based applications.

Getting acquainted with the Java utilities

The JDK comes with a slew of command line utilities that fall into the following two basic categories:

✔ Utilities that you need to use in a particular order to transform a plain text file into an executable bean (This progression of steps is called the *build* process.)

✔ Utilities that aren't strictly essential but that can serve as an invaluable part of the build process (for example, a debugging utility)

Beans don't spring into being fully formed, like Aphrodite from Zeus's head in Greek mythology; you must follow a certain set of steps to turn bean source code into an executable bean. Developers refer to these steps collectively as the *build process*. To get an overview of how the build process works, take a look at Figure 4-1. The following sections explain separately each of the utilities shown in the figure.

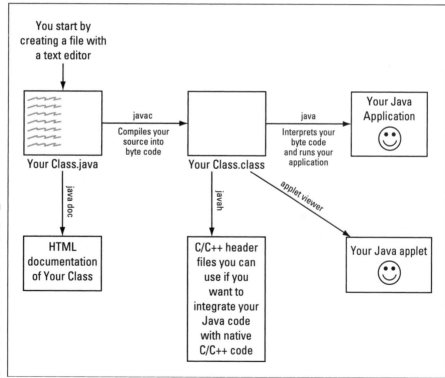

Figure 4-1: An overview of the JavaBeans build process, from source code to executable file.

The utilities in the JDK are strictly bottom-of-the-food-chain tools. That is, technically, they're all you need to create Java applets and applications, but you may want to investigate more-sophisticated ways of using the tools. Some text editors, such as WinEdit, for example, enable you to start the Java compiler simply by clicking a menu option instead of needing to switch from the editor to a command line and type **javac YourCoolClass.java**. Even more exciting are the integrated development environments, or *IDEs*, that I describe in Chapter 6. Used with the basic tools that I describe in the following sections, the IDEs automate the entire build process even more!

The compiler: javac

The name of the Java compiler is *javac*. You feed your .java source file to javac, and javac spits out compiled byte code — a file with the same prefix as the .java file you gave the compiler but with a new extension: .class. As an example, if you were to invoke the following line of code (and had a file called YourClass.java on your machine), the result would be one of two things: a compiled file, YourClass.class, or a compiler error.

```
javac YourClass.java
```

To find out what options you can specify for any utility, type the name of the utility on the command line all by itself and press Enter. You can, for example, type the following line:

```
C:\jdk-1.1\java\JavaBeansForDummies>javac
```

This line generates the following helpful tidbits:

```
use: javac [-g][-O][-debug][-depend][-nowarn][-verbose][-
          classpath path][-nowrite][-d dir][-J<runtime
          flag>] file.java...
```

The tester: appletviewer

The *appletviewer* utility is a handy tool for testing Java applets. Instead of invoking your favorite Java-enabled Web browser and then loading the .html file that embeds an applet, all you need to do to view an applet in the appletviewer utility is use the following line of code:

```
appletviewer YourTestPage.html
```

The interpreter: java

The Java interpreter is known, appropriately enough, as *java*, although many developers affectionately refer to the interpreter as the *Java runtime*. (Well, technically, the Java runtime includes just a little bit more than the Java interpreter but this definition comes close enough for government work, as the ubiquitous *they* say.) If you create a Java application (as opposed to an applet), you can test your work directly by typing something similar to the following at a command prompt:

```
java YourClass
```

You can specify more than a dozen different options when you run the Java interpreter. One of the handier options, −prof (*prof* stands for *profiler*), causes the interpreter to automatically generate a file called java.prof that contains a bunch of information on exactly what was going through the interpreter's head as it interpreted the file. Here's how you specify the profiler option:

```
java −prof YourClass
```

The documenter: javadoc

After you get used to the *javadoc* utility, you may wonder how you ever lived without it. Javadoc takes the drudgery out of writing documentation by doing the job for you. (Applause, applause!) Here's how the utility works: javadoc figures out the names of your class and all its properties, and methods. Then it figures out the relationships between these items (which methods accept which properties, from which class your class derives, and so on).

Plus, whenever you add a comment to your source file surrounded by the special symbols /** and */, as shown in the following example, javadoc automatically incorporates your comment into the documentation, too:

```
/** I want this comment to appear in the automatic
           documentation */
```

You can still use regular Java comments (statements surrounded by /* */ or prefaced by //) to comment your code, as shown in the following examples; these comments just don't appear in the automatically generated documentation.

```
/* This is a plain old comment; it doesn t appear in the
          automatically generated documentation. */

// Neither does this one.
```

Then after you finish with your code and want to document it, all you need to do is this:

```
javadoc YourClass.java
```

Almost instantly, javadoc creates a handful of .html files (AllNames.html, packages.html, tree.html, and YourClass.html) containing a blow-by-blow analysis of your classes, properties, methods, and so on — and in hypertext format at that! Nifty, huh?

For example, take a look Figure 4-2, which shows partial documentation for a class called FirstJavaApplet. As you can see, Figure 4-2 shows the automatically-generated file FirstJavaApplet.html as it looks loaded into Netscape Navigator. (The content of the HTML file is the same no matter what Web browser you use to view it.)

The packager: JAR

Because beans (as all Java programs) are intended for distribution across the Internet, the Java architects knew that they needed to figure out a way to package related files together so that they could pass one file — rather than a lot of individual files — around from machine to machine. The scheme they came up with is called *JAR*, which stands for *Java ARchive*, and it saves users a lot of download time.

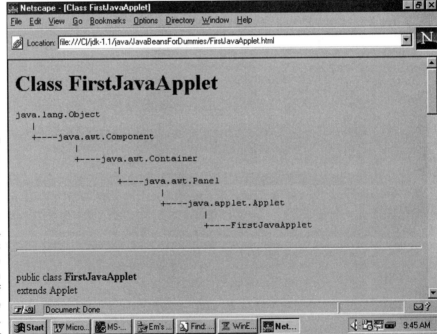

Figure 4-2:
Source code documentation in HTML format is yours in the blink of an eye if you use javadoc.

Similar to the familiar Zip compression utility, the jar utility enables you to accomplish the following tasks:

- Compress files individually.
- Group the compressed files together into a single file.

Basically, a JAR file is nothing more than a zip file with a little extra information tacked on. This extra information is called *manifest* information (similar to that of the cargo manifest on a shipment), and it gives programmers the opportunity to specify things about the zipped-up portion, such as whether or not a contained file is a bean or a resource file, the version number of each file, and similar information.

In addition to .class files, you want to package up in the same JAR file anything else a user needs on hand to run your bean-based application. Depending on how fancy you get, this package may include image files, sound files, or other resources.

You can see the jar utility in action in the section "Sticking your compiled bean in a JAR," later in this chapter; for now, here's the syntax you need to follow to run the jar utility from a command line prompt:

```
jar <some options> <name of jar file to create> <name of
              manifest file> <name of class>
```

The ink on the JAR manifest specification is barely dry. For all the latest, including a description of all the JAR options and lots of examples, check out the .html file /beans/doc/jar.html#manifest, located on this book's companion CD.

The customizer: javah

The hardy souls among you who like a challenge may be interested in knowing that you can integrate Java code with native C code. That is, you can have your Java code make a call to a function written in C to perform some low-level task that Java itself can't handle (which is most likely something that needs to be ultra-speedy or access platform-specific information). Obviously, you must write the C function yourself; the *javah* utility, however, helps out by generating some files you need to use as part of your C program. The first invocation of the javah utility in the following examples generates a header file; the second generates a stubbed-out C file.

```
javah YourClass

javah -stubs YourClass
```

You may have noticed the dreaded allusion to "platform-specific information" in the preceding paragraph. True, making calls to any other language from a Java program immediately breaks one of Java's strengths — the "write once, run anywhere" promise of true cross-platform capability. And as a rule of thumb, you want to avoid such calls like the plague. You do, however, have a couple valid reasons for using such calls, as the following paragraphs describe:

- If you're writing a Java virtual machine. (I know, fat chance, huh?)

- If you're pushing the envelope, so to speak — for example, your boss wants you to create a Java program that does *X*; the Java API that supports *X* isn't due out for three months; and you're bucking for a promotion.

The reporter: javap

Unlike the other utilities in the JDK, *javap* is more useful if you apply the utility to *other* people's Java code rather than to your own. Why? Because its job in life is to examine a compiled .class file and identify any variables or methods that you can access in that file. You already know which variables and methods *you* declared public; you may not know the same for a compiled Java file that your friend Fred sent to you. To surprise Fred and figure it out, use the following syntax:

```
javap SomebodyElsesClass
```

Batteries not included: the make utility

A *make* utility is an indispensable tool for creating real-life applications. Basically, what the make utility does is to organize the bits and pieces of the build process so that you don't need to specify stuff from scratch each time. Suppose that every time you rebuild an application, you want to clear out all the old generated files before you begin so that you're certain what the compiler produces each time is fresh and clean. To accomplish this task by hand, you need to go to the correct directory, delete the appropriate generated file(s), and then start the build process.

If you use a make utility, however, you can configure an intermediate file (called a *makefile*) to do that kind of up-front task (and a lot more besides) for you automatically. Inexplicably, as I write this chapter, the make utility is not available either as part of the JDK or the BDK. (That's surprising because traditionally, compilers come complete with make utilities.)

Fortunately, you find a copy of a make utility for your platform on the CD that comes with this book. If you're developing on UNIX, you want to use the *gnumake* utility; if you're working on Windows, *nmake* is the make utility for you.

The debugger: jdb

If you're familiar with the nice, graphical debuggers that come with most popular C/C++ compilers, I'm afraid you may be in for a bit of a disappointment when you first lay eyes on the *jdb* Java debugging utility. The jdb debugging utility is the old-fashioned kind of debugger — the kind that, after you insert some special debug APIs in your source code and invoke the debugger from the command line, requires you to type in cryptic keywords. Your reward? You get to decipher output that looks as though it were designed for somebody working on the space shuttle program.

Still, jdb is better than nothing (although, as you find out in Chapter 6, a few more alternatives to jdb than "nothing" already are available). For instructions and a brief tutorial covering the setup and use of jdb, visit one of the following URLs:

```
http://java.sun.com/products/JDK/1.1/docs/tooldocs/win32/
        jdb.html
```

```
http://java.sun.com/products/JDK/1.1/docs/tooldocs/solaris/
        jdb.html
```

Installing the JavaBeans Development Kit (BDK 1.0)

Even though the JavaBeans implementation is fully integrated into JDK version 1.1, at the time of this writing, you really need to install both the JDK *and* the BDK if you want to develop beans. (The BDK contains valuable example beans and a really useful testing utility, called the BeanBox.) After you install the JDK 1.1, you can find a copy of the BDK 1.0 both on the companion CD and at the following Web site:

```
http://splash.javasoft.com/beans/
```

After you download and install the BDK, which is refreshingly foolproof, load the README.HTML Web page you find in the /beans subdirectory. (If you install the BDK into your c:\bdk directory, for example, you find the README.HTML in c:\bdk\beans). Unlike some README files, this one really *is* worth reading! The file is your complete guide to the entire contents of the BDK, presented in a really well-organized hypertext format.

Getting acquainted with the BeanBox

A great way to get comfortable with how beans look and what they can do is to take a look at the bean-testing utility called the *BeanBox*, which comes in the BDK, and try out some of the sample beans that the kit provides. The BeanBox is an example of a container application that's designed specifically to give you a preview of the kinds of application-development tools you may see (or write!) soon.

The BDK, included on the companion CD, contains a handy overview of the BeanBox and how it works. Load `/bdk/doc/beanbox.html` and check it out!

Assuming that you install the BDK in your c:\bdk directory, here's the command you use to run the BeanBox:

```
C:\bdk\beanbox>run
```

As you can see in Figure 4-3, after the BeanBox utility springs more or less instantly to life, it displays the following three separate elements:

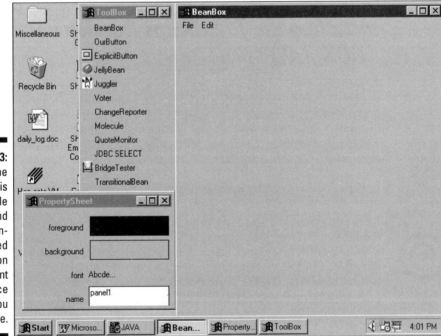

Figure 4-3: The BeanBox is an example of the kind of bean-based application development interface that you can create.

✔ The **BeanBox** proper, which isitself made up of two parts: a composition window, and a bean container bean onto which you can drop other beans

✔ A **ToolBox**, which is a palette containing all the available sample beans

✔ A **PropertySheet** window, which always displays the customizable attributes of whichever bean has *focus* at any given time (A bean gains focus when you click on it and loses focus when you click somewhere else.)

If you select View⇨Disable Design Mode from the BeanBox menu, the ToolBox and PropertySheet windows will disappear. Not to worry, though; if you want to bring them back, just select View⇨Enable Design Mode from the BeanBox menu.

If you get a chance, take a few minutes to play around with the BeanBox. Here are a few things that you may want to try:

✔ Click one of the beans in the ToolBox, position your mouse somewhere on the BeanBox, and then click again to drop the bean onto the BeanBox container bean.

✔ Select the newly added bean by clicking it and then notice how the PropertySheet display changes.

✔ Click one of the property values in the PropertySheet and customize the bean by specifying values for the various blanks that appear.

✔ Add some more beans to the fray; move them around, resize them, cut them, and paste them back onto the BeanBox bean again.

✔ Try out some of the BeanBox menu items such as File⇨Save, Edit⇨Report, or View⇨Disable Design Mode.

At the time of this writing, running the BeanBox utility messes up your *classpath* variable — which means that any bean utility you run after BeanBox is likely to fail. If you're developing on a Windows platform, a good idea is to close your MS-DOS session window and start up a new one after you finish running the BeanBox. (Starting up a fresh MS-DOS window resets your *classpath* variable to the way it's supposed to look — the way it appears in your AUTOEXEC.BAT file.)

Creating Your First Bean

I'm assuming that on your very first attempt at bean development, you merely want to dip your toes in the bean juice instead of just diving in face-first — so this section is short, sweet, and to the point. You see how to inherit bean properties, declare properties and methods, and as a by-product, you also become intimately familiar with the build process, starting from the first line of Java code and ending up at a fully tested, correctly packaged bean.

Reading is a great way to learn, but nothing quite hammers a concept home as good old-fashioned trial-and-error. If you want, feel free to follow along with the text and create your own bean as you read through this section.

Creating a bean source file

First off, you need to create a JavaBean source file. (Any old text editor you have lying around is sufficient for the job.)

If you don't have access to a text editor, you can get a trial copy of WinEdit from this book's companion CD.

Naming your baby bean

You need to heed only the following three rules in naming your bean source file:

- ✔ The file prefix must be the same (both in spelling and capitalization) as the name of the public class you define in your source. (You get only one public class per source file.) If the name of your class is `FlavoredJellyBean`, for example, you must name your file FlavoredJellyBean.java.

- ✔ The file extension must be .java.

- ✔ If you intend to place the class into a package, the class's position in its package must mirror the source code file's position in your directory hierarchy.

  If, for example, you put a statement at the top of the FlavoredJellyBean.java file that reads `package my.demo.test`, you need to make sure that you place the FlavoredJellyBean.java file in the *directory_you_intend_to_compile_from*/my/demo/test directory.

  (The example in this section doesn't use the package statement, so you can put your source file wherever you want.)

The good stuff: Bean source code

The upcoming code listing contains the source code for your very first bean. Take a look at this example and notice the comments. I cover bean-related Java syntax in detail in Chapter 7; for now, just try to get a feel for how bean source appears.

You can find the source code in Listing 4-1 on the companion CD that comes with this book. The name of the file is FlavoredJellyBean.java.

Here is the source code for FlavoredJellyBean.java, which inherits from an existing bean called JellyBean.

```
import java.awt.*;
import java.beans.*;
import sunw.demo.jelly.*;

public class FlavoredJellyBean extends JellyBean {

/** The FlavoredJellyBean class inherits all of
    JellyBean s properties and methods and then adds
    one property (flavor) and two accessor methods */

    public String getFlavor() { // getter

    /** getFlavor() is a very simple  get
        accessor method. */
        return flavor;
    }

    public void setFlavor(String newFlavor) { // setter

    /** In a real-life program, there would probably be
        some checking going on here to make sure someone
        doesn t try to set the flavor to  123  or
        something equally silly. */

        flavor = newFlavor;
    }

    private String flavor =  licorice ;//private property

}
```

See how the FlavoredJellyBean file inherits from JellyBean? The only difference between the two is that FlavoredJellyBean contains one more property (called `flavor`) and two more methods (`getFlavor()` and `setFlavor()`) than JellyBean does.

Compiling your bean

A common first-time compiler error message is Package <some package> not found in import. If you get this error message, check the value for your classpath environment variable. (The quickest way to do so in Windows is to type **echo %CLASSPATH%** at a command line prompt.) As you can see in the following formula, one of the directories in the classpath — plus one of the import statements in your source file — needs to add up to the fully qualified filename of the class you're trying to import; otherwise, you get this error every time!

classpath entry + the import statement in your file = full directory name

c:\bdk\demo + \sunw\demo\jelly = c:\bdk\demo\sunw\demo\jelly

Suppose that you're trying to import the package sunw.demo.jelly. Because Java class names are also directory names, what you're actually telling the Java compiler to do is to look for classes in the directory /sunw/demo/jelly. Depending on how you installed the BDK, this directory might be anywhere on your machine, so you need to make sure that your classpath statement provides the other half of the equation. On my machine, for example, the /sunw/demo/jelly directory is located at **c:/bdk/demo**/sunw/demo/jelly. My classpath variable, therefore, must include the directory c:/bdk/demo/.

After the FlavoredJellyBean.java source code file actually exists, you can run the compiler against it. Type the following at the command line to compile FlavoredJellyBean.java:

```
javac FlavoredJellyBean.java
```

The JDK release 1.1 contains lots of new improvements over the preceding releases. Due to these improvements, however, some methods that used to work in the earlier releases don't (or soon won't) work in release 1.1. Fortunately, the Java compiler catches any calls your bean makes, directly or indirectly, to these old-fashioned, soon-to-be-obsolete methods (called *deprecated methods*) and alerts you so that you can change them to the new-and-improved way of doing things.

For example, here's what you might see when you try to compile FlavoredJellyBean.java:

```
javac FlavoredJellyBean.java
    Note: FlavoredJellyBean.java uses a deprecated API.
    Recompile with -deprecation for details.
    1 warning
```

Unfortunately, at the time of this writing, some of the sample beans that shipped with the BDK include calls to deprecated methods, so there's not a lot you can do to keep the warning message you see above from appearing — short of rewriting the sample code. If you're curious, though, check out the following URL; it contains a list of all the deprecated methods and tips for upgrading Java source from pre-JDK 1.1 to post-JDK 1.1.

```
http://www.javasoft.com/products/jdk/1.1/docs/guide/awt/
                    HowToUpgrade.html
```

Some text editors enable you to run the Java compiler from inside an editing session, which can really cut down on the time you need to hop from editing a file to compiling the file. You can choose WinEdit⇨Project⇨Compile from the menu bar after you save your .java file, for example, and it runs javac for you automatically (after you specify javac as the Project⇨Configure⇨Compile command).

If the compiler doesn't find any coding errors, it generates the file FlavoredJellyBean.class.

One of the special comment statements (/ ** * /) generated the text below the getFlavor() method

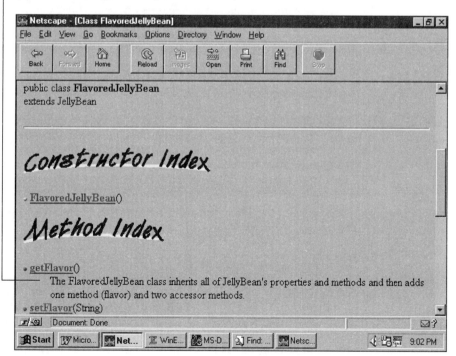

Figure 4-4:
This screen shows what one of the generated files, Flavored Jelly Bean.html, looks like.

Writing up your bean

With a utility such as javadoc, you really have no reason not to create good-looking documentation for every bean you create! Here's how:

```
javadoc FlavoredJellyBean.java
```

You can see the result of the preceding command directive in Figure 4-4, which shows one of the automatically generated documentation files.

Sticking your compiled bean in a JAR

The standard format for flinging beans around the Web isn't the compiled format; instead, you use the *JAR* format. The JAR format enables you to bundle related beans (beans that are already compiled, that is) and resource files together and then squish that bundle into the smallest possible volume.

In order to stick a bean into a JAR, you first need to create a file called a *manifest* file. The following example shows you what a bare-bones manifest file should look like. The name of the manifest file is the name of the class followed by a .mf (for "manifest") extension, so in this example, the name of the file is FlavoredJellyBean.mf.

```
Manifest-Version: 1.0
Name: FlavoredJellyBean.class
Java-Bean: True
```

The following command-line directive is a typical invocation of the jar utility. The cfm options tell the jar utility to create a new JAR file named flavored.jar and put it in the /jars folder, using the information it finds in the manifest file named FlavoredJellyBean.mf.

```
jar cfm jars\flavored.jar FlavoredJellyBean.mf
FlavoredJellyBean.class
```

Putting your bean to the test

After you safely tuck away your compiled bean in a JAR, you're ready to test the bean out! The quickest way to take a bean for a test drive is to add your bean to the BeanBox palette.

To do so, first move the JAR file for the bean that you want to test into the official /jar directory, like this:

```
copy FlavoredJellyBean.jar c:/bdk/jars
```

Then, in the /bdk/beanbox directory, type the following command if you're developing in Windows:

nmake run

If you're developing in UNIX, use the following command:

gnumake run

Voilà! The preceding command directive adds your new bean to the ToolBox palette and then automatically runs the BeanBox utility. You should see something similar to what appears in Figure 4-5: FlavoredJellyBean, in all its glory! (See "FlavoredJellyBean" at the bottom of the Toolbox window? That means you can drag an instance of `FlavoredJellyBean` onto the `BeanBox` and play around with it.)

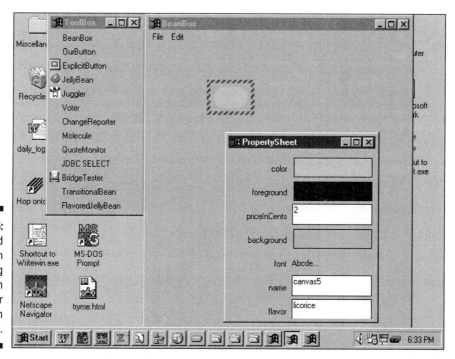

Figure 4-5:
Flavored
JellyBean
is playing
nicely with
all the other
little bean
examples.

Chapter 5

Getting Started II: Using an Existing Bean

. . . .

. . . .

Chapter 4 is devoted to describing how to create a bean, but that's only half the bean story. The other half is figuring out how to combine beans to create nifty bean-based applications. After all, beans were designed to be reused, right? This chapter shows you how to go about doing just that — reusing premade beans as building blocks to create your own custom applications.

Here, Beanie, Beanie, Beanie!

So where can you go to beg, borrow, steal, rent, or (if everything else fails) lay out hard cold cash for beans to use in your applications? Well, as you know, the beans API is barely out of beta as of the time of this writing. Yes, you're well ahead of the curve on this one! And that's good news — and bad news. The good news is that after you finish reading *JavaBeans For Dummies*, you know more about beans than anybody else on your cyberblock. The bad news is that, as I write, no Web repositories chock-full of ready-made beans currently exist.

By the time you read this book, however, my crystal ball tells me that beans o'plenty should be floating around the Web (just as scores of Java applets and applications are available for download today). Listed in the following paragraphs are a couple of premiere Java-resource-clearing-house-type Web sites that should be among the first to feature beans on their menus.

EarthWeb's Gamelan site is the official directory of all things Java. Check it out at the following URL:

```
http://www.gamelan.com/pages/Gamelan.programming.html
```

Jaze, the Java e-zine from PartBank, offers an ever-expanding list of Java applets and applications at the following address:

```
http://www.partbank.com/jaze/
```

Fortunately, as you can see in Table 5-1, the Bean Developer Kit contains more than a dozen ready-made beans on which you can cut your teeth — sample beans that you can use as-is or as a starting point for your own beans. In the following sections, you see how to customize each of these beans, connect the beans via events to form a mini-application, and then package the whole thing up and send the package to your mom for her birthday.

Table 5-1	Sample Beans in the JavaBean Developer Kit
Name of Bean	*Description*
BeanBox	You can drop other beans onto this container bean.
BridgeTester	Test different data types for properties by using this bean.
ChangeReporter	Use this bean to test bound properties.
EventMonitor	This bean enables you to monitor event notification as a source bean fires 'em off.
ExplicitButton	This bean is nothing more than a souped-up push button.
JDBC SELECT	You need JDBC on your machine to use this database-access bean.
JellyBean	A simple, basic bean that appears as an oval jelly-beanlike shape.
Juggler	An animation bean. (Guess what the Juggler juggles? Beans!)
Molecule	This 3-D bean enables you to manipulate a 3-D image of a molecule.
OurButton	This basic push button bean shows you how to derive beans from AWT components. (Chapter 7 contains additional information on AWT components.)
Orange Button	Because this (otherwise unremarkable) orange button implements the `serializable` interface, check it out to see an example of how to make your own beans persistent.

Name of Bean	Description
QuoteMonitor	A remote access bean, the QuoteMonitor uses something called the *Java RMI* to display a stream of pretend stock quotes. (Check out Chapter 7 for details on the RMI.)
SorterBean	This bean, which graphically displays a sorting algorithm after you click it, is also a plain old applet.
TickTock	Take a look at the TickTock bean to see how to create a very (very!) simple invisible bean.
TransitionalBean	This dead-simple bean is backward-compatible with JDK 1.0.2., so that you can use it with Version 3.0 of both Netscape Navigator and Microsoft Internet Explorer.
Voter	Use this bean to process vetoable change requests. (See Chapter 3, for more information about vetoable change requests.)

17-bean salad

The BeanBox utility isn't magic. Quite the contrary; it's a bean-based application. As you may expect, you have a BeanBox bean, a ToolBox bean, and a PropertySheet bean. In addition to these beans, however, the developers added to the utility a bunch of other beans that, together, form the complete BeanBox utility. The following table contains a complete listing.

Bean name	Description
BeanBox	This bean is a container bean so that you can drop other beans onto it.
BeanBoxFrame	This bean is, in essence, the BeanBox utility. You get only one of these, no matter how many beans (including BeanBox beans) you load. This bean is an overall manager that handles the BeanBox menu and keeps track of which bean has the focus (that is, which bean a user most recently selected with a mouse click) at any given time.
CustomizerDialog	This bean is responsible for the consistent look of all the customizer dialogs.
EditedAdaptor	The PropertySheet bean uses this bean to hook up the property editors and their corresponding beans.
ErrorDialog	Just what you'd think — a bean that presents consistent (but customized) pop-up error messages to the user. (Try starting the QuoteMonitor without first opening a mock quote server and you see what I mean.)

(continued)

(continued)

EventTargetDialog	A bean that walks BeanBox users through the process of hooking up an event on a bean source to a method on a bean target.
HookupManager	This bean generates files that start with ___Hookup and places them in the \beanbox\tmp directory. These generated Java source files help implement events.
PropertyCanvas	This bean displays the little rectangle around property values (and enables you to change the property values).
PropertyDialog	The bean responsible for displaying properties.
PropertyHookup	This bean manages the connections between bound properties and the beans interested in those properties.
PropertyNameDialog	This bean displays the dialog boxes that enable you to customize properties. (You can see the bean if you choose Edit⇨Bind Property from the BeanBox menu bar.)
PropertySelector	This bean is the property editor bean for a choice field.
PropertySheet	This bean manages the PropertySheet window that you see.
PropertyText	The property editor bean for a text field.
ToolBox	This bean manages the ToolBox window that you see while you run the BeanBox utility.
Wrapper	The bean you use to surround a selected bean (a bean that has focus) with a nice black border.

Not only is the BeanBox utility a mini-application development tool that you can use to test your beans, but the classes that comprise the BeanBox (which you find in c:\bdk\beanbox\sun\beanbox) also are excellent examples themselves of how to go about performing all kinds of useful tasks — handle menus, save to disk, lay out graphics, cut/copy/paste, and so on.

One Size Rarely Fits All

JavaBeans components were designed to be customizable so that you can reuse them in lots of different applications. The ExplicitButton bean that comes in the BDK, for example, has a default label marked *press*. Well, who in the heck wants to put a button marked *press* in an application? I mean, okay, the label says it all, I guess, but what if you decide to add two buttons to your application — and the labels on both read *press?* Wouldn't that look a little silly? Clearly this is a job for customization!

Customizing with the BeanBox utility

The BeanBox utility makes customizing beans a snap. All you need to do is select the bean you're interested in customizing, and the PropertySheet window associated with that bean appears. Click the property you want to customize (the property value, not the property name — for example, select the values press or Abcde, not the property names label or font); make the change — either by typing over the old information or following the instructions in the property editor that appears — and bingo! That's all you need to do. Your change takes place immediately. Check out Figure 5-1 for a candid before-and-after shot of the ExplicitButton bean.

To save your changes, choose File⇨Save from the BeanBox menu bar and give your new, improved, better-tasting bean any file name that you want. The next time you run the BeanBox, you can retrieve your saved file (which represents a snapshot of how the BeanBox and the ExplicitButton looked at the time you saved them) by choosing File⇨Load from the BeanBox menu bar.

If you load the file and don't see your modified bean after a minute or so, try clicking at random in the BeanBox — that should do the trick.

How the BeanBox supports customization

Just clicking a few buttons and having stuff happen is all well and good (and is my favorite part of programming, actually), but understanding *why* the stuff happens is even better. And in the case of bean development, your understanding the behind-the-scenes machinations that the BeanBox is going through is essential. Why? Because, at present, the BeanBox isn't expected to develop into a full-fledged development environment — or even to continue to exist, for that matter. (Luckily, Chapter 6 explores several tools that *are* designed as full-fledged development environments.) The bad news is that you can't depend on the BeanBox for all your development needs. You *can* depend on your ability to re-create the function of the BeanBox, however, after you understand how beans work — which is exactly what this section is all about.

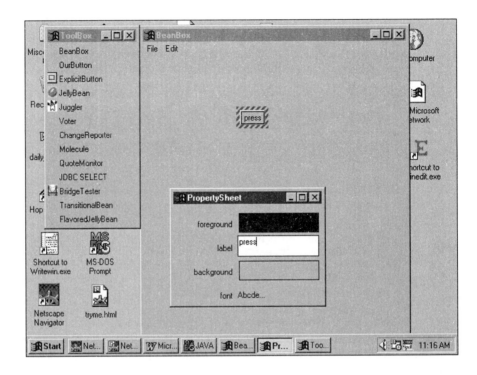

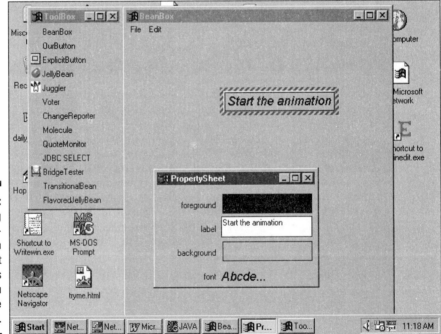

Figure 5-1:
Customizing
a push-
button bean
label's font
and text is
easy if you
use the
BeanBox.

As you customize the bean

While you're busy changing the text and font associated with the ExplicitButton's label, the BeanBox is busy, too. Here's what the utility does:

✔ The BeanBox displays a property editor (PropertyText) that presents you with the opportunity to change the label's attributes based on the ExplicitButtonBeanInfo class. (You see an example of four different property editors in Figure 5-2: the property editors associated with the foreground, the label, the background, and the font properties.)

✔ Alerted by events associated with the property editor, the BeanBox calls the appropriate setter accessor methods on ExplicitButton (setForeground(), setLabel(), setBackground(), or setFont(), depending on which property you're customizing) and then displays the new property values.

As you save the bean

After you choose File⇨Save, the BeanBox creates a file on your hard disk with the name you provide by implementing the java.io.Serializable API. (You find out more about this API in Chapter 13.) Although you can name this file anything you want (and probably did), the convention is to create a file with the .ser suffix, which is short for *serialization* — for example, MyApplication.ser.

The saved, or *pickled*, file (and I'm not making this one up — *pickled* is a real term!) contains all the beans in the BeanBox utility at the moment you click File⇨Save, which in this case includes the following beans:

✔ The BeanBox bean (the BeanBox bean comes up by default every time you run the BeanBox utility so that you have a place to drop other beans).

✔ The ExplicitButton bean that you customize.

As you resurrect the bean

After you choose File⇨Load from the BeanBox utility menu to reload your saved file, the BeanBox utility opens the specified file (which contains an example of the BeanBox bean as well as the modified example of ExplicitButton), deserializes the beans, and reconstitutes them.

Cooking Up a Pot of Beans

Earlier sections of this chapter all concern individual beans. In this section, you find out how to connect beans together to create a mini-application. Figure 5-2 shows what the completed application should look like.

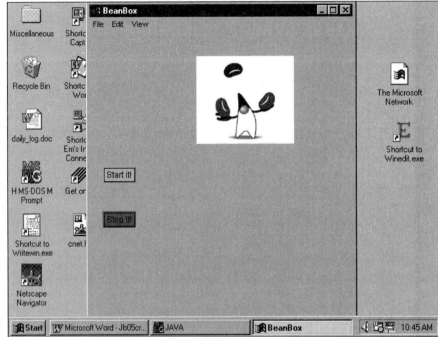

Figure 5-2:
This mini-
application
may not
wow 'em at
COMDEX,
but it does
demonstrate
the basics
of bean-
based
application
development!

Connecting beans with the BeanBox utility

The purpose of the mini-application described in this section is to provide
application users with an animation, a button to press if they want to start
the animation, and a button to press if they want to stop it. Simple? Absolutely! Follow these steps to create this mini-application (and take a look at
Chapter 4 if you need tips on completing one or more of the following steps):

1. **Run the BeanBox.**

2. **Drop an ExplicitButton bean onto the BeanBox and customize the
   ExplicitButton bean by changing its label from** *press* **to** *Start.*

3. **Drop another ExplicitButton bean onto the BeanBox and change this
   bean's label from** *press* **to** *Stop.*

4. **Drop a Juggler bean onto the Bean Box.**

5. **Switch the focus to the Start button by selecting (clicking) that
   button.**

6. **Choose Edit⇨Events⇨button push⇨actionPerformed from the
   BeanBox menu bar.**

7. **Drag the stretchy line that appears to the Juggler bean and click the Juggler bean once.**

8. **In the EventTargetDialog box that appears, select the** `startJuggling` **target method and choose OK.**

9. **Click the Stop button.**

10. **Choose Edit⇨Events⇨button push⇨actionPerformed from the BeanBox menu bar.**

    Your BeanBox resembles the one shown in Figure 5-3.

11. **Drag the stretchy line that appears to the Juggler bean and click the Juggler bean once.**

12. **In the EventTargetDialog box that appears, select the** `stopJuggling` **target method and click OK.**

Complete those 12 easy steps and you should have a tasty plate of beans on-screen in front of you. Click Start, and the animation should start; click Stop, and — you guessed it! — the animation should stop immediately. Look good? Then choose File⇨Save from the BeanBox menu bar and call your new application miniapp.ser.

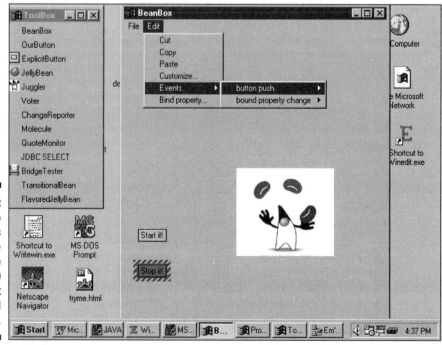

Figure 5-3:
Hooking up the buttons to the animation (Juggler) bean: Just point and click.

How the BeanBox supports bean connections

If you read Chapter 3, you see how an event that happens to one bean can trigger a method call on another bean.

In the case of the BeanBox, the adapter code to hook up an event on one side (clicking the push button) with a method call on the other side (starting and stopping the Juggler animation bean) is generated automatically if you follow the steps in the preceding section. The following code listing is an example of the automatically generated code on my machine after I hooked the Start push button up to the startJuggling method of the Juggler.

As you look through the code, notice the actionPerformed() method, which tells the Java runtime that a push button was clicked.

ActionListener extends the java.util. EventListener interface ⎯⎯

ActionEvent inherits indirectly from java.util. EventObject

```
// Automatically generated event hookup file.

package sun.beanbox;

public class ___Hookup_32b646a6 implements
            java.awt.event.ActionListener,
            java.io.Serializable {

  public void setTarget(sun.demo.juggler.Juggler t) {
    target = t;
  }

  public void actionPerformed(java.awt.event.ActionEvent
                              arg0){
    target.start(arg0);
  }

  private sun.demo.juggler.Juggler target;
}
```

The following list gives you a slow-motion instant replay of exactly how the Start button (the ExplicitBean button, which derives from the OurButton bean) connects to the Juggler bean. Keep in mind that the OurButton bean, as do all good beans that want to keep others apprised of the events that happen to them, defines an addActionListener method.

1. **You make the connection in the EventTargetDialog bean (by following Steps 5 through 8 in the preceding section).**

2. **The EventTargetDialog bean creates the adapter and then invokes the adapter's** setTarget() **method — sending the Juggler as a parameter which connects the adapter to the Juggler.**

3. **Then the EventTargetDialog invokes the** addListener() **method of OurButton on behalf of the Juggler (which connects the adapter to OurButton, completing the connection).**

Clicking the Start button invokes the OurButton's fireAction() method, which in turn, invokes the actionPerformed() method on the adapter — which itself in turn, calls the Juggler's start() method — and the Juggler animation begins. Tables 5-2 illustrates this process.

Table 5-2	The Cast of Characters!	
"Start" button (OurButton source)	*Adapter (__Hookup)*	*Juggler (target)*
defines addActionListener()	defines setTarget(Juggler)	
calls actionPerformed() → → →	defines actionPerformed{	
	target.start() → → →	start(ActionEvent){
	}	startJuggling();
		}

Canning Your Beans

In Chapter 4, you find out how you to put your beans in a JAR. In this section, the process is a little different: You must put the beans — the ExplicitButton, the BeanBox, and the Juggler — in a JAR file, all right, but you also must include the *pickle* and any automatically generated event-handling classes that you create as part of the customization process. (A pickle, as you may recall from the section "As you save the bean," earlier in this chapter, is what high-tech programmers with a propensity to snack a lot call an application's instance data. Think of a pickle as a snapshot of an application taken at a particular point in time — what choosing File⇨Save from the BeanBox menu generates.)

Unfortunately, at the time of this writing, the BeanBox menu doesn't contain a Box-This-Puppy-Up-and-Tie-a-Ribbon-around-It command, which enables you to hand someone an executable file that automatically kicks off the BeanBox utility preloaded with your bean-based application. So back to the old-fashioned command line you must go. The upcoming steps describe the procedure you need to use to package your custom application by hand.

Any bean-based application development tool worth its salt automates the process that I describe in the following steps. (Performing a bunch of repetitive steps such as these is the kind of thing that computers are much better at handling than are humans.) Check out Chapter 6 for the lowdown on several bean-based development tools.

To package your custom application by hand, however follow these steps:

1. **Figure out what beans you need to include in the JAR file.**

   In this example, you need to include the ExplicitButton, BeanBox, and Juggler beans, because those are the beans you combined to create your mini-application. You also need to include any other files neces-sary to instantiate these beans at runtime (for example, the series of .gif files that make up the juggling animation). No sweat! Java makes the process easy. All the files you need are in the /buttons, /beanbox, and /juggler directories, as follows:

   c:\bdk\demo\sunw\demo\buttons

   c:\bdk\beanbox\classes\sun\beanbox

   c:\bdk\demo\sunw\demo\juggler

2. **Figure out what events you need to include.**

   Take a look at the c:\bdk\beanbox\tmp\sun\beanbox directory. You should see two files with weird names that start with __Hookup_. Those files are your automatically generated event classes.

   If you have more than two ___Hookup_ files in your /tmp directory, the extra files result from other event connections you made as you were becoming familiar with how the BeanBox works. No problem! If you can't figure out which two belong to the World-Famous Mini-App based on the files' timestamps, take a look at the files with a text editor. Because the ___Hookup_*.java files contain the automatically-generated source code for your adapter, you can pick out which ones contain references to the connections you made inside the BeanBox utility. You can tell, for example, that the following code snippet is from an adapter that connects a push button to the startJuggling() method of the Juggler:

```
public void setTarget(sunw.demo.juggler.Juggler t) {
    target = t;
}
```

```
public void actionPerformed(java.awt.event.ActionEvent
        arg0) {
    target.startJuggling(arg0);
}
```

3. **Make a note of the filename under which you saved your customized application.**

   The name I suggested (in the section "Connecting beans with the BeanBox utility," earlier in this chapter) was miniapp.ser.

4. **Copy all the files — the .class files, the ___Hookup_ files, and the .ser file — into a temporary directory.**

   This step isn't technically necessary, but performing this step makes your life a lot easier.

5. **Run the jar utility.**

   In Step 4, you copied all the files into a subdirectory you named C:\myDirectory. The `jar` statement that you type at the command line looks as follows:

   ```
   jar cf miniapp.jar C:\myDirectory
   ```

   You may notice that the preceding `jar` command doesn't include a manifest file declaration similar to the example in Chapter 4. Right now, the manifest file format isn't fully documented. Manifests may be optional, but they're a darn good idea, and my guess is the documentation should be done by the time you read this book. For all the latest information, I encourage you to visit the following URL:

   ```
   http://java.sun.com/products/JDK/1.1/designspecs/jar/
                   manifest.html
   ```

   Unfortunately, the BeanBox doesn't support the deserialization of a bean-based application at the time of this writing (that is, the utility doesn't enable you to load a JAR file containing a serialized, or *.ser*, file, like the one you just created). The BeanBox included in the next release of the BDK, however, is most likely to support this feature. Until then, check out Chapter 13, which explains the ins and outs of serialization and deserialization at the API level.

Chapter 6

Beware the IDEs (Interactive Development Environments)

● ●

In This Chapter

▶ Understanding the benefits of an IDE

▶ Exploring some popular IDEs

▶ Picking an IDE that fits your needs

● ●

1 f you installed the JDK 1.1 and the BDK 1.0, you have all that you need to create beans and bean-based applications. Still (as you may have noticed if you've had a chance to read Chapters 4 and 5), these tools were designed to make bean development possible — not necessarily to make it easy!

Fortunately, tools *are* available to make the task of creating and using beans easy. These tools are called *IDEs,* or *integrated development environments.* Several IDEs are already available at this writing, varying from low-budget, bare-bones utilities to sophisticated graphical environments with built-in debuggers. A few WYSIWYG ("what you see is what you get") bean authoring tools are available, too, promising to enable users to create beans and bean-based applications visually, without having to write a lick of code.

Some online magazines, such as *PC Magazine,* conduct product reviews of Java IDEs as soon as they hit the street. For an example, check out the following URL, which contains an in-depth comparison of several of the IDEs listed in this chapter:

```
http://www.pcmagazine.com/features/javatool/_open.htm
```

As you know, JavaBeans is brand-spanking-new. Some of the IDEs detailed in this chapter fall into the "heads-up" category — they're full-fledged Java IDEs that have publicly announced support for JavaBeans but haven't implemented it at this writing (but may well have done so by the time you read this chapter).

IDEs: The best of times, the worst of times

The good thing about IDEs is that most of these tools work right out of the box — that is, they're integrated with all the runtime and development support supplied in the Java Developers Kit and JavaBeans Development Kit, so developers who install one of the IDEs don't have to download and configure the JDK and BDK separately.

The not-so-good thing is that most of these IDEs are industrial-strength tools designed for professional developers, and they require a decent machine to perform at peak capacity.

(Individual requirements differ from IDE to IDE, as you see later in this chapter, but count on at least a 100MHz Pentium, a hefty 24MB of RAM, and lots of extra disk space.)

IDEs are produced by a variety of software vendors, so each IDE provides unique strengths (and also imposes different hardware requirements). This chapter gives you an overview of some of the most popular IDEs to help you decide which — if any — to add to your collection.

AppletAuthor

Unlike VisualAge for Java (covered later in this chapter), a Java-based development tool that's coming soon from the folks at IBM, AppletAuthor is aimed at the nonprogrammer market: graphic artists, communication specialists, and marketing types. Because AppletAuthor was designed to help non-developers construct simple Java applications, this software is often referred to as an *authoring* tool (as opposed to a development tool).

AppletAuthor extends the drag-and-drop model that was responsible for spawning all those HTML WYSIWYG editors a while back to include bean-based Java applets. With AppletAuthor, you can create Web pages that include customized JavaBeans as easily as you can create fancy documents with a word processing application.

Because AppletAuthor was designed for nontechnical users, it's delivered as a complete Java-in-a-box kit, including all the necessary Java development and runtime executables. Therefore, you don't have to have installed and configured the JDK first to get AppletAuthor up and running.

At this writing, the beta of version AppletAuthor is available for Windows 95 and Windows NT.

AppletAuthor requires the following minimum system setup:

- A Pentium processor
- Microsoft Windows 95 or Microsoft Windows NT 4.0

Always first with the latest styles — the JDK

The JDK is sometimes referred to as the *reference* Java/JavaBeans implementation. That's because new function appears in the JDK first, and other vendors (who licensed the rights to the Java source code from JavaSoft) *refer* to the JDK as they incorporate the new function into their own products.

- 24MB RAM
- 10MB free hard-disk space
- VGA display

A beta copy of AppletAuthor is available on the companion CD-ROM.

To keep up with the latest AppletAuthor developments, visit

```
http://www.ibm.com/java/appletauthor/html/
           appletauthor_home.html
```

Many of the tools in this chapter are themselves written entirely in Java. Toss out *that* bit of information when a coworker tries to tell you that Java isn't a "real" programming language!

VisualAge for Java

IBM's VisualAge for Java is the latest addition to the popular VisualAge family of application-development products. As you might expect from a company like IBM, VisualAge for Java is a full-featured development environment with drag-and-drop application construction, a spiffy editor, a code debugger, and a multitude of built-in database-access services. VisualAge for Java is optimized for developers who want to create Java-based applications to interact with the applications that they already have lying around (you know — the mainframe ones that everybody gripes about but have actually been working with day in and day out for the past 15 years).

VisualAge tools for other languages — including C++, Smalltalk, and COBOL — have gained quite a following for their focus on what IBM likes to refer to as *the enterprise,* which is an important-sounding word that means "really big companies whose computer-development staffs absolutely have to make stuff work, or HEADS WILL ROLL." So although the generally available, bean-including version of VisualAge for Java isn't expected to hit the streets until early 1997, odds are that when it appears, it'll be well worth the wait.

At this writing, VisualAge For Java is expected to require the following minimum system setup:

- ✔ A Pentium processor
- ✔ Microsoft Windows 95, Microsoft Windows NT 4.0, or OS/2 Warp 4.0
- ✔ 32MB RAM
- ✔ 100MB free hard-disk space

For the latest details pertaining to VisualAge for Java, visit

```
http://www.software.ibm.com/ad/vajava/index1.htm
```

Mojo

Mojo, from Penumbra Software, Inc., is actually two seamlessly integrated tools for the price of one:

- ✔ Mojo Designer
- ✔ Mojo Coder

A visual WYSIWYG tool, Mojo Designer's intent is to hide implementation details so that even developers who have modest Java skills can create working Java components quickly and easily. (Some people say that Mojo Designer's interface is reminiscent of Microsoft Visual Basic.) As their coding skills improve, developers can switch to Mojo Coder, which provides direct access to the Java code generated by the Designer via a built-in editor and class browser.

Mojo comes complete with a whole bunch of standard beans grouped in categories such as drawing, multimedia, business, networking, and database. If you build your own beans, you can add those to the Mojo palette, too.

Mojo 2.0, which is available at this writing, hasn't yet incorporated support for JavaBeans. But Penumbra Software has announced explicit bean support for its next release.

Mojo 2.0 requires the following minimum system setup:

- ✔ A 75MHz Pentium processor
- ✔ Windows 95 or Windows NT 3.51+
- ✔ 32MB RAM
- ✔ 60MB free hard-disk space

An evaluation copy of Mojo 2.0 is included on the CD-ROM that comes with this book. Check it out!

You can visit Penumbra Software's Mojo pages at

```
http://www.PenumbraSoftware.com/mojos.htm
```

JFactory

JFactory, from Rogue Wave Software, is a cross-platform Java application-development environment that comes with a collection of prebuilt components. This IDE includes such nonstandard goodies as automatic `javadoc`-compliant comments (check out Chapter 4 for details on the javadoc utility), automatic menu handling, and context-sensitive help. JFactory also bills itself as being an open IDE, which means that you can integrate your own text editor (and other tools, such as bitmap editors and debuggers) directly into the tool, if you have a strong preference. (JFactory provides the default tools, in case you don't have a preference.)

JFactory Version 1.1 runs on an impressive array of platforms, as described later in this section. Bean support, although it has not been expressly announced at this writing, is widely rumored to be included in the next major release.

In addition to the following minimum system setups, JFactory 1.1 requires you to download, install, and configure the JDK 1.0.2. (This requirement is expected to change to JDK 1.1 before you know it.)

For Windows 95/NT, the minimum requirements for JFactory are

- A 486 processor
- 16MB of RAM
- 25MB of free hard-disk space

For Sun SPARC Solaris 2.4 or 2.5, the minimum requirements are

- X11R5
- 30MB of free hard-disk space

For HP-UX 10.01, the minimum requirements are

- X11R5
- 30MB of free hard-disk space

For OS/2 Warp, the minimum requirements are

- A 486 processor
- 4MB of RAM
- 25MB of free hard-disk space

Interested in JFactory? Check it out for yourself at

`http://www.roguewave.com/products/jfactory/jfactory.html`

Java Workshop

From the people at Sun Microsystems Inc. who brought you Java (now regrouped into their very own division, called JavaSoft) comes Java Workshop. Java Workshop's visual interface is based on the Web browser model, so if you're used to surfing the Web with a browser such as Netscape Navigator or Microsoft Internet Explorer, you'll feel comfortable with Java Workshop right away.

Java Workshop includes all the stuff that you'd expect to find in a first-class development environment: a WYSIWYG wizard, a version-control editor, a class browser, an integrated testing utility, and a debugger. The product is also heavy on how-to stuff (always a plus, in my book), with a relatively thorough tutorial and online help scattered throughout.

Java Workshop 1.0 is available for Solaris 2.4 or later, Windows 95, and Windows NT 3.51. Explicit support for JavaBeans isn't included in the Version 1.0 release, but it's expected to be there, with bells, sometime in early to mid-1997.

Java Workshop 1.0 imposes the minimum requirements (depending on your system) described in the following sections.

For Windows 95 and NT 3.51, the minimum requirements for Java Workshop are

- Intel 486 or Pentium processor (100 MHz)
- 24MB RAM
- 15MB free hard-disk space

For Solaris 2.4 (or later), the minimum requirements are

- ✔ Sun SPARC, Intel 486, or Pentium processor (100 MHz)
- ✔ 32MB RAM
- ✔ 15MB free hard-disk space
- ✔ OSF/Motif 1.2.3-compliant windowing system

A 30-day free evaluation copy of Java Workshop is included on the companion CD-ROM.

For online information about Java Workshop, load this URL:

```
http://www.sun.com/workshop/java/tnb/
```

Visual Café

Visual Café, from Symantec, is a full-featured Java IDE that gives you a choice: You can develop Java components visually, or you can code straight to the metal with the Java-syntax-sensitive text editor.

Aimed at the professional-developer crowd, Visual Café is another top-of-the-line contender. The product comes with a native high-performance compiler that's reported to be jillions of times faster than the compiler that comes with the JDK. Visual Café also boasts a debugger with support for multithreaded applications, and at this writing, it's the only IDE that includes a JIT compiler. (*JIT* stands for *just in time*, and it replaces the slower Java interpreter included in the JDK so that Java applications run lickety-split.)

Visual Café currently is the only IDE that's available for the Macintosh *and* Windows 95/NT. This one's worth a good long look, if for no other reason than the fact that it's the current darling of the industry press.

Visit the following URL for details:

```
http://www.pcmagazine.com/features/javatool/javas1.htm
```

For Macintosh System 7.5, the minimum requirements for Visual Café are

- ✔ A PowerPC processor
- ✔ 24MB RAM
- ✔ 30MB free hard-disk space

For Windows 95/NT, the minimum requirements for Visual Café are

- ✔ Intel 386 processor
- ✔ 16MB RAM
- ✔ 30MB free hard-disk space

Visual Café Pro (for Windows 95/NT only) combines Visual Café with Symantec's dbANYWHERE technology to yield a Java IDE with built-in JDBC support for Sybase SQL Anywhere and Microsoft SQL Server! For details, take a look at Chapter 10. Then visit

```
http://www.symantec.com/product/index_devtools.html
```

Part III
Advanced Bean Recipes

The 5th Wave   By Rich Tennant

"HONEY! OUR WEB BROWSER GOT OUT LAST NIGHT, AND DUMPED THE TRASH ALL OVER MR. BELCHER'S HOME PAGE!"

In this part . . .

*P*art III takes you deeper into the Java jungle. You become familiar with the portion of the Java language that's most applicable to bean development. Each bean-essential API (*application programming interface*) is explored in detail with an eye toward practical application.

You also get a firsthand look in this part at how JavaBeans components can be incorporated with other technologies, including the ActiveX and OpenDoc component models, relational databases, and data servers (both Java and non-Java). Integrating beans with these other technologies enables you to create powerful, state-of-the-art Web-based applications. (Java: It's not just for browser animation anymore!)

Chapter 7

Java Language Overview

. . . .

In This Chapter

▶ Taking advantage of Java's object-oriented nature

▶ Becoming acquainted with the Java virtual machine

▶ Deciphering Java's approach to exception handling

▶ Making the most of Java's built-in security features

▶ Understanding how the Java APIs are packaged

. . . .

*B*ecause JavaBeans is an extension to the Java language, developing JavaBeans requires that you know a little bit about Java programming in general. In this chapter, you discover how Java delivers the benefits that you've heard so much about — the benefits that together make Java the ultimate language for implementing Internet-based applications. This chapter also introduces all the Java class libraries that you need to know about (except for the `java.beans` class library, which is covered in meticulous detail in Part IV).

Basic Java Lore

I'm sure that you've heard the marketing hype. Java is

✔ So completely cross-platform that the same Java application can run on a mainframe and on one of those automatic bread-making machines that everybody has nowadays

✔ So secure that it makes ordinary fireproof safes look flimsy

✔ So easy to program that my 8-year-old niece can develop two or three Java applications between naptime and dinnertime

If there are any marketers in the audience, please cover your eyes; the rest of you are about to learn the truth about Java. Ready? OK, here goes:

✔ Java currently is available for over a dozen platforms, with support for many more expected in the near future.

However: Different companies provide the support for different platforms — that is, different companies create and deliver the Java *virtual machines* that run on the different platforms, and at this writing, these implementations have some teeny-tiny differences. The upshot is that *not* all Java programs can run identically on all Java-enabled platforms. Fortunately, the recently announced 100% Pure Java Initiative (see the upcoming sidebar, "When 99-$^{44}/_{100}$% just isn't pure enough") is intended to eliminate these differences.

✔ Java has several layers of built-in security, and incorporates the very latest in computer-security research and technology.

However: The Internet provides unprecedented opportunity for mischief. Nothing is foolproof, as the saying goes, except death and taxes.

✔ Java is object-oriented, which makes programming with it much, much simpler than with traditional languages (if you're familiar with object-oriented techniques, of course). Java also abstracts the really hard stuff — pointer manipulation and memory management, for example — that other languages force programmers to handle.

However: It took my 8-year-old niece several days to write one simple Java application.

Objects, schmobjects

All the Java class libraries are implemented as a bunch of objects — and a good thing, too, because you can inherit from them to create your own objects, which cuts way down on the code that you have to write. (Applause!) Entire books have been written about object-oriented programming, which is a fairly hefty topic. Still, you don't need to know tons to get started programming with JavaBeans; all that you need to know, you can find right here, in this section.

You can't read three pages of Java documentation without stumbling across the words listed in Table 7-1, so you might as well learn them now.

Table 7-1	Programming Shoptalk
Term	**Definition**
class	A type (or *class*) of object. `Dog` is a class, for example; `Lassie` is a concrete instance of the `Dog` class.
constructor	A special kind of method used to create instances of a class.
encapsulation	The practice of declaring all of an object's data `private`, which forces other developers to access it in an orderly fashion, via publicly declared methods.
event	An occurrence; something that happens to an object (a mouse click, for example).
inheritance	The capability to take all the methods and properties from one class, add some new stuff, and create an entirely new class in the blink of an eye — without having to reimplement the stuff from the first class.
instance	Also referred to as an *object*, an *instance* is a particular representation of a class. `Button` is a class, for example; `myDownloadButton` is an instance.
instantiate	Creating an instance of a class is also known as *instantiating* the class.
interface	A group of abstract methods (you can think of it as being an abstract class). Because many classes can implement the same interface, interfaces provide support for multiple inheritance.
method	A behavior associated with a particular object. `click()`, for example, is a method associated with any push button.
object	A software representation of a real-life thing; includes data (properties) and behavior (methods). An object is sometimes called an *instance*.
property	A characteristic of a particular object; something that describes the object. A property is sometimes referred to as an *attribute* or *field*.

Got the concepts pretty well under your belt? Great! The following examples show the terms in Table 7-1 applied to actual snippets of Java code.

Here is a selected portion of the `JellyBean` class definition:

extends
lets you take
advantage
of inherit-
ance

Defining
a class

This class
implements the
Serializable
interface

A
constructor

A method

An event
notification
being sent to
other beans

```
package sun.demo.jelly; // the package name (and
                // directory structure)

import java.awt.*; // importing the AWT class library
import java.beans.*; // importing the Java Beans library

public class JellyBean extends Canvas
    implements Serializable{
// The JellyBean class is inheriting from the
// Canvas class

  public JellyBean() { // a constructor method
    resize(60,40);
  }

  public void paint(Graphics g) { // a method
    g.setColor(ourColor);
    g.fillArc(5, 5, 30, 30, 0, 360);
    g.fillArc(25, 5, 30, 30, 0, 360);
    g.fillRect(20, 5, 20, 30);
  }

  // a method to get the value of the ourColor property
  public synchronized Color getColor() {
    return ourColor;
  }

  // a method to set the value of the ourColor property
  public void setColor(Color newColor) {
    Color oldColor = ourColor;
    ourColor = newColor;

    // firing an event
    changes.firePropertyChange( color , oldColor,
                               newColor);
    repaint();
  }

  // a method to get the value of the
  // ourPriceInCents property
  public synchronized int getPriceInCents() {
    return ourPriceInCents;
  }
```

```
// a method to set the value of the ourPriceInCents
// property; this method throws an exception
// if the price can't be set for some reason
public void setPriceInCents(int newPriceInCents)
            throws PropertyVetoException {
  int oldPriceInCents = ourPriceInCents;

    ...

}


// All properties are defined below. Notice
// they're all declared private?

private Color ourColor = Color.orange;
private int ourPriceInCents = 2;
}
```

Encapsulation (private data),

ourColor — and ourPriceInCents are both properties

The following example shows an example of another bean that uses the class definition described in the preceding example to create an object.

```
import sun.demo.jelly;
...
JellyBean myJellyBean = new JellyBean();
```

myJellyBean- is an instance of the JellyBean class

Java is platform-independent . . . or is it?

Java's most compelling claim to fame is its platform-independence. You can develop a Java program on one platform, and somebody clear across the planet, running a completely different platform, can download and execute your Java program — no questions asked. Quite a unique feat, isn't it? Read on to see how it's accomplished.

Q. Compiled or interpreted? A. Both!

As you probably know, a *compiler* is a tool that turns human-readable source code into computer-readable compiled code. Traditional compilers produce compiled code that must be executed by specific hardware. If you compile C++ source code with a Windows 95 C++ compiler, for example, the resulting compiled code is executable only in Windows 95. The Java compiler, though, is a little different — it produces architecture- and operating-system-neutral code, called *bytecode*, that can be executed by *any* Java virtual machine in existence.

An *interpreter* translates human-readable code into computer-readable code, too, but there's a difference: Whereas a compiler does all its translations at the same time, an interpreter does its translations one line of code at a time. The result? Compiled code typically runs faster than interpreted code. Some languages (such as C and C++) are compiled; others (such as JavaScript) are interpreted. Java uses a two-step approach; it's both compiled *and* interpreted.

1. **Compiling Java code.**

   Suppose that you create a Java program. First, you create a source file and name it something like `MyClass.java`. Then you compile the source file by running the javac compiler, like this:

   ```
   javac MyClass.java
   ```

   The output of the compiler (assuming that it didn't encounter any errors) is a compiled bytecode file called `MyClass.class`.

2. **Interpreting the code.**

   The Java runtime (which you can invoke either by typing **java MyClass.class** at a command-line prompt, if your program is a Java application, or by loading a Web page into a Java-enabled Web browser if your program is a Java applet) runs the completed code. Technically, the runtime passes `MyClass.class` off to the Java virtual machine, which *interprets* the compiled code, one line at a time, into machine-specific instructions.

Why did the Java designers create a language that is both compiled and interpreted, instead of one or the other? Two reasons. One reason is so that Java programs can be run on multiple platforms. The other reason is that two processing steps means two opportunities to perform security checks.

Java JIT: It's not shorthand for "Jitters"!

Although interpreters have many good points (they offer flexibility, for example, because interpretation is line-by-line as opposed to a pass/fail proposition), they also have a reputation for being . . . well, turtlelike. So several companies are developing a new tool, called the Just-In-Time (JIT) compiler. A JIT compiler compiles bytecode into executable code on the fly, all at once. (You still need the first compile step to convert Java source code to compiled bytecode, though.)

Although JITs are relatively new, they've been widely reported to run more than 25 times faster than a plain old interpreter. Symantec is one tool provider that bundles a JIT compiler with its IDE, called Visual Café. (Refer to Chapter 6 for a comparison of Java IDEs.)

VrrrooM! VrrrooM! The Java virtual machine (VM)

The Java virtual machine (or VM) makes Java portable across multiple hardware configurations and operating systems. Think of the VM as being a software version of a CPU that uses compiled Java bytecode as its instruction set. (A CPU, or *central processing unit*, is also referred to as a *microprocessor chip.*) That's why the VM is called a virtual machine!

A VM comprises three things:

- A **class loader** (discussed in the "Security pays" section later in this chapter)

- A **bytecode verifier** (also discussed in the "Security pays" section)

- An **execution unit**, which is a fancy name for "something that executes the compiled bytecode." Today, this something can be either an interpreter or a JIT compiler.

Each Java-supporting platform has at least one implementation of the Java VM. Several VMs are currently available, all of them developed by different companies that have one thing in common: They forked over the necessary licensing fees to Sun Microsystems.

Java-enabled Web browsers have Java VMs built right in, so users don't have to go to any special trouble to load Java-enabled Web pages.

Who's running the show?

Sun Microsystems came up with the Java language specification, and its implementation (the JDK that you know and love so well) is often referred to as the *reference implementation,* because it was the first, and all the other implementations "refer" to it. When a company licenses Java from Sun, however, to some extent it's no longer Sun's baby. The licensing company can port the Java language to a different platform; it can add special features to its VM implementation to make its own implementation faster or more capable than those from other companies; it can even include pieces of the Java runtime in its for-sale products. (Many of the IDEs listed in Chapter 6 do just that.)

Now, I'm sure that the first thing that popped into your mind when you read the preceding paragraph was, "Yeah, right — 10 different companies with 10 different development teams are all going to implement the Java specification *identically*? I'm on a team, and when our weekly staff meeting rolls around, we can't even agree on what kind of doughnuts to have delivered!" Human nature being what it is, the possibility does exist that different development teams may implement the Java VM differently. Fortunately, the 100% Pure Java Initiative was devised to help developers stay on track (see the next sidebar, "When 99-$^{44}/_{100}$% just isn't pure enough").

Security pays

Security is a big issue in Internet circles, especially where Java's concerned. When you load a Java-enabled Web page, for example, what actually happens is that the Java applet is downloaded from who knows where and executes locally — on your machine. For widespread use of Java applications to take off, users need to feel comfortable that the Java code they download can't do any mischief, either by damaging their machines (hardware, software, or data) or by reporting unauthorized information that it finds on their machine back to its leader. Java has several built-in security features that guard against all these brands of mischief.

Security is a big deal, and this section just skims the tip of the iceberg. Even if this chapter contained an exhaustive description of all the current security features, it would be out of date by the time you read it; Java security is becoming more and more sophisticated at an astonishing pace. (As I write, a new API, `java.security.*`, is nearing completion.) To keep up on the latest developments in Java security, visit the following URL:

```
http://www.javasoft.com/products/JDK/1.1/docs/guide/
security/JavaSecurityOverview.html
```

When 99-44/100% just isn't pure enough

In theory, Java is completely cross-platform. (I discuss how cross-platform capability works in the section titled "VrrrooM! VrrrooM! The Java virtual machine (VM)" in this chapter.) In reality, though, developers have the ability to create Java programs that contain extensions to Java. (An *extension* can be a formalized thing, such as Microsoft's Raw Native Interface, or just a call to a non-Java program).

Typically, when developers start talking about extensions, cross-platform capability flies right out the window (although JavaSoft's newly proposed standard for handling Java extensions, called the Java Native Interface, may change all that). After all, Java may be cross-platform, but chances are that the extension you wrote in heaven-only-knows-what-other language probably isn't.

Recognizing the need for a concerted focus on cross-platform issues, dozens of industry leaders got together to support something called the 100% Pure Java Initiative. Basically, these companies got together and threw some money into a hat to provide the following:

✔ **Education and technical support programs** to teach interested developers how to write completely cross-platform Java code

✔ **A validation program** to help developers verify that their code truly does run identically on every single Java-enabled platform

Visit the following URL to see how you can get involved in the 100% Pure Java Initiative:

```
http://www.javasoft.com/100per-
cent/index.html
```

Security in the language itself

The Java language eliminates two of the easiest ways to booby-trap (whether on purpose or by accident) a Java program:

✔ **Lack of pointer arithmetic.** In C or C++, if you don't know an object's name, you can guess at a place in memory, and if you guess correctly, you can access the object anyway. You can't do that in Java; all references to objects are via symbolic names.

✔ **Automatic garbage collection.** Manipulating memory directly can cause problems in two ways:

- You can forget to discard some memory when you finish with it, which can cause the application to leak memory like a sieve and eventually use up the user's machine's resources.

- You can discard the same piece of memory twice, which can cause all manner of goofy results.

You can't make either of these errors in Java, because the Java language itself takes care of deleting memory that's no longer in use (also referred to as *automatic garbage collection*).

In addition to eliminating the error-prone features described in the preceding list, Java also increases a developer's ability to write secure applications by including a special security-related class called `java.lang.SecurityManager`, which you can subclass to implement your own security policy for a specific class — or for the entire Java system. (A *security policy* is whatever you want it to be. You may forbid all Java programs from writing to users' hard drives, for example, but allow certain programs to read certain files on their hard drives.)

Netscape Navigator already implements a SecurityManager, which by default keeps any Java applet from doing anything roguish (load libraries, define native method calls, start other programs on the client — those kinds of things).

The following code listing shows you how to implement the `SecurityManager` class to create your own custom `SecurityManager`. As you can see if you look at the two `checkAccess()` methods, security is being added in this listing for two classes: `Thread` and `ThreadGroup`.

```
...
import java.io.*;

class SecretPasswordSMgr extends SecurityManager {

  private String password;

  SecretPasswordSMgr(String password) {
    super();
    this.password = password;
  }

  private boolean accessOK() {
    int c;
    DataInputStream dis = new DataInputStream(System.in);
    String response;

    System.out.println("What's the secret password?");
    try {
      response = dis.readLine();
      if (response.equals(password))
        return true;
      else
        return false;
    } catch (IOException e) {
      return false;
    }
  }
  public void checkAccess(Thread g) {
    if (!accessOK())
      throw new SecurityException("Not!");
  }
  public void checkAccess(ThreadGroup g) {
    if (!accessOK())
      throw new SecurityException("Not Even!");
  }
}
...
// Installing the new SecurityManager (this needs to be
// done in a separate file from the declaration
// of the new SecurityManager). You can only
// substitute one SecurityManager per session (for
```

The added security method for the Thread class

The added security method for the ThreadGroup class

```
// security reasons, of course!)
try {
   System.setSecurityManager(new
      SecretPasswordSMgr( MySecurityManager ));
 } catch (SecurityException aSecurityException) {
   System.out.println( SecurityManager already set! );
}
```

The code in the preceding example represents two files. The first file defines a new class called SecretPasswordSMgr, which is based on (or which, as the object-oriented gurus like to say, *derives from*) the standard security class named SecurityManager. The new class contains a checkAccess() method that uses another method — accessOK() — to determine whether a user's password is valid. (The Java runtime calls checkAccess() to see whether it's OK to process a request.) If the password isn't valid, access is denied, and the class throws a security exception.

Code in the second file installs the new security manager (SecretPasswordSMgr) in place of the old one.

To see a complete step-by-step tutorial on creating and installing a custom SecurityManager class, visit

```
http://www.beanie.com/java/tutorial/networking/security/
writingSMgr.html
```

Security in the compiler

The following well-known tricks might work in C or C++, but they won't make it past the Java compiler:

- ✔ Trying to access a private or protected variable or method without proper authority
- ✔ Trying to pull off an illegal cast or data conversion
- ✔ Trying to access the value of an uninitialized local variable

Security in the VM

Three things make up the Java VM: a class loader, a bytecode verifier, and an execution unit. (An execution unit can be either an interpreter or a JIT compiler.) Both the class loader and the bytecode verifier boast their own security features:

- ✔ **Class loader:** A class loader's job in life is to load compiled bytecode (.class files) from the local disk or (more likely) from somewhere on the Internet. The class loader keeps the loaded .class files from different servers separate from one another and from local .class files, so that they can't interfere with one another.

✓ **Bytecode verifier:** When a class loader loads a .class file from across the Internet, the bytecode verifier gets a whack at it (four whacks, actually). The bytecode verifier scans through the bytecode four times, looking for different things each time. If all four passes complete successfully, the file has the correct format and doesn't contain any instructions that could corrupt memory when it is executed. (Don't ask me how the verifier does this; the answer has something to do with theorem provers, structural constraints, and other stuff that hurts my head.)

Another security "feature" is a result of the availability of the source code for the Java compiler and interpreter. At this very moment, thousands of university students around the world are trying their best to defeat Java's security measures so that they can present their bug reports to JavaSoft and be acknowledged in the next Java release.

I Take Exception to That!

In the kinder, gentler '90s, *errors* are called *exceptions*. Java, because it's object-oriented, uses a popular object-oriented model for handling exceptions, called the *try-throw-catch* model. Here's how it works: You write a block of Java code that you want the VM to *try* to execute. If an exception (which can be any abnormal condition) occurs, whatever method call first detected the exception *throws* it, and your block of code *catches* it and deals with it appropriately.

Look at the following code to see how the try-throw-catch model is implemented in Java:

```
try {
  Thread.sleep(30000);
} catch (InterruptedException aCaughtException) {
  System.out.println("Rats, my sleep was rudely
         interrupted.");
}
// The code from here on down in the file will execute,
// whether or not an exception occurred.

...
```

Imagine that while the statement Thread.sleep(30000); is being executed, something goes wrong, and for some reason, this statement can't complete its job successfully. As soon as it's interrupted, the sleep() method throws an exception of the type InterruptedException, the preceding code snippet catches it — and all the statements in the catch block are executed. In this case, the catch block has only one statement, which is

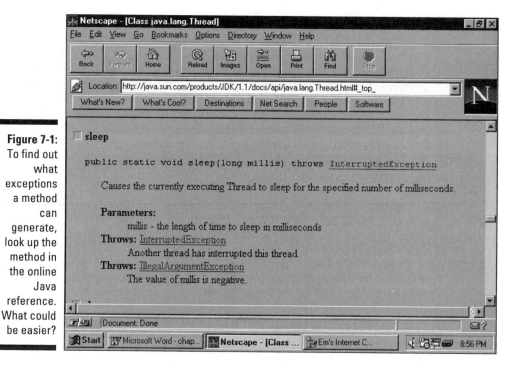

Figure 7-1:
To find out
what
exceptions
a method
can
generate,
look up the
method in
the online
Java
reference.
What could
be easier?

```
System.out.println( Rats, my sleep was rudely
    interrupted. );
```

Handling exceptions is fairly simple, after you get used to the syntax. The hard part is knowing what kind of exception a method that you're trying to call is going to throw when it croaks — and that's not really so hard. All you have to do is look up the method signature (that's the method exactly as you intend to call it — in this case, with one parameter) in the online Java API reference. As you can see in Figure 7-1, the online reference documentation spells out exactly which exceptions this method call is capable of tossing your way.

Load this URL and you see the entire Java API reference, alphabetized for your convenience:

```
http://java.sun.com/products/JDK/1.1/docs/api/AllNames.html
```

Java Class Libraries

When you're developing JavaBeans components, having at least a passing knowledge of the nonbean-related Java class libraries is essential, because

✔ Many of the classes that you need to use when you develop beans are implemented in nonbean-related Java class libraries.

✔ You need to be aware of what each library contains, so that you can refer to the correct libraries in your source code. (Java classes are organized in libraries, or *packages,* according to the kind of function that they provide: all the graphical elements in one library, all the classes that deal with data input/output in another, and so on.) If you want to use a Text element, for example, you need to include the following statement near the top of your source file:

```
import java.awt.*;
```

So because even bean developers don't live by java.beans alone, the following sections are devoted to a discussion of the nonbean-related Java API. (The java.beans package is covered in excruciating detail in Part IV, so it's not included here.)

You can look up the latest information on any of the packages described in this chapter by loading the following URL:

```
http://java.sun.com/products/JDK/1.1/docs/api/packages.html
```

Fundamental Java classes: java.lang

Unlike the other packages discussed in this chapter, java.lang doesn't require you to load it implicitly; the Java compiler does that for you automatically.

The classes that you'll find implemented in the JDK 1.1 version of java.lang are bare-bones building-block classes, things like the following:

Boolean	Object
Character	String
Number	System

For a complete class listing for the java.awt package, look at

```
http://java.sun.com/products/JDK/1.1/docs/api/
Package-java.lang.html
```

Basic graphical interface components: java.awt

The Abstract Window Toolkit (or AWT) contains all the classes that you could possibly want for creating basic graphical user interfaces. Here's a sample of the kinds of classes that you'll find in java.awt:

Button	Label
Canvas	List
Checkbox	MenuItem
Color	Scrollbar
Event	TextField
Font	

To get access to any of the classes in this package, include the following statement near the top of your Java source file:

```
import java.awt.*;
```

For a complete class listing for the java.awt package, look at

```
http://java.sun.com/products/JDK/1.1/docs/api/
Package-java.awt.html
```

Keep the java.awt documentation page bookmarked; most of the beans that this book describes are derived from AWT components.

Java input/output classes: java.io

java.io contains just about every class you can imagine capable of dealing with data input or output. Here's an abbreviated list:

BufferedInputStream	OutputStream
BufferedOutputStream	PrintStream
FileInputStream	RandomAccessFile
FileOutputStream	StreamTokenizer
InputStream	StringBufferInputStream
LineNumberInputStream	

To get access to any of the classes in this package, include the following statement near the top of your Java source file:

```
import java.io.*;
```

You'll become intimately familiar with the `java.io` package when you investigate persistence in Chapter 13.

You can find the complete contents of the `java.io` package at

```
http://java.sun.com/products/JDK/1.1/docs/api/
Package-java.io.html
```

Java communication classes: `java.net`

The classes packaged in `java.net` have to do with high-level communication protocols such as Internet addressing, TCP/IP, MIME, and WWW. Here's a smattering:

DatagramPacket	ServerSocket
HttpURLConnection	Socket
InetAddress	URL

To get access to any of the classes in this package, include the following statement near the top of your Java source file:

```
import java.net.*;
```

To see a complete class listing for `java.net`, look at

```
http://java.sun.com/products/JDK/1.1/docs/api/
Package-java.net.html
```

You can find lots more information about the `java.net` package in Chapter 10.

Java utilities: `java.util`

The `java.util` package is kind of a grab-bag of useful classes that don't belong in any other category. A few of the classes that you'll find in `java.util` are

Date	Random
Dictionary	TimeZone
GregorianCalendar	

To get access to any of the classes in this package, include the following statement near the top of your Java source file:

```
import java.util.*;
```

You can see the full description of `java.util` at

```
http://java.sun.com/products/JDK/1.1/docs/api/
Package-java.util.html
```

The `java.util` class also comes into play when you implement event handling, which I discuss in Chapter 12.

Chapter 8

Java APIs of Particular Interest to Bean Developers

. . . .

In This Chapter

▶ Introspecting beans by using the Java Core Reflection API

▶ Persisting beans by using the Object Serialization API

▶ Cutting and pasting beans by using the Java AWT API

▶ Packaging beans by using the Java Archive API

▶ Distributing beans by using the remote method invocation API

. . . .

Some of the ideas that the JavaBean architects came up with — such as reflection, serialization, packaging, and distribution, all of which are covered in this chapter — have broader applicability than just JavaBeans. Because of this wide applicability, these concepts were implemented in the core Java API, where they're available to all Java-based developers, whether they're developing beans or not. (But of course, why wouldn't they be?)

This chapter explores each of these areas in detail, with special emphasis on the issues that are relevant to bean developers. API syntax for the bean-related items in each of these packages is provided in Part IV.

Introspection without Therapy: The Java Core Reflection API

Introspection is so intimately tied to customization in the JavaBeans model that you may even say it's the reason why JavaBeans is customizable. Think about it: To customize a bean, you need to know what to customize, right?

Suppose that you want to add a generic, off-the-shelf (or off-the-Web) download bean to your electronic Todd Rundgren fan club so that fellow fans around the world can download the cache of Todd-related personal, historical, and musical trivia that you've compiled. For the bean to work in your application, you need to customize it somewhat. At the very least, you want to specify the following:

- Which files contain the trivia (and where they're located)
- The descriptions that you want to display next to your files
- A form that users can fill out (while their data is being downloaded) to get on your monthly fan-letter distribution list

If you're building your application inside an IDE, the chances are good that the tool designer did all the hard stuff, and you can customize the download bean easily via some nice graphical interface.

If *you* are the tool designer, however, it's *your* job to figure out automatically what properties, methods, and events the download bean supports (not to mention the hundred or so other beans that users may connect with your tool). How do you figure out what interface the download bean supports if you shipped your product before the download bean was created?

Face it — the value of an application-building tool is that it enables users to drop in their own custom beans (or a package of beans that they bought at We Be Beans) and hook them together to build applications. The only way users can do that is if you, the tool builder, have some way of automatically inspecting each bean's insides at design time. Fortunately, such a process exists; it's called *introspection*.

The following two categories of introspection are possible:

- Reflection
- Explicit specification

The low-budget approach: Reflection

As a developer, you can use the classes and methods in the `java.lang.reflect` package to make intelligent guesses about a bean's properties, methods, and events, based on something that the bean architects called design patterns (see Table 8-1).

By default, the reflection API reports only public bean members (*members* include properties and methods), but you can extend this policy to include nonpublic members by providing a custom `SecurityManager` for a particular class. Refer to Chapter 7 for tips on how to create your own `SecurityManager`.

Table 8-1   Classes Available in the `java.lang.reflect` Package

Class	Description
Array	Enables you to create and access arrays dynamically
Constructor	Enables you to access and inspect class constructors dynamically
Field	Enables you to access and inspect class and instance fields dynamically
Method	Enables you to access and inspect class and instance methods dynamically (even abstract methods)
Modifier	Enables you to figure out whether a method or property is public, private, or any of several other modifiers

To see the entire contents of the `java.lang.reflect` package, see this book's companion CD.

Design patterns

You can successfully apply simple rules called *design patterns* (actually, a more accurate term is *standard naming conventions*) to JavaBeans code — that is, the `java.lang.reflect` classes and methods report a bean's contents correctly — only if bean developers are consistent in the conventions that they use for naming bean properties, methods, and events.

For plain old properties, each property should be accompanied by two accessor methods: one to get the value and the other to set the value. First, take a look at the syntax for the accessor methods:

```
// getter & setter syntax
public <PropertyType> get<PropertyName>()
public void set<PropertyName>(<PropertyType> x)
```

And now take a look at a couple examples:

```
// getter and setter examples for a property called
// firstName
```

(continued)

(continued)

```
public String getFirstName(){
   // Code to return firstName
}


public void setFirstName(String inputName) {
// Code to set the value of FirstName
}
```

If the property is Boolean (that is, if it can hold only the value `true` or `false`), you should provide a slightly different accessor method than the one shown in the preceding section to get the value.

Here's the syntax for naming a getter accessor method for a Boolean property:

```
// getter syntax
public boolean is<PropertyName>()
```

And here's an example of the syntax in action:

```
// example accessor method to get the value of a property
// called female
public boolean isFemale() {
    // Code to return true or false depending
    // on the value of female
}
```

For indexed properties (properties that are arrays), both accessor methods should look slightly different, as shown in the following syntax:

```
// getter & setter syntax
public <PropertyElement> get<PropertyName>(int x)
public void set<PropertyName>(int x,
    <PropertyElement> y)
```

Now take a look at a real-life example:

```
// example getter & setter accessor methods for a
// property called jobCandidateList[]
public Candidate getJobCandidateList(int index) {
    // Code to return an array
}
```

```
public void setJobCandidateList(int index,
    Candidate inputCandidate) {
  // Code to set the value of an array
}
```

For each event that you want a bean to broadcast to the world (called a *multicast* event), you need to provide two methods that other beans can call to register their interest in hearing about the event.

Following is the syntax you need to follow in creating methods that add and remove event listeners. (Chapter 12 explains how these methods fit into the overall JavaBeans event-handling scheme.)

```
// syntax for adding and removing event listeners
public void add<EventListenerType>(<EventListenerType> x)
public void remove<EventListenerType>(<EventListenerType> x)
```

And here's a real-life example involving a type of event called MyChange:

```
// examples of adding and removing event listeners
public void addMyChangeListener(MyChangeListener
        aMyChangeListener) {
  // Code to add an event listener
}
public void removeMyChangeListener(MyChangeListener
aMyChangeListener){
  // Code to remove an event listener
}
```

Just make sure that the EventListenerType you pick actually ends in the word Listener and that whatever you call your EventListenerType, it extends the java.util.eventListener interface, as follows:

```
public interface MyChangeListener extends
    java.util.EventListener {
  // Your code here
}
```

If, for some reason, you want to restrict a bean's event-notification activities to just one listener (called a *unicast* event), make sure that the add method throws something called a TooManyListenersException if more than one bean registers interest, as follows:

```
public void addMyChangeListener(MyChangeListener
aMyListener) throws java.util.TooManyListenersException
```

Chapter 12 discusses events and event handling in detail. For details on exception handling, refer to Chapter 7.

Java code examples

Assuming that a bean developer conscientiously followed the naming conventions described in the preceding section, you can inspect that developer's beans with impunity. You can inspect beans in either of two ways:

- ✔ You can use methods of the `Introspector` class, as described in Chapter 11.
- ✔ You can use the built-in methods of `java.lang.Class`, as described in the next paragraph.

Suppose that you want to get a list of all the methods defined for a particular class and then inspect each of the methods. All you need to do is invoke the `getMethods()` method on the class, as follows:

```
// First, get a list of methods
Method[] listOfMethods =
   AnObject.getClass().getMethods();
```

Then, for each of the methods returned, you can call any of the methods defined for the `java.reflect.Method` object, including `getName()`, `getParameterTypes()`, `getReturnType()`, and even `invoke()`! Take a look at the following Java statement for an example of how you may call `getName()` on a method to determine the method's name:

```
// Next, inspect one of the methods
String nameOfFirstMethod = listOfMethods[0].getName();
```

Leaving nothing to chance: Explicit specification

If you aren't comfortable with the idea of letting Java methods guess at your bean's innermost secrets, you can always provide an implementation of the `BeanInfo` interface. The `BeanInfo` interface enables you to specify certain details about your bean's members (such as whether a property is bound or constrained or whether an event is unicast).

The java.beans.BeanInfo interface, along with a basic implementation of BeanInfo called SimpleBeanInfo, is covered in Chapter 11. For now, just be aware that you have the option to spell out details about your bean's properties, methods, and events if you so desire.

The Introspector class of the java.beans API, which you find out about in Chapter 11, first looks for an implementation of the BeanInfo interface for a bean that it's inspecting. If the Introspector doesn't find one, it uses the classes and methods in java.lang.reflect to do its best to figure out the bean's properties, methods, and events.

Persistence Really Pays Off: The Object Serialization API

Serializing an object essentially means "flattening an object into a serial stream of data and saving the whole thing to disk in a recognizable state so it can be restored later." (And no, I don't know why they didn't just call it "the object-saving API"!) Basically, the JavaBeans architects wanted to provide a couple of ways to save (or *persist*) beans, as follows:

✔ **Serialization** is a quick-and-dirty way to save simple beans that's fairly easy to use, if not exactly ultra-practical. If you reconstitute a bean, the process is called *deserialization*.

✔ **Externalization** is a way to specify precisely what, when, and how bean information is saved. (This approach is much harder to implement than plain serialization is, so save it for when you're really feeling frisky.)

Because the externalization mechanism is so closely related to serialization, only persistence via serialization is covered in this chapter. (Chapter 13 covers the externalization API in detail, if you're interested.)

The Java database connectivity mechanism (the *JDBC*) isn't considered to be a serialization technique, but it *is* another way to make beans persistent. Check out Chapter 10 for a discussion of the JDBC and how you can use it to store your beans in relational databases.

The theory

If you want to save a bean's data, your bean's class definition needs to implement java.io.Serializable or java.io.Externalizable, as in the following example:

```
public class MyBean extends YourBean implements
   Serializable {
```

Implementing either the `Serializable` or `Externalizable` interface marks your class as savable, but that's all it does; it's still up to your bean (well, to you, actually) to define when you want your bean's data to be saved — and how, too, if you're implementing the `Externalizable` interface.

The `java.io.*` package gives you many choices, but the easiest approach is to save beans by calling the `writeObject()` method of the `ObjectOutputStream` object. If you want to reconstitute your beans, call the corresponding `readObject()` method of the `ObjectInputStream` object.

Confused? You won't be after you see Listing 8-1 in the following section, which shows an example of serializing and deserializing that should be familiar to you if you've horsed around with the BDK at all: the File⇨Save and File⇨Load options from the `BeanBox` menu.

Chapter 13 describes the `java.io` package in much greater detail than this persistence-overview section does.

Java code examples

A few things about the code snippet in Listing 8-1 are worth noting:

- ✔ The statement import `java.io.Serializable;` is necessary so that you can refer to the `Serializable` interface in the class definition, as follows:

```
public class BeanBox extends Panel implements
        Serializable {
```

- ✔ The `save()` method, as you may expect, is where all the code to serialize the `BeanBox` container bean (as well as all the beans that have been added to the `BeanBox`) is located.
- ✔ The `load()` method contains the logic to deserialize (or load) the saved state of the `BeanBox` — and any beans that the `BeanBox` contained when it was saved — back into memory.

Listing 8-1   The BeanBox: An Example of Serialization
Using `writeObject()` and `readObject()`

```
import java.io.Serializable;
...
public class BeanBox extends Panel implements
    Serializable {

...
/**
```

```
 * This implements the "save" menu item and stores the
 * current state of the BeanBox to a named file.
 */
```

This method executes after you choose File⇨Save from the BeanBox menu

```
public void save() {
  FileDialog fd = new FileDialog(getFrame(),
    "Save File", FileDialog.SAVE);
  ...
  fd.setFile(defaultStoreFile);
  fd.show();
  String fname = fd.getFile();
  if (fname == null) {
    return;
  }

  try {
    java.io.FileOutputStream f = new
      java.io.FileOutputStream(fname);
    java.io.ObjectOutput s = new
      java.io.ObjectOutputStream(f);
    int count = countComponents();
    s.writeObject(new Integer(count));
    for (int i = 0; i < count; i++) {
      Component c = getComponent(i);
      s.writeObject(c);
    }
    s.flush();
    f.close();
  } catch (Exception ex) {
    error("Save failed", ex);
  }
}
```

This statement serializes the BeanBox

This statement serializes the beans contained in the BeanBox

```
...
/**
 * This implements the "load" menu item and loads
 * the BeanBox state from a named file.
 */
```

This method executes after you choose File⇨Load from the BeanBox menu

```
private void load() {
  removeAll();
  FileDialog fd = new FileDialog(getFrame(),
    "Load File", FileDialog.LOAD);
  ...
```

(continued)

(continued)

```
fd.setFile(defaultStoreFile);
fd.show();
String fname = fd.getFile();
if (fname == null) {
  return;
}

try {
  java.io.FileInputStream f = new
    java.io.FileInputStream(fname);
  java.io.ObjectInput s = new
    java.io.ObjectInputStream(f);
  Integer x = (Integer) s.readObject();
  int count = x.intValue();
  for (int i = 0; i < count; i++) {
    Component c = (Component) s.readObject();
    add(c);
  }
  f.close();
} catch (Exception ex) {
  error( Load failed , ex);
}
}
```

Deserializing the BeanBox bean

Deserializing each bean inside the BeanBox bean

Miscellaneous Bean Stuff: AWT Extensions

AWT stands for *Abstract Windowing Toolkit*. The AWT library defines many useful GUI components — things such as labels, buttons, and panels. (*GUI*, which is pronounced "gooey," is an acronym for *graphical user interface*.) The AWT was part of the Java implementation long before JavaBeans came along. After beans hit the scene, however, the AWT was beefed up to include a couple of great features that are especially useful for bean developers:

✔ Data-transfer capability, including support for Clipboard activities (available in JDK 1.1) and drag-and-drop (not available at this writing)

✔ A bang-up event model

The JavaBeans event model is implemented in `java.awt.event`. The event model is covered in Chapter 2, so the focus of this section is on data transfer between beans by means of your soon-to-be-old-friend Mr. Clipboard.

The theory

You know how, if you're running several applications in Windows (or Mac or OS/2, or NeXT or . . .), you can cut some text out of one application and paste it into another? The official term for this capability to transfer data from one application to another is, appropriately, *data transfer*. You can achieve data transfer in a couple of ways, but as I write this chapter, the latest JDK (version 1.1) provides support for only one: cut-and-paste via something called the Clipboard.

You can think of the Clipboard as being a huge blackboard. Whenever you cut or copy text from one application, the computer writes all the text on the blackboard in the blink of an eye. If you paste the text into another application, the computer copies the text from the blackboard into the new application. The Clipboard is kind of like a halfway house for data, and it's not limited to Java programs. Because you interact with the native platform's own one-size-fits-all Clipboard, you can transfer data between Java and non-Java applications at will.

Clipboard support is provided in the `java.awt.datatransfer` package. You can find complete documentation for this package on the CD that comes with this book:

The players are as follows:

- ✔ `Clipboard getSystemClipboard()`

  This method returns the one Clipboard that's shared among all the applications running on a platform.

- ✔ `java.awt.datatransfer.ClipboardOwner`

  Any class that wants to write to the Clipboard needs to implement this interface.

- ✔ `java.awt.datatransfer.Clipboard`

  You can create multiple examples of the `Clipboard` class.

- ✔ `void setContents(Transferable content, ClipboardOwner owner)`

  You can use this `Clipboard` method to write data to the Clipboard.

- ✔ `Transferable getContents(Object requestor)`

  You can use this `Clipboard` method to read data from the Clipboard.

A security issue is implied in a Java program's capability to access the one-and-only systemwide Clipboard. (What if the Java program is malicious?) If you want to take advantage of the systemwide Clipboard, you need to provide explicit support for it in a custom `SecurityManager` implementation; refer to Chapter 7 for details. Alternatively, you can create your own private Clipboards, if you want, and bypass the system Clipboard altogether.

Java code examples

The example code shown in Listing 8-2 creates an object called `ClipboardTest`, which defines a `Copy` button, a `Paste` button, and a text field. After a user clicks the `Copy` button, the contents of the text field are saved to the system Clipboard. After a user clicks the `Paste` button, the contents of the Clipboard are pasted into the text field.

You may help your understanding of the entire data-transfer process if you keep the following points in mind as you peruse the code in Listing 8-2:

- ✔ The program begins when a new `ClipboardTest` object is created (see the `main()` method near the bottom of the listing?) and the new `ClipboardTest` object's `show()` method, inherited from its dear old parent `Frame`, is called.

- ✔ `ClipboardTest` implements `ClipboardOwner`, so it's okay for `ClipboardTest` to write to the system Clipboard that it grabs hold of as soon as it's instantiated. Here's the line that grabs the system Clipboard:

```
Clipboard clipboard =
    getToolkit().getSystemClipboard();
```

- ✔ After a user clicks the `copyButton`, the `setContents()` method writes data to the Clipboard. Notice in the following code example that `contents` is of type `StringSelection`? That's no accident; data that's going to pass to and from the Clipboard must be of type `Transferable` (as you know from having seen the `setContents()` signature in the preceding section), and `StringSelection` conveniently implements the `Transferable` interface.

```
StringSelection contents = new
    StringSelection(srcData);
clipboard.setContents(contents, this);
```

- ✔ After a user clicks the `pasteButton`, the `getContents()` method retrieves data from the Clipboard. Notice in the Java statement that follows the `contents` variable is of type `Transferable`? This choice of data type is no accident; `getContents()` expects the `contents` variable to be of type `Transferable`.

```
Transferable content = clipboard.getContents(this);
```

As soon as the data is retrieved from the Clipboard by the preceding statement, it's pasted into the text field as shown in the following example.

```
String dstData =
    (String)
        content.getTransferData(DataFlavor.stringFlavor);
dstText.appendText(dstData);
```

Listing 8-2	Fun with Clipboards

```
import java.awt.*;
import java.awt.datatransfer.*;

public class ClipboardTest extends Frame implements
  ClipboardOwner {

  TextArea srcText, dstText;
  Button copyButton, pasteButton;
  Clipboard clipboard =
    getToolkit().getSystemClipboard();

  public ClipboardTest() { // constructor
    super("Clipboard Test");
    …

    copyButton = new Button("Copy Above");
    …
    add(copyButton);

    pasteButton = new Button("Paste Below");
    pasteButton.disable();
    …
    add(pasteButton);

    …
  }
```

Get the ——— system Clipboard

(continued)

(continued)

```
public boolean action(Event evt, Object arg) {
    if (evt.target == copyButton) {
        // Implement Copy operation
        String srcData = srcText.getText();
        if (srcData != null) {
            StringSelection contents = new
                StringSelection(srcData);

            clipboard.setContents(contents, this);
            pasteButton.enable();
        }
        return true;

    } else if (evt.target == pasteButton) {
        // Implement Paste operation
        Transferable content =
            clipboard.getContents(this);

        if (content != null) {
            try {
                String dstData =
                    (String)content.getTransferData(
                    DataFlavor.stringFlavor);

                dstText.appendText(dstData);
            } catch (Exception e) {

            System.out.println( Couldn t get contents
                in format:   +
                DataFlavor.stringFlavor.getHumanPresentableName());
            }
        }
        return true;
    }
    return false;
}

public void lostOwnership(Clipboard clipboard,
    Transferable contents) {
    System.out.println( Clipboard contents replaced );
}
```

Write data to — the Clipboard

Read data — from the Clipboard

A new ———
Clipboard is
created

```
public static void main(String[] args) {
    ClipboardTest test = new ClipboardTest();
    test.show();
}
}
```

You can find this example on the CD in this book.

Packaging Beans with the Java Archive (JAR) API

If you read either Chapter 4 or Chapter 5, you pick up a taste for how you can use the JAR utility to bundle bean-based application files. This section pokes its fingers a little farther into the jar and comes up with guidelines for the following:

✔ Modifying the HTML <APPLET> tag to load JAR files automatically

✔ Using the JAR API directly

The theory

JAR files are stored in a compact, platform-independent format. By using the jar utility, you round up all the files associated with a Java-based application (.class files as well as auxiliary files such as sounds and images), stuff them all into a JAR file, and distribute them via HTTP in one fell swoop. Remember that I'm talking about the Internet here, so you realize considerable benefit from transferring, say, 10 files at the same time instead of opening 10 separate connections and transferring the files one at a time.

You also realize great benefit by keeping files as small as possible, which is why the JAR format compresses files based on the de-facto "zip" compression standard.

To create JAR files, you have a couple options:

✔ You can invoke the jar utility from the command line, as illustrated in Chapters 4 and 5 (the common approach).

✔ You can use the classes and methods defined in the java.util.zip package to create JAR files dynamically (the uncommon approach).

Creating JAR files dynamically is technically nonbean-related. For information about how to create JAR files dynamically by using the `java.util.zip` package, check out the CD that comes with this book.

As demonstrated in the following section, all you must do to load JAR files that already exist is to add a parameter clause to the HTML `<APPLET>` tag to specify that applet-related bean files are to load automatically from a particular JAR file.

Soon, applet authors can sign JAR entries digitally to prove (or *authenticate*) who contributed the entries and when. To keep up on the latest security issues related to JAR files, keep an eye on this URL:

```
http://java.sun.com/products/JDK/1.1/docs/guide/jar/
manifest.html
```

Java code examples

The HTML code in the following example shows you how to specify a JAR file inside the `<APPLET>` tag. As you may expect, the JAR filename (`jars/animator.jar` in this case) is relative to the directory that contains the HTML code snippet.

```
<APPLET CODE=Animator.class
WIDTH=460 HEIGHT=160>
<ARCHIVES= jars/animator.jar >
</APPLET>
```

Contrary to popular belief, the most-requested data flavor isn't vanilla

A *data flavor* is a format that transferable data can be massaged into, and any given transferable object can have multiple data flavors associated with it. If you load a really spiffy Web page in either Netscape Navigator or Microsoft Internet Explorer, for example, and then attempt to save it, you're given the choice of two data flavors: plain text and HTML.

`StringSelection`, which implements the `Transferable` interface, is associated with the `Java.lang.String` data flavor. The next release of the JDK is expected to provide some additional handy classes, such as `StringSelection`, that come with some default flavors for common data types.

The name of the ARCHIVES attribute may change in the near future to ARCHIVE, so don't be surprised if you create an HTML file containing code similar to the preceding example and the line with the ARCHIVES directive causes an error. Just change ARCHIVES to ARCHIVE and load the page again.

Java on the Server, Java on the Client: The Remote Method Invocation (RMI) API

Developers can create distributed applications based on JavaBeans with the Java remote method invocation (RMI) APIs. Distributed applications can be fairly involved, so Chapter 10 is devoted entirely to that subject. For now, just be aware that the following RMI packages are devoted to distributed application development:

- ✔ java.rmi
- ✔ java.rmi.dgc
- ✔ java.rmi.registry
- ✔ java.rmi.server

If you'd like to browse the RMI packages and get familiar with their contents before checking out Chapter 10, see the CD that comes with this book.

Chapter 9

Integrating JavaBeans with Other Component Models

In This Chapter

▶ Linking beans with ActiveX components

▶ Combining beans with JavaScript and plug-ins via Netscape Navigator's LiveScript

▶ Integrating beans with LiveObjects (OpenDoc components)

*T*he JavaBeans component model isn't the only component model in town. At this writing, three others are on the market: ActiveX, LiveScript, and OpenDoc. Although each of these architectures has its strengths (check out the rest of this chapter for details), none is identical to JavaBeans.

Because one of the overriding goals of the JavaBeans architects was to make JavaBeans components completely portable and open, they devised a way to integrate JavaBeans components with each of these other component models. Although the integration isn't fully implemented at this writing, this chapter explores how it's expected to work after it's available — and shows you where to look for the latest information online so that you can be the first on your block to take advantage of it after it hits the streets.

ActiveX

ActiveX is a popular component model for the Windows platform. Currently, ActiveX is implemented not only in Microsoft Internet Explorer, but also in many client-side Windows applications (such as Visual C++, Microsoft Word 97, and Microsoft Excel 97).

And they said it would never happen!

In the past, ActiveX was available only for computers running Windows. At this writing, however, an implementation of ActiveX for the Macintosh has been announced, as well as a plug-in to make ActiveX components compatible with Netscape Navigator. Industry critics are skeptical of claims that these newly announced ActiveX systems will be equivalent to the original implementation in terms of function or speed, but time will tell.

One thing's for sure: The times, they are a'changing!

For details on the ActiveX SDK for the Macintosh and the ActiveX plug-ins for Navigator, respectively, visit these Web sites:

```
http://www.microsoft.com/intdev/
    sdk/mac/
```

```
http://www.ncompasslabs.com/
    products/scriptactive.htm
```

Years ago, ActiveX components began life as OLE (*Object Linking and Embedding*) controls; you may also have heard OLE controls referred to as OCXs. In its infancy, this technology was less a full-fledged component model than a dynamic data-exchange mechanism. Now, however, the technology has evolved to incorporate something called COM, which is Microsoft's own *Component Object Model*. The reason why you can cut and paste data from one Windows application (or ActiveX component) to another without so much as a backward glance is that the developers of each of these applications implemented OLE/COM in their products.

You know how, after you get familiar with something and figure out how to use it really well, you tend to keep on using it? The same is true of many of the developers who programmed ActiveX in its earlier incarnations now that ActiveX is all grown up. At this writing, more than 100 ActiveX components are already available — and the number is growing. Proponents also point to ActiveX's overall performance characteristics as being an advantage over JavaBeans if you throw in beans' dependence on still-poky-at-times-depending-on-the-implementation Java virtual machines.

You can find ActiveX components in many places on the Web, including this one:

```
http://www.microsoft.com/activex/gallery/
```

Notice that unlike JavaBeans components, ActiveX components are at this writing compatible only with Microsoft Internet Explorer running under Windows. This situation appears to be changing, however (see the sidebar "And they said it would never happen!" for details).

At this writing, JavaSoft is developing (or should I say building?) a bridge between the JavaBeans model and the ActiveX model. This *bridge*, implemented as a native Windows OCX, is to stand between a JavaBean and the ActiveX model. You can think of a bridge as being a translator if you like. The job of this bridge is to stand between a bean and the ActiveX environment (as shown in Figure 9-1) and to do the following:

✔ Intercept all the calls that a bean makes to the JavaBeans API and transform them into equivalent ActiveX calls

✔ Intercept all the ActiveX calls directed back toward the bean and transform them into calls that the bean can understand

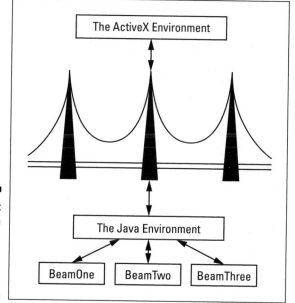

Figure 9-1:
Between
bean and
eternity:
the ActiveX
Bridge.

The only additional step you need to take to make your beans interact directly with ActiveX components is to run a special installation program to register the beans with the ActiveX environment. The installation program uses introspection (hey, it's coming in handy already!) to figure out which bean methods the ActiveX environment is going to need to be ready to map to ActiveX methods — kind of a "heads up; we've got another bean coming, and here's what it looks like!" situation.

The bean-to-ActiveX bridge is expected to be available sometime early in 1997. To keep up on the latest developments, visit the following URL:

`http://splash.javasoft.com/beans/bridge/`

LiveConnect

LiveConnect is the technology that enables Netscape Navigator's JavaScript implementation to interact directly with Java applets and plug-ins. At present, Netscape Navigator's LiveConnect provides the only available implementation that enables direct JavaScript-to-plug-in interaction. In addition, although HTML support for Java applets is provided both by Navigator and Internet Explorer, JavaScript-to-applet interaction is currently supported only by Navigator. LiveConnect is implemented only in Netscape Navigator (version 3.0 and later).

The good folks at JavaSoft and Netscape are putting their heads together as I write to make sure that JavaScript interacts as seamlessly with JavaBeans in the future as it does with Java applets today.

For more details regarding LiveConnect, visit this URL:

```
http://splash.javasoft.com/beans/bridges.html
```

If you're interested in JavaScript-to-JavaBeans interaction, check out a copy of *JavaScript For Dummies*, also published by IDG Books Worldwide, Inc.

OpenDoc

OpenDoc is a cross-platform, vendor-neutral component-software architecture developed by Apple and promoted by CI Labs, a not-for-profit consortium that involves several industry-leading companies (see the sidebar "CI Labs and Live Objects"). OpenDoc was designed to be the be-all, end-all, everything-including-the-kitchen-sink component software model, so by today's standards, its support for standard component services such as layout, persistence, and event handling is very sophisticated.

In addition (and this feature is pretty cool), OpenDoc uses a simple, standards-based language called IDL (for *interface definition language*) that theoretically can map C, C++, Java, Smalltalk, or any other programming language directly to OpenDoc. Yes, you read that correctly. Write a program in any of these languages, say the magic incantation, and poof! — out pops an OpenDoc executable. (Well, okay, the process isn't *quite* that simple, but that's the theory.)

Language independence is like world peace: Everybody thinks that it's a great idea, but somehow, it's always a little harder to pull off than it seems. OpenDoc was implemented in C++, and although it's true that language

Oh, you meant the *other* cross-platform!

Although the OpenDoc *architecture* is cross-platform, the OpenDoc API is not — and a big difference exists between an architecture and an implementation. Suppose that you develop an OpenDoc-based application on a Macintosh and want to port it to Windows so that users running Windows can use your application. Because the OpenDoc architecture is cross-platform, the way that your application is organized stays the same. Because the OpenDoc API isn't cross-platform, however, you'll have to rewrite parts of it (the parts that rely on native platform services).

bindings are available to translate IDL files to stubbed-out files implemented in other languages, here's the honest truth: Currently, developing OpenDoc programs in any language other than C++ is going to cost the developer a significant amount of extra effort.

At this writing, OpenDoc has just become generally available for Windows 95, Windows NT, OS/2, and AIX/6000. Although OpenDoc has already made quite a splash on the Macintosh platform, the adoption curve to date has been slightly lower on the other supported platforms. As a result, few tools are available to help developers create and maintain OpenDoc-based applications.

Similar to the JavaBeans-to-ActiveX bridge, a JavaBeans-to-OpenDoc transformer to enable two-way communication between beans and OpenDoc components has been announced. At this writing, the implementation details are still under wraps, but if you keep an eye on this URL, you can access the latest facts as they develop:

```
http://www.cilabs.org/About/roadmap.html
```

The transformer is expected not only to map JavaBeans APIs to OpenDoc APIs but also to expose native OpenDoc interfaces that have no Java equivalent. Exposing native OpenDoc interfaces means that JavaBeans developers can make calls directly to OpenDoc APIs if they feel so inclined.

Although at this writing no firm availability date for the JavaBeans-to-OpenDoc transformer has been announced, you can keep your finger on the OpenDoc pulse by visiting the following URLs:

```
http://opendoc.apple.com/
http://www.software.ibm.com/clubopendoc/
```

CI Labs and Live Objects

You may have noticed that the entire premise of component software rests on the developers' capability to play nice and create components that actually work together. Recognizing the inherent difficulties that a single company would experience in creating and promoting the standards necessary to support this scheme, several important players in the software industry came together and agreed to contribute representatives to CI Labs (a shortened version of *Component Integration Laboratories*). CI Labs is a vendor-neutral body charged with promoting cross-platform component-software interoperability.

One of CI Labs' offerings is a validation program for what it calls Live Objects. Live Objects are OpenDoc/Java-based applications that have passed a battery of tests designed to ensure that they are fully compliant with other OpenDoc/Java-based applications.

For more details, see this URL:

```
http://www.cilabs.org/
    LiveObjects/
```

Chapter 10

Distributing Beans

● ●

In This Chapter

▶ Defining "distributed" beans

▶ Connecting beans to database servers by using JDBC

▶ Linking beans to CORBA-compliant servers by using IIOP and IDL

▶ Attaching beans to Java servers by using RMI

● ●

Given that Java and JavaBeans were designed specifically for Internet-application development and given that the Internet is nothing if not the biggest, most distributed network on planet Earth, it's easy to see why the JavaBeans architects made the provision for built-in distribution support. Distribution is like potato salad, however; everybody thinks he has *the* true definitive recipe (and doesn't much care for any of the others!).

This chapter explores several distributed-bean-based scenarios, ranging from low-rent to sophisticated. You find detailed instructions for integrating beans with database servers, Java servers, and non-Java servers, as well as a few handy tips to keep in mind while you're designing your distributed system.

What's a Distributed Bean, Anyway?

The bottom-line definition of a *distributed* software application is this: Part of the application runs on one machine and part runs on another. Distribution implies the existence of a *client/server model*, which sounds much more impressive and mysterious than it really is. Think about it: If you have half an application on one computer and half on the other, the two halves must talk at some point, right? Well, whichever half initiates the conversation is called the *client*; the other half (the half that answers and "serves" the request) is called the *server*.

This client/server model repeats throughout this chapter, with beans playing the role of the client and different types of applications (databases, Java programs, and non-Java programs) playing the role of the server.

The skinny on client/server configurations

The client/server model is sometimes referred to as a *two-tier model*, because two types of players are involved: clients and servers.

A *three-tier model* is one in which a third player — typically, another server — is inserted smack-dab into the middle of the process. The classic example of a three-tier model is a desktop computer (client) attached to a workstation (server) attached to a mainframe (technically a server, too, because it answers requests but traditionally called a *host*).

Three-tier applications are a great way to update old mainframe applications. Here's how:

✔ The mainframe *host* applications stay the same (old and cryptic, but hey — they were state-of-the-art 20 years ago, when they were installed).

✔ The *client* runs a user-friendly interface that talks only to the workstation server, even when requesting mainframe data.

✔ The workstation *server* acts as a go-between. If the client asks this server for data that only the mainframe has, the workstation turns around and asks the mainframe for the data itself. Before the workstation hands the data back to the client, however, it may massage it, process it, make some decisions based on it, or turn it purple — whatever is appropriate.

The three-tier approach to distributed systems extends the usefulness and life of mainframe applications while enabling users to take advantage of nice, colorful graphical interfaces on desktop machines (instead of those horrid old green terminals). One-to-one mapping between client requests and mainframe applications isn't required either. In fact, most three-tier systems revitalize existing mainframe applications by using mainframe output to provide input to newer, more sophisticated applications that reside on the server.

One of the reasons people are so excited about Java and JavaBeans is that these programs are a natural fit for developing client-side Internet applications. Suppose that you're a bank, with tons of money invested in secure, reliable mainframe applications. You'd like to enable users to tap into their bank accounts over the Internet, but you don't want to touch the stuff that you know works — the workhorse mainframe applications (sound reasoning, in my book). With Java, you don't need to! You can create a platform-independent, bean-based application that connects, via one of the servers described in this chapter, to your existing mainframe applications. You end up needing to develop the bean-based client and the server, but you don't need to mess with the mainframe applications at all. Talk about recycling!

Making Beans Talk to Database Servers

Just about any nontrivial application accesses a database at some point. Databases have been around for quite some time, and they're indispensable in terms of storing and retrieving data. This section explains how you can replace the default persistence mechanism discussed in Chapter 8 (the `java.io.Serializable` API) with a full-fledged database-management system (or DBMS). Assuming that you have a DBMS available, you need only the following two things to make your beans communicate with it:

✔ The JDBC (Java database connectivity toolkit); which I discuss in detail in the following section

✔ One database driver for every DBMS that you want to talk to

JDBC

Think of the JDBC (Java database connectivity toolkit) as an adapter that plugs into your beans on one side and to your favorite relational database, via a JDBC driver, on the other side.

What, exactly, is a database server?

A *database server* is a nothing more than a plain old database application, also called a *DBMS* (*database-management system*). The name *server* is contextual; DBMSes are called database servers if client programs (bean-based applications, for example) contact them to ask them for services.

Several types of DBMSes are on the market. Hierarchical (used mostly on mainframes), relational, and object-oriented DBMSes are the biggies. Relational databases currently are the most popular for new application development because they work well, they're available for many platforms, and they're robust. (*Robust* is

a computer term that means "doesn't fall apart every couple of hours.")

Object-oriented databases are coming on strong and may well represent the next generation of database development. For now, however, many developers consider these databases to be a little slow and a little too new, so relational DBMSes are the most prevalent. (The JDBC, which you read about in the surrounding section, enables communication only between Java and relational databases.)

Access, Informix, Oracle, and Sybase are some popular relational DBMSes.

Baby, you can drive my database

A JDBC *driver* is a piece of software that serves as a mediator between the database and the JDBC. Like a printer driver (the software that sits between your printer and a word processing program, translating back and forth whenever you need to print something), a JDBC driver translates between a particular DBMS and the JDBC.

The JDK should eventually come bundled with the following JDBC-related components:

- ✔ The JDBC driver manager
- ✔ The JDBC driver test suite (available separately right now; see the section "The JDBC driver test suite," later in this chapter, for details on where to get it)
- ✔ The JDBC-ODBC bridge

JDBC driver manager

The JDBC driver manager (`java.sql.DriverManager`) is the backbone of the JDBC architecture. The driver manager is actually quite small and simple; its primary function is to connect Java applications to the correct JDBC driver and then stand back out of the way.

To see the class definitions for the `DriverManager`, visit the following Web site:

```
http://www.javasoft.com/products/JDK/1.1/docs/api/Package-
        java.sql.html
```

The JDBC driver test suite

The purpose of the JDBC driver test suite is to help you test the JDBC drivers that you're interested in to make sure that they work. The test suite validates that a driver implements all the JDBC classes and methods and that it contains all the functions required for JDBC compliance.

As of Spring 1997, the JDBC driver test suite is still in beta form. Download it from the following URL:

```
http://splash.javasoft.com/jdbc/
```

Bridge across the river JDBC–ODBC

Just in case you haven't gotten your minimum daily requirement of abbreviations yet, here's another: ODBC. *ODBC* stands for *Open Database Connectivity*, and it's somewhat similar to JDBC in that both ODBC and JDBC connect applications to various relational databases. Be aware of one big difference, however: ODBC is available only for Windows platforms (although support for Macintosh has been announced and is expected soon).

JavaSoft and Intersolv are in the process of codeveloping the JDBC–ODBC bridge. The bridge, implemented in the `sun.jdbc.odbc` package, translates JDBC method calls to ODBC function calls so that applications based on JavaBeans can use ODBC drivers just as they can JDBC drivers.

Why bother with a bridge? Why not just require developers to use JDBC drivers? One reason is that applications that rely on ODBC have already been developed. Why make developers write them again?

Another reason is that ODBC drivers have been implemented for more than 50 DBMSes to date. Without a bridge, developers would need to create an additional 50 DBMS drivers for JDBC — and chances are that a couple of the DBMSes aren't exactly winning any popularity contests, which would mean that either

- ✔ Someone would need to implement a JDBC driver for the few people who wanted it, or

- ✔ The few people who wanted it couldn't access JDBC at all.

Drivers and putters

In theory, a JDBC driver is a piece of software that enables a bean, via the JDBC, to talk to a specific DBMS. In practice, a JDBC driver is a Java class that implements the `java.sql` package for a particular DBMS. Then JavaBeans can instantiate and call this Java class whenever they want to use it to communicate with a particular database.

Four flavors of JDBC drivers

As they say, there's more than one way to skin a cat (my apologies to the cats in the audience), and JDBC drivers are no exception. This section describes the four implementations of JDBC drivers that you're most likely to encounter:

✔ **JDBC-ODBC bridge plus ODBC driver**. In this case, ODBC binary code — and, in many cases, database client code — must be loaded on each client machine involved. As a result, this kind of driver is most appropriate for use in a corporate intranet in which client installations are controlled with an iron fist. Fortunately, that description fits the profile of current ODBC-based applications.

✔ **Half-native DBMS API and half-Java driver**. This kind of driver converts JDBC calls to calls on the client API for Oracle, Sybase, Informix, DB2, or some other DBMS. Like the bridge driver, this type of driver requires some binary code to be loaded on each client machine.

✔ **JDBC-to-network-protocol 100 percent Java driver**. This category of driver translates JDBC calls into a DBMS-independent network protocol, which a server then translates into a specific DBMS protocol. Because this kind of driver needs to handle stuff such as client/server security and firewall access, several database middleware vendors are adding it to their existing products that are already set up to handle these tasks.

✔ **Native-protocol 100 percent Java driver.** This driver is the classic, by-the-book driver — the one that you probably envisioned as you read the JDBC overview earlier in this chapter. Because JDBC calls head straight for the database server, expect these drivers to be implemented by the DBMS companies themselves instead of by third-party vendors. (After all, who could be more expert in how to communicate with a DBMS than its creators?)

As time passes and the Java technology matures, the third and fourth drivers listed are likely to predominate. Both drivers are pure Java, which means that they're completely cross-platform. These drivers also are the most flexible of the bunch; unlike the first two, these drivers don't require any extra hassle on the client with these approaches.

The following site contains a list of available and in-progress JDBC drivers:

    http://splash.javasoft.com/jdbc/jdbc.drivers.html

Real-life example

So much for theory; now it's time to get down to business! In the following example, you see how one IDE vendor — Symantec — has integrated JDBC support into its product, Visual Café Pro 1.0. You also see how to connect Sybase SQL Anywhere version 5.0 (a relational database server that comes bundled with Visual Café Pro) to a Java applet via the Visual Café Pro development environment.

The following separate components you can deliver by using Visual Café Pro:

- ✔ The Visual Café Pro development environment
- ✔ A JDBC driver from Symantec called dbANYWHERE
- ✔ The Sybase SQL Anywhere 5.0 database engine

After you install all three of the components described in the preceding list, you can follow these steps to connect a database to a Java applet by using Visual Café Pro:

1. **Create a database.**

   Visual Café Pro comes with some sample databases with which you can experiment, so you don't need to create your own right off the bat.

2. **Register the database with dbANYWHERE.**

   Part of the Sybase database product is a tool called the ODBC Administrator. You use the ODBC Administrator to describe the database from Step 1 to dbANYWHERE.

3. **Create a database-aware Java applet.**

   Visual Café Pro comes with a built-in wizard that makes creating a simple database-aware applet really easy. With just a few mouse clicks, you can create an applet containing some of (or all) the fields in the database from Step 1.

4. **Run the applet.**

   As you probably know, the Sybase SQL database server and dbANYWHERE must be up and running before you run the applet. (In a real-life bean-based application, both of these programs would be running on a machine somewhere else on the Internet.)

   Bingo! Your applet automatically accesses your database via the JDBC (dbANYWHERE) and fills the database fields you included on your applet with real, live data.

Because Visual Café Pro supports the JDK 1.02 at the time of this writing, it doesn't yet include built-in support for JavaBeans. Fortunately, as far as the JDBC goes, the example in this section works the same whether you're connecting a relational database to an applet or (soon) to a bean.

For the latest information on Symantec's Visual Café Pro 1.0 visit the following Web sites:

```
http://www.symantec.com/vcafeprowin/guide/overview.html
```

```
http://www.microsoft.com/msaccess/
```

Making Beans Talk to CORBA-Compliant Servers

Partly because the phrase is so much fun to say, *CORBA-compliant ORBs* are popular with developers who spend a great deal of time creating distributed applications. Beans, of course, are optimized for distributed applications, especially ones distributed across the Internet. Therefore, integrating ORBs and beans makes good sense. The following sections tell you all you need to know to understand when, why, and how to integrate your bean-based applications with a CORBA-compliant ORB.

CORBA

CORBA (or *Common Object Request Broker Architecture*) is a standards-based specification that describes how to build distributed ORBs (literally, *object request brokers*, but you can think of them as being plain old objects for now) that can talk to one another. CORBA was designed in response to the huge proliferation of computer languages, hardware platforms, operating systems, application-development environments, and communications protocols — none of which (as you may already have noticed, if you work with computers regularly) seems to work with any of the others without such a standard!

CORBA is promoted by an industry consortium called the Object Management Group (OMG). The good folks who participate in the OMG figured that if they came up with the definitive specification for an ORB, any object implemented to the specification could run on any platform, talk to any other object written in any other language residing on any other platform, and interface to any communications protocol known (or knowable) to humankind. (Esperanto, anyone?)

More than 500 companies, large and small, participate in the OMG, making it the largest standards body in existence. Visit the following URL to keep up with the group's activities:

```
http://www.omg.org
```

Many developers agreed that creating an object-interaction standard was, indeed, a good idea, and implemented ORBs to the CORBA specification. A few of the best-known ORBs are IBM's SOM (System Object Model), Iona's Orbix, Object-Oriented Technologies' DOME (Distributed Object Management Environment), and Sun Microsystems' Solaris NEO, but many more are on the market. The following sections show you what you need to do to create a bean-based application that can talk to objects developed in any of these environments.

CORBA IDL

All the CORBA implementations understand at least two languages:

- ✔ IDL (the *interface definition language* defined by the CORBA specification)
- ✔ One other language (C, C++, Java, Smalltalk, and so on)

IDL is kind of a pidgin language (almost a "real" programming language, but much simpler) that developers use to describe their classes and methods; then they use an actual programming language to complete the implementation.

All of a CORBA-based object's interfaces (methods, properties, and events), for example, are declared in an IDL file and then implemented in a separate file. This second file can be C, C++, Java, Smalltalk, or whatever other CORBA-compliant language the object's developer decides is the best one for the job. Figure 10-1 illustrates how this process works.

Look at Figure 10-1 and then at Listing 10-1, which shows a real live IDL file describing a GuestBook interface. Notice in Listing 10-1 that the register() method has no guts; that stuff comes later, in the implementation file.

Listing 10-1	guest.id

```
module sunw {
module idl {
module demo {
module guest {

// A guestbook
interface GuestBook {
  string register(in string sig, in string message);
};
};
};
};
};
```

Listing 10-2 shows an example Java implementation for the IDL source file shown in Listing 10-1.

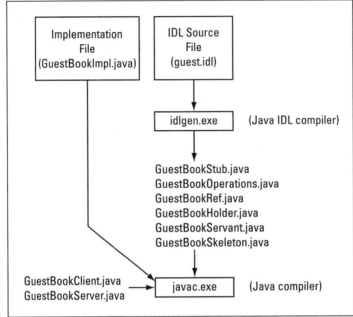

Figure 10-1:
The role
that IDL
plays in the
entire
development
process.
Look at all
the stuff
that's
generated
for you!

Listing 10-2   `GuestBookImpl.java`

Here's the
implementation
of the
`register()`
interface
declared in the
IDL file.

```java
package sunw.idl.demo.guest;

public class GuestBookImpl implements GuestBookServant {
  synchronized public String register(String sig,
    String message) throws
         sunw.corba.SystemException {
    String host = sunw.door.Orb.getCallerHostName();
    System.out.println("-------------");
    System.out.println(host + ": " + sig + "\n");
    System.out.println(message);
    System.out.println("-------------");

    String response;
    if (message.length() > 2) {
      response = "Thanks for the comments.";
    ...
    }
    return (response);
  }
  static java.io.OutputStream out;
}
```

Listing 10-2 shows you how the interface declared in Listing 10-1 may be implemented. Notice that the `register()` method throws a special ORB exception (`sunw.corba.SystemException`)?

Other vendors besides JavaSoft have Java-to-CORBA implementations in the works. Visit the following URL for a partial list:

```
http://nugget.cs.ucla.edu:8001/~lidu/java.corba.html
```

CORBA IIOP

IIOP (or *Internet Inter-ORB Protocol*) is a special protocol designed to enable ORBs to communicate over the Internet, much as HTTP enables Web-page distribution. Every CORBA-compliant ORB must, by definition, support IIOP.

IIOP is a fairly involved animal, but fortunately, you don't need to know much about it unless you're interested in developing an ORB yourself. Bean developers need only know how to use it, which is the topic of the following section.

As this book goes to press, IIOP is still in development. Another protocol, called *Doors*, is graciously standing in until IIOP is ready — but Doors enables communication only between Java clients and Java servers. The best way to handle Java-to-Java communication is to use something called remote method invocation (RMI), which is explained in the section "Making Beans Talk to Java Servers," later in this chapter.

Not-ready-for-prime-time example

As I write, the Java IDL specification is still in flux, and the latest implementation release is alpha-level. (*Alpha* is Greek for "Let's just put this thing out and see what kind of feedback we get.")

Rather than present a detailed working example of an implementation that's sure to change by the time you read this chapter, I instead describe the basic steps that you need to follow to communicate to a CORBA-compliant ORB from a bean, from start to finish. I also include some code snippets to help you get a feel for the level of complexity involved.

You can find the complete code for this example on the companion CD, but be sure to check the following URL for updates:

```
http://splash.javasoft.com/JavaIDL/pages
```

Here are the steps you need to follow if you want to make your bean talk to a

CORBA-compliant ORB via IIOP:

1. **Download the alpha version of Java IDL from** `http://splash.javasoft.com/JavaIDL/pages/`, **install it, and configure it according to the directions displayed on the download page.**

   Eventually, the client-side portion of the Java IDL should be bundled into the JDK, but for now, it's available separately.

2. **Create an IDL file (see Listing 10-3 later in this chapter for an example) declaring a single interface (**`GuestBook`**) and a single method:** `register()`.

3. **Run the IDL compiler (**`idlgen`**) against the IDL source code to generate tons of useful Java source files, called *stub* files.**

   One of the six files generated appears in Listing 10-6, later in this chapter.

4. **Create the source code for a Java applet.**

   Add code to the applet source to connect the applet to the `GuestBookServer` automatically (that is, as soon as the browser invokes the `start()` method) and transmit the user's Internet address and comments after the user clicks the Submit button (as shown in Listing 10-5, later in this chapter).

5. **Create the source code for a Java server (see Listing 10-7, later in this chapter).**

6. **Run the** `javac` **compiler against all the Java source code.**

Developers often invoke a compiler indirectly by running a *make file*, which organizes the many source files involved and compiles them in the correct order. After you download the Java IDL, you see that it comes with a *make* file for you to use in conjunction with the *make* utility provided on the companion CD-ROM.

Remote object interface file

The code snippet shown in Listing 10-3 shows an interface file that a developer may code. The file defines what classes and methods should be available (not how they should work).

Listing 10-3	`guest.idl`

```
// The IDL interfaces for a simple demo  echo  server.
// Echo is in the module sunw::idl::test

module sunw {
module idl {
module demo {
module guest {
```

```
// A guestbook
interface GuestBook {
  string register(in string sig, in string message);
};
};
};
};
};
```

See the keyword `module` in the listing? Each Java package is mapped to a corresponding IDL module, so the following code corresponds to the `sunw.idl.demo.guest` package:

```
module sunw {
module idl {
module demo {
module guest {
```

You can see the complete `guest.idl` file at the following URL:

```
http://splash.javasoft.com/JavaIDL/pages/idl-guest-
        idl.html#source
```

Remote object implementation file

When you have an interface file, you can create a corresponding implementation file. Listing 10-4 shows the `GuestBookImpl` file that a developer may code. Notice the reference to the generated class `GuestBookServant`.

Listing 10-4	GuestBook.Impl

```
package sunw.idl.demo.guest;

public class GuestBookImpl implements GuestBookServant {
    synchronized public String register(String sig,
      String message) throws
            sunw.corba.SystemException {

    String host = sunw.door.Orb.getCallerHostName();
    System.out.println(               );
    System.out.println(host +  :   + sig + \n );
    System.out.println(message);
    System.out.println(               );
```

Here's the ——
implementation
of the register
method.

(continued)

Listing 10-4 *(continued)*

```
   String response;
   if (message.length() > 2) {
     response = "Thanks for the comments.";
     ...
   }
   return (response);
 }
 static java.io.OutputStream out;
}
```

See how the `register()` method is implemented in the file?

You can see the entire file excerpted in the preceding example at the following URL:

```
http://splash.javasoft.com/JavaIDL/pages/idl-guest-
            impl.html#source
```

Client source file

Listing 10-3 and 10-4 show the interface and implementation of a remote object. (In real life, the remote object may be coded by another developer in another CORBA-compliant language.) By contrast, Listing 10-5 shows the source code for a client program called `GuestBookClient.java`.

Listing 10-5 **GuestBookClient.java**

```
// A simple Java applet that can run in a
// Web page and connect to an Echo server
// running on a named machine.

package sunw.idl.demo.guest;

import java.awt.*;
import java.applet.Applet;
...
public class GuestBookClient extends Applet {

  ...
  public void start() {
    // (Re)start the applet.

    ...
    showStatus("Connecting to server at " + url);
    ...
```

This is where the client program makes a call to the server object ———

Here, the ——— identity of the server object is being verified

```
    try {
      // Resolve the target URL
      try {
        // Create a holder
        target = GuestBookStub.createRef();
        // resolve the name into the holder
        sunw.corba.Orb.resolve(url, target);
      } catch (Exception ex) {
        System.err.println("Couldn't resolve " + url + " :
            " + ex);
      ...
    } catch (Throwable th) {
      ...
      throw new Error("GuestBookClient.start failed : " +
          th);
      ...
    }

  public boolean action(Event evt, Object arg) {
    if (evt.target == submitButton) {
      try {
        if (target != null) {
          String sig = sigField.getText();
          if (sig.length() > 1000) {
            sig = sig.substring(0, 1000);
          }
          String comment = comments.getText();
          ...
          response = target.register(sig, comment);
        }
      } catch (Exception ex) {
        System.err.println("Caught exception while invoking
            Echo: " + ex);
        ...
    }
    ...
  GuestBookRef target;
  String url;
}
```

Here's the call ——— on the remote server object

As you can see, the client program contacts the server, asks it for some information (you could say that it requests a service), and goes on its merry way after it gets the requested information.

The preceding snippet was taken from at the following URL:

```
http://splash.javasoft.com/JavaIDL/pages/idl-guest-
                client.html#source
```

Stub and skeleton files

The stub and skeleton files generated by idlgen are ugly, ugly, ugly — but necessary. Both stub and skeleton files define classes and methods (client- and server-side proxies, respectively) that the other files depend on to make the communication leap between the client and the server.

Listing 10-6 shows an example of the generated file GuestBookStub.java, which contains the definition of the GuestBookStub class and two of GuestBookStub's methods: createRef() and register().

Listing 10-6	GuestBookStub.java

Here's the implementation of the register method —

```
public class GuestBookStub
    extends sunw.corba.ObjectImpl
    implements sunw.idl.demo.guest.GuestBookRef {
public String register(String sig, String message)
    throws sunw.corba.SystemException {
    try {
      sunw.orb.MarshalBuffer __mb =
            representation().getMarshalBuffer();
      representation().invokePreamble(__mb,
            __registerOperationDescriptorInstance);
      if (sig != null) {
        for (int __at = 0 ; __at < sig.length() ; __at +=
            1) {
          if (sig.charAt(__at) > \u00ff ) {
            throw new sunw.corba.CharacterRangeException();
          }
        }
      }
      __mb.putString(sig);
      if (message != null) {
        for (int __at = 0 ; __at < message.length() ; __at
            += 1) {
          if (message.charAt(__at) > \u00ff ) {
            throw new sunw.corba.CharacterRangeException();
          }
        }
      }
```

```
        __mb.putString(message);
        representation().invoke(__mb,
            __registerOperationDescriptorInstance);
        String __result = null;
        __result = __mb.getString();
        if (__result!= null) {
          for (int __at = 0 ; __at < __result.length() ; __at
              += 1) {
            if (__result.charAt(__at) > '\u00ff') {
              throw new sunw.corba.CharacterRangeException();
            }
          }
        }
        representation().releaseMarshalBuffer(__mb);
        return __result;
        ...
      }
    }
```

Here's the ——— `public static sunw.idl.demo.guest.GuestBookRef createRef() {`
definition of   `    return new GuestBookStub();`
the createRef()   `}`
method

Fortunately, you don't need to modify the automatically generated files in any way. (You don't even need to look at them if you don't want to!)

Got any skeletons (or stubs) in your closet?

You may be wondering what *skeleton* and *stub* files are, why you need to generate them, and what roles they play in the remote method invocation process. Well, wonder no longer — I am about to reveal all.

A *stub* is a client-side proxy for your remote interface; a *skeleton* is a server-side proxy. As you can see in Figure 10-2 in the section "RMI," later in this chapter, if a Java client wants to invoke a method on a server, the client must forward the request to the stub; then the stub must forward the request to the skeleton; and finally, the skeleton must forward the request to the server.

Why bother? Putting in these two extra layers doesn't cost anything in terms of development time (the `rmic` compiler creates both the stub and skeleton files for you automatically) and doing so pays off handsomely in terms of flexibility.

The server

Servers are management-type programs that stay running and alert for incoming requests. This server is relatively bare-bones; all it does is take note of the name of the GuestBook remote object. (The technical term for what the server is doing here is "binding the remote object in the server registry.") If a client attempts to call a method on the remote object, the server knows how to contact the remote object and pass on the request.

Listing 10-7 shows how the server (GuestBookServer.java) may be coded.

Listing 10-7 GuestBookServer.java

```java
package sunw.idl.demo.guest;

public class GuestBookServer {

  public static void main(String argv[]) {
    sunw.door.Orb.initialize(servicePort);
    sunw.door.Orb.logConnections(true);

    // Create and publish a guestbook server
    try {
      GuestBookRef o = GuestBookSkeleton.createRef(new
          GuestBookImpl());
      sunw.door.Orb.publish(pathName, o);
    } catch (sunw.door.naming.Failure ex) {
      System.err.println("Couldn't bind object: "
+ ex.getMessage());
      return;
    }

    System.err.println("setup and bound " + pathName +"
        server object OK");
  }
  ...
}
```

The preceding two lines make the GuestBook remote object available to any client that comes looking for it

Check out the source code for the server in its entirety at the following URL:

```
http://splash.javasoft.com/JavaIDL/pages/idl-guest-
       server.html#source
```

Making Beans Talk to Java Servers

If you know for sure that the remote call your bean is going to make is to a Java server, you can skip all the machinations associated with CORBA compliance and use a simpler scheme instead: RMI, or *remote method invocation*.

Why would you want to use RMI instead of CORBA IDL? Well, for one thing, RMI is a bit easier, as you see in the following sections. In fact, making a call to a Java program residing on a server across the ocean is just as easy as calling one on the same machine.

Using RMI can be much faster than using CORBA IDL, too, because you don't need to play Twenty Questions each time you make a remote call. ("Hmm . . . let's see, what kind of ORB are you? Okay, you're an implementation of SOM. Now, let me remember how I call a SOM ORB. . . . Are you implemented in C? Yes? Okay. . . . Got it! Hey, **SOM!**") Instead, you can cut to the chase, because you know that Java's at the other end.

Because this approach is useful only if you know that the service you're requesting is on a Java server, it's most useful if you're the one who's coding the server.

RMI

All the classes that you need to implement remote method invocation are contained in the following two packages:

- ✔ `java.rmi`
- ✔ `java.rmi.server`

In addition to the classes provided in `java.rmi` and `java.rmi.server`, two utilities that you need to implement RMI — `rmic` and `rmiregistry` — are supplied in the JDK.

You can find a great RMI primer from the folks at JavaSoft at the following URL:

```
http://chatsubo.javasoft.com/current/doc/rmi-spec/rmi-
           objmodel.doc.html
```

Figure 10-2 gives you an overview of how the RMI process works.

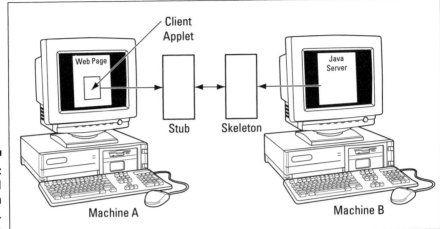

Figure 10-2:
The RMI
process in
all its glory.

rmic

The `rmic` utility is the RMI compiler. The compiler takes compiled `.class` files as input and spits out *SomeInterface*_stub.class and *SomeInterface*_skel.class files, which are stub and skeleton files, respectively (see the sidebar "Got any skeletons (or stubs) in your closet?" for a description of stub and skeleton files).

rmiregistry

The `rmiregistry` utility enables you to create something called a *remote object registry*. Think of a registry as like a waiting list at a restaurant: All remote objects need to register themselves with the remote object registry so that clients (the wait staff) can look them up.

Creating a distributed Java-to-Java application

Following are the basic steps for creating a distributed Java-to-Java application (check out the following section to see these steps in action):

1. **Write the necessary Java and HTML source files:**

    A. *A Java remote interface.* Create a file containing a generic description of what this type of remote object should look like.

    B. *A Java remote object (server).* This file is an implementation of the remote interface in 1.A.

    C. *A Java applet* that invokes a method on the remote server (1.B.) and an HTML file to embed the Java applet,

or

A Java application that invokes a method on the remote server (1.B.).

2. **Compile Java source files and copy the resulting executables to the appropriate executable directory.**

   A. Run the Java compiler, `javac`, against the `.java` source files to generate `.class` files.

   B. Run the RMI compiler, `rmic`, against the compiled `.class` files to generate stubs and skeletons (automatically generated `.class` files that create one client-side and one server-side proxy for each of your remote interfaces).

   C. Make the executables visible to one another by copying them to a directory that's listed in the server machine's `CLASSPATH` environment variable. This process is often referred to as *pushing public*, because you're pushing (okay, copying, if you want to get technical) files from your private development directories to public directories so that other programs can access them.

3. **Start the remote object registry.**

4. **Start the server.**

5. **Start the client.**

   That is, either load the Web page that contains the client Java applet or start the Java client application.

Real-life example

This section presents an example application created by the steps outlined in the preceding section. This example is simple, but it gives you a taste for the mechanics of developing distributed Java applications. The example merely prints "Hello there, World!" but (and here's the cool part) it does that by performing the following tasks:

✔ Installing a remote object, or Java server, that contains a `sayHello()` method

✔ Running a client on the same machine that contacts the server and invokes the server's `sayHello()` method

You may wonder what benefit you can get from implementing a client/server application on one machine, as this example shows. What's the point? Well, in real-life applications, you probably want to keep your client on one machine and your server on another. That arrangement is fine, but for testing purposes, putting both components on the same machine is easier. That way, you don't need to worry about getting access to another machine until the noncommunication-related bugs are all worked out.

A version of this example that communicates from a client on one machine to a server on another machine is available on the Web at the following URL:

```
http://java.sun.com/products/JDK/1.1/docs/guide/rmi/
                    getstart.doc.html
```

Step 1A: Create the source-code file for a Java interface

Directory structure is important if you're programming with Java; it must match package structure exactly, or all hell breaks loose. (Okay, nothing that extreme actually happens, but your programs don't compile or run.)

All the source-code files in Listing 10-8 were stored in the `c:/jdk-1.1/java/JB4D/examples/hello` directory. As you scan this section, notice how this directory name matches up with the `package` statements in each source-code file and also with the command-line directives.

`Hello.java`, shown in Listing 10-8, is available on the companion CD-ROM.

Listing 10-8	`Hello.java`

```
package examples.hello;

public interface Hello extends java.rmi.Remote {
  String sayHello() throws java.rmi.RemoteException;
}
```

In the preceding example, one interface (`Hello`) is declared. `Hello` in turn declares one method (`sayHello()`), which throws a special kind of exception called a `RemoteException`.

Distributing applications introduces a new category of potential problems — namely, the communication between the Java client and the Java server could fail at any time for any of a hundred or so reasons. To trap this kind of exception, every remote interface that you declare needs to throw a `RemoteException` (in addition to any application-specific exceptions that you feel the urge to handle).

Step 1B: Create the source-code file for the implementation of a Java interface

Listing 10-9 shows an example of a Java interface implementation, also called a *remote object* or a *remote server* (`HelloImpl.java`). The full example is available on the companion CD.

Listing 10-9	HelloImpl.java

```
package examples.hello;

import java.rmi.*;
import java.rmi.server.UnicastRemoteObject;
```

The HelloImpl class extends the Hello interface

```
public class HelloImpl extends UnicastRemoteObject
                      implements Hello {
  private String name;

  public HelloImpl(String s) throws RemoteException {
    super();
    name = s;
  }
```

This is the implementation of the sayHello() method defined in the interface

```
  public String sayHello() throws RemoteException {
    return  Hello there, World! ;
  }
```

The program starts right here

```
  public static void main(String args[]) {

    // Create and install a pre-fab security manager
    // so no one can mess with the registry or
    // the remote object about to be created
    System.setSecurityManager( new RMISecurityManager());

    try {
      HelloImpl remoteObject = new
          HelloImpl( HelloServer );
```

The preceding two statements create an instance of the remote object (server) and bind it to its name (HelloServer)

```
      Naming.rebind( /HelloServer , remoteObject);
      System.out.println( HelloServer was just added to the
          registry... );
    } catch (Exception e) {
      System.out.println( HelloImpl croaked. Here s why:
          + e.getMessage());
      e.printStackTrace(); // as though this is going to be
          readable!
    }
  }
}
```

A couple things in the preceding code are worth paying special attention to:

✔ The Hello class and the SayHello() method that were declared in Hello.java are being implemented in HelloImpl.java.

✔ As soon as the Java program starts, it creates an instance of the server, names it "HelloServer", and puts the name in the registry so that the remote client can find it whenever the client looks for the name.

Step 1.C: Create a client Java application that invokes a method on the remote server

Listing 10-10 shows the implementation for a Java client (cleverly named theClient.java). For your convenience, theClient.java is available on the companion CD.

Listing 10-10   theClient.java

```
package examples.hello;

import java.awt.*;
import java.rmi.*;

public class theClient {
    public static void main(String args[]) {

        String message =   ; // initialize the message

        try {
            // Naming is a bootstrap object that s
            // used to look up a server immediately

            Hello anObject = (Hello)Naming.lookup( /
                HelloServer );
            message = anObject.sayHello();
            System.out.println( And here s the message:
                    + message);
        } catch (Exception e) {
            System.out.println( Client exception:   +
                e.getMessage());
            e.printStackTrace();
        }

    }
}
```

The client process begins right here

The client looks for a remote object called "HelloServer"

The client now calls the HelloServer's method sayHello()

The first thing that theClient tries to do is to look up a Java server called HelloServer . If theClient finds this server, it calls the method sayHello() on that server object.

In Listings 10-9 and 10-10, you can see that the name of the remote object being inserted into the registry (and subsequently being called on to perform) is `/HelloServer`. This name is called a *nonqualified* name because it doesn't specify the precise host machine on which the object is installed. (You don't need to spell out the host machine unless it's a different machine from the client.)

If the code that registers the object *were* on a different machine from the client, the name being looked up would need to include the protocol, host, and (optionally) the port, as follows:

```
rmi://someHost/HelloServer
```

Step 2A: Run the Java compiler

To compile the `.java` files created in Step 1 into `.class` files, run the Java compiler from the `c:/jdk-1.1/java/JB4D` directory, as follows:

```
javac -d c:\jdk-1.1\java\JB4D Hello.java HelloImpl.java
             HelloApplet.java
```

The `-d` option asks the compiler to put all the output files generated (`Hello.class`, `HelloImpl.class`, and `HelloApplet.class`) in the base directory, `c:\jdk-.1\java\JB4D`. (Later, in Step 2.C, you refer to this directory.)

Step 2B: Run the RMI compiler

To generate stub and skeleton files based on the compiled `.java` files, invoke the RMI compiler, as follows:

```
rmic -d c:\jdk-1.1\java\JB4D examples.hello.HelloImpl
```

Again, the `-d` option tells the compiler where to put all the output files generated (in this case, `HelloImpl.stub` and `HelloImpl.skel`).

Step 2C: Make the executable files visible

As you do in any development effort (not just in Java), after you create executable files, you must stick them in a directory that's visible to the rest of the system. So you need to make sure that the `CLASSPATH` environment variable contains a reference to the base directory — which, in this example, is `c:\jdk-1.1\java\JB4D`. (If you installed the JDK, you're no doubt familiar with the `CLASSPATH` environment variable and know how to define it.)

Errors caused by misplaced executables are far and away the most common — and most annoying — aspects of any development effort (which is why `make` files were invented). Often, these errors take the form `Can t find so-and-so file` and appear whenever you try to run either the client or the server program. If this situation happens to you, make sure that your `.class` files are located in the directory where your CLASSPATH expects them to be.

Step 3: Start the remote object registry

So far in this exercise, you've seen the three (necessary but boring) Cs of development: coding, compiling, and configuring. Now it's time to rock 'n' roll! The next thing that you need to do is kick off the remote object registry. (A *remote object registry,* as you may recall, is a special list that contains all the names of remote objects available and explains where to find them.)

The registry doesn't need human intervention to do its job after it's up and running, so you can start it in background — that is, you can start the registry and tell it immediately to go hide in a corner and wait for further instructions. Here's how to start the remote registry in background:

- ✔ Windows: `start rmiregistry`
- ✔ UNIX: `rmiregistry &`

Make sure that the remote registry is up and running nicely, as shown in Figure 10-3, before you minimize it to get it the heck out of your way.

The registry keeps track of all the remote objects that are registered. Obviously, if you register a remote object (as you see in Step 4) and then mess around with the remote object — change it, recompile it, or whatever — without bringing the registry down and then back up again, the registry is damaged, the result of which is probably a `java.net.SocketException: Socket read failed` error after you attempt to start the server. Rule of thumb: Bounce the registry (in software parlance, to *bounce* means to bring a server or other program down and then back up again) every time you recompile *anything.*

Step 4: Start the server

To start the server in background mode, Windows users should type something similar to the following at the command-line prompt:

```
start java -Djava.rmi.server.codebase=c:/jdk-1.1/java/JB4D/
                examples.hello.HelloImpl
```

Make sure that you include the trailing forward slash after the `codebase` value in the preceding command; it's required.

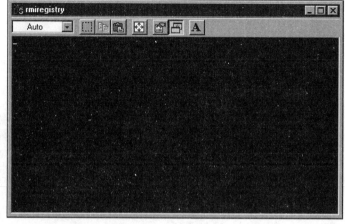

Figure 10-3:
The remote
registry,
successfully
started.

UNIX users should append the ampersand to the end of the command and leave off the start, as follows:

```
java -Djava.rmi.server.codebase=c:/jdk-1.1/java/JB4D/
                 examples.hello.HelloImpl &
```

The -D option preloads the server's codebase property with the base directory (the directory that contains all the .class files).

Figure 10-4 displays the result that you should see.

Step 5: Start the client

After the remote object registry and the Java server are running, it's time to kick off the Java client. From the c:/jdk-1.1/java/JB4D directory, type the following URL:

```
java theClient
```

Figure 10-5 displays the reward that you should receive for your efforts.

Depending on your hardware and software configuration (and on your patience, or lack thereof), the time it takes for the client to contact the server may seem interminable. Distributing applications always add a degree of processing overhead; that's the nature of the beast. As the Java environment matures, however, the lag should become much less notice-able. After all, Java was designed for the Internet, and the Internet is, by its very nature, distributed. Rest assured that some really smart folks are already working on this problem.

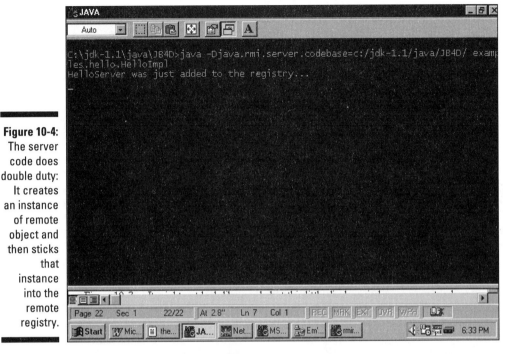

Figure 10-4:
The server code does double duty: It creates an instance of remote object and then sticks that instance into the remote registry.

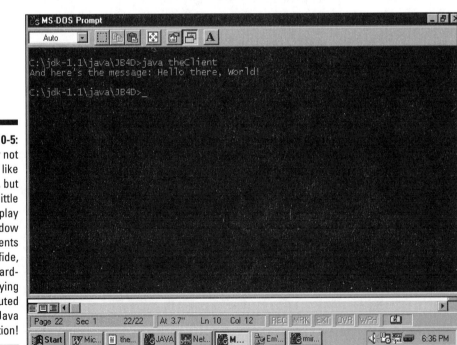

Figure 10-5:
It may not look like much, but this little display window represents a bona fide, card-carrying distributed Java application!

Part IV

The Nitty Gritty: The JavaBeans API (java.beans)

The 5th Wave   By Rich Tennant

PROGENITORS TO THE JAVA PROGRAMMING LANGUAGE

Lava | Developed in Hawaii, objects would suddenly erupt into a hot flowing stream of information.

Guava | Objects "grew" on computers tree structure which users could convert to a data jam to be spread across the Web.

Jabba "The Hut" | Named after the developer, objects tended to get lost in cyberspace.

Fava | Objects were referred to as "beans", but would repeat themselves when overused.

In this part . . .

The information in this reference part is essential for serious bean development! In this part, you find detailed descriptions of all of the APIs you need to understand to create JavaBeans components, organized not by package (that organization scheme can be found in the Index), but instead by the way you, as a developer, most likely want to use them: by function. I've created separate chapters devoted to introspection, customization, event handling, and persistence. (I've even thrown in a "Miscellaneous" chapter that lists the few odds-and-ends that didn't quite fit in the other categories.)

Chapter 11

Introspection Makes for Happy, Well-Adjusted Beans

● ●

In This Chapter

▶ Interface publishing: Spelling out your own bean details

▶ Interface discovery: Accessing other developers' bean details

● ●

*T*he process that an application-development tool uses to determine what properties, methods, and events are associated with another bean is called *introspection*. There are two major categories of introspection: *reflection* and *explicit specification*. Chapter 8 describes the support for introspection through reflection provided by the core Java API (java.lang.reflect). This chapter completes the picture by detailing the bean-specific classes, interfaces, and methods (all packaged in the java.beans API) that are devoted to explicit definition of a bean's vital statistics.

The BDK, a copy of which is on the companion CD-ROM, contains hypertext documentation that covers all the classes, interfaces, and methods presented in this chapter. To check it out, load the HTML file /bdk/doc/apis.html.

The Least You Need to Know about Introspection

There are two sides to the introspection coin: interface publishing and interface discovery. On the one side, bean developers are responsible for publishing their beans' interfaces. On the other side, application developers who want to use those beans are responsible for discovering the beans' interfaces.

Interface publishing

Bean developers, at their sole discretion, may choose to provide one or more descriptor classes to accompany each bean that they create. (A *descriptor class* is nothing more than a class that contains some descriptive information.) Special descriptor classes exist for events, parameters, methods, and properties — every aspect of a bean's life. Along with creating these descriptor classes, developers who want to describe their beans explicitly must create a class that implements the BeanInfo interface (similar to the SimpleBeanInfo class).

Interface discovery

When another developer wants to get familiar with the contents of your bean, all she needs to do is create an instance of the Introspector class and invoke its getBeanInfo() method, passing your bean's class as an argument. getBeanInfo() returns an instance of your implementation of BeanInfo (whew, that was a mouthful!). When she has your bean's associated implementation of BeanInfo, the other developer can call methods that return all the descriptor information associated with your bean.

 The most logical place for interface discovery to be is inside an application development tool. In such a scenario, the developer clicks on a button labeled something like "Display bean contents." Clicking the button does all the dirty work: creating the instance of the Introspector class, calling the getBeanInfo() method, and displaying the bean's members for the application developer in a nice graphical display window.

Classes

You use the classes in this chapter when you want to do one of the following:

- ✔ Publish your bean's interface
- ✔ Discover what the interface for somebody else's bean looks like

The following sections organize all the classes related to bean introspection alphabetically. For each class, I provide a description, a pedigree (a list of the class's parent, grandparent, and so on), and a list of related methods, along with some handy hints on how, when, and why you'd want to use each method.

Although constructors technically are methods, too (they're methods that you use to construct instances of a class), I broke them into their own little category so that they'll be easy to spot.

The "Pedigree" sections that appear throughout this chapter show what superclasses each class inherits from — a mighty handy thing to know. By default, every class inherits all of its predecessors' methods, so any given class contains not only the methods that are listed for it, but all the methods listed for each of its superclasses as well.

The properties of these classes aren't listed because (in keeping with sound object-oriented principles) they're not _exposed_ — that is, you can't get to them directly. The only way to access properties is through accessor methods, and the accessor methods _are_ listed.

BeanDescriptor

A BeanDescriptor provides global information about a bean, such as the name of its class and the properties defined in FeatureDescriptor, which is BeanDescriptor's parent class. BeanDescriptor is just one of the many kinds of descriptor objects that a BeanInfo object returns; it also returns descriptors for properties, methods, and events.

Pedigree

```
java.lang.Object
   ➪ java.beans.FeatureDescriptor
      ➪ java.beans.BeanDescriptor
```

Constructors

The BeanDescriptor class defines two constructors: one that accepts one argument, and one that accepts two arguments.

BeanDescriptor(String beanClassName)

This constructor uses reflection to create a BeanDescriptor for a bean that doesn't have an associated customizer. (See Chapter 15 for details on the Customizer class.)

Signature:

```
public BeanDescriptor(String beanClassName)
   throws IntrospectionException
```

Example:

```
DownloadDescriptor myDownLoadDescriptor = new
   BeanDescriptor(DownloadBean);
```

`BeanDescriptor(String beanClassName,`
`String customizerClassName`

This constructor creates a `BeanDescriptor` for a bean that has an associated customizer. (See Chapter 15 for details on the `Customizer` class.)

Signature:

```
public BeanDescriptor(String beanClassName,
           String customizerClassName)
  throws IntrospectionException
```

Example:

```
BeanDescriptor myDownLoadDescriptor = new
   BeanDescriptor(DownloadBean, DownloadCustomizer);
```

Methods

Only two methods are directly associated with the `BeanDescriptor` class.

`getBeanClass()`

This method returns the `Class` object associated with the bean.

Signature:

```
public Class getBeanClass()
```

Example:

```
someBeanDescriptor.getBeanClass();
```

`getCustomizerClass()`

This method returns the `Class` object of the bean's customizer. If the bean has no customizer, this method returns `null`. (See Chapter 15 for details on the `Customizer` class.)

Signature:

```
public Class getCustomizerClass()
```

Example:

```
someBeanDescriptor.getCustomizerClass();
```

EventSetDescriptor

An `EventSetDescriptor` describes a group of events that a bean can fire on a single event listener.

If you're not comfortable with all the various parts that make up the event model, check out Chapter 2 for an overview of the event-handling process.

Pedigree

```
java.lang.Object
    ⇨ java.beans.FeatureDescriptor
        ⇨ java.beans.EventSetDescriptor
```

Constructors

You can construct an `EventSetDescriptor` in four ways. You can use any of these constructors, although your choice often depends on two things:

- ✔ What information you have available to pass in when you're ready to create an `EventSetDescriptor`
- ✔ How closely you adhere to standard Java method-naming conventions

The first two constructors, for example, set descriptor values based on names you provide them (the constructors), so you can use these constructors even if you haven't followed standard Java naming conventions.

The second two constructors use reflection to set the descriptor values, so to use these constructors, you must already have implemented all the methods that make up an event and named the methods properly. (Refer to Chapter 3 for a description of standard method-naming conventions.)

EventSetDescriptor(Class, String, Class, String)

This constructor creates an `EventSetDescriptor` by making some assumptions. When you pass it a value for `eventSetName`, the constructor assumes the following things:

- ✔ Your listener interface is named `EventSetNameListener`.
- ✔ The class of your event is named `EventSetNameEvent`.

✔ Your registration method is named addEventSetNameListener.

✔ Your deregistration method is named removeEventSetNameListener.

If, for example, you decide to name your event set propertyChange, this constructor logs the listener interface as PropertyChangeListener, the event class as PropertyChangeEvent, the registration method as addPropertyChangeListener(), and the deregistration method as removePropertyChangeListener().

Signature:

```
public EventSetDescriptor(Class sourceClass,
            String eventSetName,
            Class listenerType,
            String listenerMethodName)
    throws IntrospectionException
```

In the preceding syntax:

✔ sourceClass is the name of the bean's class (the class that fires the event).

✔ eventSetName is the name by which you want this EventSetDescriptor to be known. The name should start with a lowercase character.

✔ listenerType is the name of the type of listener involved — in other words, the name of the interface that's allowed to listen to, or receive, events (also called a *target* interface).

✔ listenerMethodName is the name of the method on the target interface that is invoked when the target interface receives the event.

Example:

```
EventSetDescriptor anESD = new
        EventSetDescriptor(my.package.BeanClass,
        propertyChange ,
        java.beans.PropertyChangeListener.class,
        propertyChange );
```

```
EventSetDescriptor(Class, String,
Class, String[], String, String)
```
This constructor makes fewer assumptions than the first constructor makes, so instead of allowing the constructor to guess the names of your methods, you must specify the names explicitly.

Signature:

```
public EventSetDescriptor(Class sourceClass,
         String eventSetName,
         Class listenerClass,
         String listenerMethodNames[],
         String addListenerMethodName,
         String removeListenerMethodName)
  throws IntrospectionException
```

In the preceding syntax:

- ✔ sourceClass is the name of the bean's class (the class that fires the event).
- ✔ eventSetName is the name by which you want this EventSetDescriptor to be known. The name should start with a lowercase character.
- ✔ listenerClass is the name of the type of listener involved — in other words, the name of the interface that's allowed to listen to, or receive, events (also called a *target* interface).
- ✔ listenerMethodNames is an array of strings. Each string represents the name of one of the methods that is called when the event is delivered to its target listener interface.
- ✔ addListenerMethodName is the name of the registration method.
- ✔ removeListenerMethodName is the name of the deregistration method.

Example:

```
EventSetDescriptor anESD = new
        EventSetDescriptor(beanClass,
         propertyChange ,
        java.beans.PropertyChangeListener.class,
           listOfMethodNamesToCall[],
            mySpecialAddPCLMethod ,
            mySpecialRemovePCLMethod );
```

EventSetDescriptor(String, Class, Method[], Method, Method)

This constructor uses reflection to create an EventSetDescriptor. In other words, the constructor looks at the names of the various event-related methods and logs them into the descriptor.

Signature:

```
public EventSetDescriptor(String eventSetName,
          Class listenerType,
          Method listenerMethods[],
          Method addListenerMethod,
          Method removeListenerMethod)
  throws IntrospectionException
```

In the preceding syntax:

- ✔ eventSetName is the name by which you want this EventSetDescriptor to be known. The name should start with a lowercase character.

- ✔ listenerType is the name of the type of listener involved — in other words, the name of the interface that's allowed to listen to, or receive, events (also called a *target* interface).

- ✔ listenerMethods[] is an array of Method objects describing each of the event-handling methods in the target listener.

- ✔ addListenerMethod is the registration method.

- ✔ removeListenerMethod is the deregistration method. (This method is directly related to the preceding addListenerMethod method.)

Example:

```
String eventName;
Class listenerType;
Method methodList[];
Method addMethod;
Method removeMethod;

...
// logic to assign each of the variables above with
// the appropriate value
...
EventSetDescriptor anESD = new
    EventSetDescriptor(eventName,
               listenerType,
               methodList,
               addMethod,
               removeMethod);
```

EventSetDescriptor(String, Class,
MethodDescriptor[], Method, Method)

This constructor is nearly identical to the preceding one, in that this constructor also creates an EventSetDescriptor using the Class and Method objects. The difference? This constructor throws in a reference to the MethodDescriptor class instead of a list of methods (handy if you happen to have a MethodDescriptor defined).

Signature:

```
public EventSetDescriptor(String eventSetName,
    Class listenerType,
    MethodDescriptor listenerMethodDescriptors[],
    Method addListenerMethod,
    Method removeListenerMethod)
  throws IntrospectionException
```

In the preceding syntax:

- eventSetName is the name by which you want this EventSetDescriptor to be known. The name should start with a lowercase character.

- listenerType is the name of the type of listener involved — in other words, the name of the interface that's allowed to listen to, or receive, events (also called a *target* interface).

- listenerMethodDescriptors[] is an array of MethodDescriptor objects describing each of the event-handling methods in the target listener.

- addListenerMethod is the registration method.

- removeListenerMethod is the deregistration method.

Example:

```
String eventName;
Class listenerType;
MethodDescriptor methodDescriptorList[];
Method addMethod;
Method removeMethod;
...
// logic to assign each of the variables above with
// the appropriate value
...
```

(continued)

(continued)

```
EventSetDescriptor anESD = new
    EventSetDescriptor(eventName,
                listenerType,
                methodDescriptorList,
                addMethod,
                removeMethod);
```

Methods

The following nine methods are directly associated with the
`EventSetDescriptor` class.

getAddListenerMethod()

This method returns the listener-registration method implemented
on an event source. By default, this method takes the form of
`addEventNameListener`. For an event named `PropertyEvent`, for example,
this method returns `addPropertyEventListener()`.

The registration method for an event is set when an `EventSetDescriptor`
object is created. For details, see the constructors for
`EventSetDescriptor`.

Signature:

```
public Method getAddListenerMethod()
```

Example:

```
someEventSetDescriptor.getAddListenerMethod();
```

getListenerMethodDescriptors()

This method returns an array of `MethodDescriptor` objects associated with
the methods that are called when events are fired on a target listener
interface. This array of `MethodDescriptor` objects is set whenever an
`EventSetDescriptor` object is created (see the constructors associated
with `EventSetDescriptor` for details).

Signature:

```
public MethodDescriptor[] getListenerMethodDescriptors()
```

Example:

```
someEventSetDescriptor.getListenerMethodDescriptors();
```

```
getListenerMethods()
```
This method returns an array of `Method` objects representing methods within a target listener interface that are called when events are fired.

Signature:

```
public Method[] getListenerMethods()
```

Example:

```
someEventSetDescriptor.getListenerMethods();
```

```
getListenerType()
```
This method returns the `Class` object implemented for a target listener interface (`PropertyChangeEvent`, for example). As you may have guessed, this `Class` object is set as when an instance of `EventSetDescriptor` is created.

Signature:

```
public Class getListenerType()
```

Example:

```
someEventSetDescriptor.getListenerType();
```

```
getRemoveListenerMethod()
```
This method returns the listener deregistration method implemented on an event source. By default, this method takes the form of `removeEventNameListener`. For an event named `PropertyEvent`, for example, this method returns `removePropertyEventListener()`.

Signature:

```
public Method getRemoveListenerMethod()
```

Example:

```
someEventSetDescriptor.getRemoteListenerMethod();
```

isInDefaultEventSet()

Use this method to determine whether an event is in the default set. It may change in future JavaBeans implementations, but for now, categorizing an event as being part of the default set is just a way to mark the event so that you can retrieve it later (see `setInDefaultEventSet()`). `isInDefaultEventSet()` returns `true` if the event set is in the default set and `false` if it's not.

By default, the value returned by this method is `true`.

Signature:

```
public boolean isInDefaultEventSet()
```

Example:

```
someEventSetDescriptor.isInDefaultEventSet();
```

isUnicast()

Use this method to determine whether an event is unicast. Unlike multicast events, which can be sent to many listeners, event sources can send unicast event notifications to one target only. The average, everyday event is multicast, but you have the option to create (via `setUnicast()` and some fancy codework) a unicast event, if you ever feel the need. This method returns `true` if the event is unicast and `false` if it's multicast.

Signature:

```
public boolean isUnicast()
```

Example:

```
someEventSetDescriptor.isUnicast();
```

setInDefaultEventSet(boolean)

Use this method to mark an event as being part of the default set. Categorizing an event as being part of the default set is just a way to mark it so that you can retrieve it later; for more information, see the section that describes `isInDefaultEventSet()`.

Signature:

```
public void setInDefaultEventSet(boolean
   inDefaultEventSet)
```

Example:

```
someEventSetDescriptor.setInDefaultEventSet(false);
```

`setUnicast(boolean)`

Use this method to describe an event as unicast. Unlike multicast events, which can be sent to many listeners, event sources can send unicast event notifications to only one target. (The average, everyday event is multicast, but you have the option to detect (via `isUnicast()`) a unicast event.

Signature:

```
public void setUnicast(boolean unicast)
```

Example:

```
someEventSetDescriptor.setUnicast(false);
```

FeatureDescriptor

`FeatureDescriptor` is the base class (also called the *parent class* or *superclass*) of several other classes: `EventSetDescriptor`, `MethodDescriptor`, and `PropertyDescriptor`. As a result, these other classes inherit all of `FeatureDescriptor`'s methods free of charge!

Pedigree

```
java.lang.Object
   ↪ java.beans.FeatureDescriptor
```

Constructors

`FeatureDescriptor` defines one constructor, but you rarely call it directly. Instead, you call the constructors of the classes that inherit from `FeatureDescriptor`s: `EventSetDescriptor`, `MethodDescriptor`, and `PropertyDescriptor`.

`FeatureDescriptor()`

This constructor is about as simple as they come; it requires no parameters.

Signature:

```
public FeatureDescriptor()
```

Example:

```
FeatureDescriptor aFD = new FeatureDescriptor();
```

Methods

FeatureDescriptor boasts 13 methods. The following sections list those methods in alphabetical order:

attributeNames()

Returns an Enumeration containing the names of any attributes that were set with the setValue() method (described later in this chapter).

An Enumeration is nothing more than a collection of objects. Any class that implements the java.util.Enumeration interface must implement these two methods: hasMoreElements() and nextElement().

Signature:

```
public Enumeration attributeNames()
```

Example:

```
someFeatureDescriptor.attributeNames();
```

getDisplayName()

Returns a string representing the display name associated with a descriptor (see setDisplayName() later in this chapter). If no display name is set with setDisplayName(), this method returns the same value that getName() returns.

Signature:

```
public String getDisplayName()
```

Example:

```
someFeatureDescriptor.getDisplayName();
```

getName()

Returns the short programmatic name (as opposed to the nice long display name) of the descriptor set via setName().

Signature:

```
public String getName()
```

Example:

```
someFeatureDescriptor.getName();
```

getShortDescription()

Returns the short description associated with a feature via the
setShortDescription() method. If no short description is defined for the
feature, this method returns the same value as getDisplayName().

Signature:

```
public String getShortDescription()
```

Example:

```
someFeatureDescriptor.getShortDescription();
```

getValue(String)

Given an attribute name associated with a feature, this method returns the
value that's paired with that attribute. (See setValue() for details.) If no
value is associated with the specified attribute name for a feature, this
method returns null.

Signature:

```
public Object getValue(String attributeName)
```

Example:

```
someFeatureDescriptor.getValue( myAttribute );
```

isExpert()

Returns true if this feature is flagged as expert via the setExpert()
method; otherwise, returns false. (The expert flag is used to denote
features that are intended for expert users rather than plain old normal
users.)

Signature:

```
public boolean isExpert()
```

Example:

```
someFeatureDescriptor.isExpert();
```

isHidden()

Returns true if this feature is flagged as hidden via the setHidden() method; otherwise, returns false. (The hidden flag is used to mark features that are intended for use by application-development tools rather than human beings.)

Signature:

```
public boolean isHidden()
```

Example:

```
someFeatureDescriptor.isHidden();
```

setDisplayName(String)

Use this method to set the display name for a descriptor. You can use getDisplayName(), described earlier in this chapter, to retrieve the display name.

The difference between a display name and a normal, or programmatic, name is that a display name is meant for human eyes, whereas a programmatic name is intended for use inside a program. For this reason, display names generally are longer and more descriptive than programmatic names.

Signature:

```
public void setDisplayName(String displayName)
```

Example:

```
someFeatureDescriptor.setDisplayName( My Special Display
       Name );
```

setExpert(boolean)

Use this method to flag a feature as expert. (The expert flag marks features that are intended for use by expert users.) You can retrieve this value via the getExpert() method.

Signature:

```
public void setExpert(boolean expert)
```

Example:

```
someFeatureDescriptor.setExpert(true);
```

setHidden(boolean)

Use this method to flag a feature as hidden. (The hidden flag denotes features that are intended for use by application-development tools rather than human beings.) You can retrieve the Boolean value set by this method by using the isHidden() method.

Signature:

```
public void setHidden(boolean hidden)
```

Example:

```
someFeatureDescriptor.setHidden(true);
```

setName(String)

Use this method to associate a programmatic name (as opposed to a display name) with a descriptor. To retrieve the programmatic name, use the getName() method.

Signature:

```
public void setName(String name)
```

Example:

```
someFeatureDescriptor.setName( myName );
```

setShortDescription(String)

Use this method to associate a short description with a feature. (In this case, *short* means fewer than 40 characters.) You can use getShortDescription() to retrieve an existing short description.

Signature:

```
public void setShortDescription(String text)
```

Example:

```
someFeatureDescriptor.setShortDescription( Here is my
          description. );
```

setValue(String, Object)

Use this method to associate an attribute–value pair with a feature. You can use `getValue()` and `attributeNames()` to retrieve the attribute–value pair.

Signature:

```
public void setValue(String attributeName,
          Object value)
```

Example:

```
someFeatureDescriptor.setValue( myAttribute , myObject);
```

IndexedPropertyDescriptor

An `IndexedPropertyDescriptor` is a special kind of `PropertyDescriptor`. `IndexedPropertyDescriptor` describes an indexed property, which is a property that acts like an array and therefore has an indexed read method (and possibly an indexed write method) defined to allow access to specific elements of the array.

Pedigree

```
java.lang.Object
    ⇨ java.beans.FeatureDescriptor
        ⇨ java.beans.PropertyDescriptor
            ⇨ java.beans.IndexedPropertyDescriptor
```

Constructors

The `IndexedPropertyDescriptor` class defines three constructors.

IndexedPropertyDescriptor(String, Class)

This constructor constructs an `IndexedPropertyDescriptor` for a property with a bare minimum of information required from the caller. Because little information is passed from the caller, the constructor has to make an assumption — namely, that the accessor methods for this property follow the standard Java naming conventions (`getPropertyName()` and `setPropertyName()`).

Signature:

```
public IndexedPropertyDescriptor(String propertyName,
                Class beanClass)
  throws IntrospectionException
```

In the preceding syntax:

- ✔ propertyName is the programmatic name of the property.
- ✔ beanClass is the Class object of the bean that contains the property.

Example:

```
IndexedPropertyDescriptor anIPD = new
    IndexedPropertyDescriptor( FileList ,
                my.package.DownLoadBean);
```

IndexedPropertyDescriptor(String, Class,
String, String, String, String)
This constructor accepts the name of a property, as well as method names
for reading and writing the property, so the constructor doesn't have to
guess (for those times when getPropertyName() and setPropertyName()
just won't do the job).

Signature:

```
public IndexedPropertyDescriptor(String propertyName,
                Class beanClass,
                String getterName,
                String setterName,
                String indexedGetterName,
                String indexedSetterName)
  throws IntrospectionException
```

In the preceding syntax:

- ✔ propertyName is the programmatic name of the property.
- ✔ beanClass is the Class object of the bean that contains the property.
- ✔ getterName is the name of the method used to retrieve the property
  values as an array. This value may be null if the property is write-only
  or must be indexed.

✔ setterName is the name of the method used to write the property values as an array. This value may be null if the property is read-only or must be indexed.

✔ indexedGetterName is the name of the method used to read an indexed property value. This value may be null if the property is write-only.

✔ indexedSetterName is the name of the method used to write an indexed property value. This value may be null if the property is read-only.

Example:

```
IndexedPropertyDescriptor anIPD =
    new IndexedPropertyDescriptor( somePropertyName ,
                    my.package.SomeClass,
                    null,
                    null,
                      someIndexedGetter ,
                      someIndexedSetter );
```

IndexedPropertyDescriptor(String, Method, Method, Method, Method)

This constructor accepts the name of a simple property and a bunch of Method objects (instead of a bunch of strings representing method names, as the preceding constructor does) for read/write methods.

Signature:

```
public IndexedPropertyDescriptor(String propertyName,
                Method getter,
                Method setter,
                Method indexedGetter,
                Method indexedSetter)
    throws IntrospectionException
```

In the preceding syntax:

✔ propertyName is the programmatic name of the property.

✔ getter is the method used to read the property values as an array. This value may be null if the property is write-only or must be indexed.

✔ setter is the method used to write the property values as an array. This value may be null if the property is read-only or must be indexed.

> ✔ `indexedGetter` is the method used to read an indexed property value. This value may be `null` if the property is write-only.
>
> ✔ `indexedSetter` is the method used to write an indexed property value. This value may be `null` if the property is read-only.

Example:

```
addProperty(new IndexedPropertyDescriptor(
    decapitalize(someName.substring(3)),
    null,
    null,
    null,
    someMethod));
```

Methods

There's not much to describe with respect to an indexed property, so only three methods are associated with the `IndexedPropertyDescriptor` class.

getIndexedPropertyType()

This method returns the Java class of the indexed property.

Signature:

```
public Class getIndexedPropertyType()
```

Example:

```
someIndexedPropertyDescriptor.getIndexedPropertyType();
```

getIndexedReadMethod()

This method returns the method used to read an indexed property value. If the associated property isn't indexed or is write-only, this method returns `null`. No explicit `setIndexedReadMethod()` method exists. The value retrieved by this method is set when an `IndexedPropertyDescriptor` is created.

Signature:

```
public Method getIndexedReadMethod()
```

Example:

```
someIndexedPropertyDescriptor.getIndexedReadMethod();
```

getIndexedWriteMethod()

This method returns the method used to write an indexed property value. If the associated property isn't indexed or is read-only, this method returns null.

Signature:

```
public Method getIndexedWriteMethod()
```

Example:

```
someIndexedPropertyDescriptor.getIndexedWriteMethod();
```

IntrospectionException

An IntrospectionException is a special kind of exception that's thrown only when an exception occurs during introspection. (You may have noticed that many of the methods in this chapter throw one of these puppies.)

If you're a little fuzzy on exception handling, refer to Chapter 7, which contains a simple description of the overall exception-handling process.

Typical causes for this exception to be thrown include:

- Specifying a string class name that doesn't match up with a Class object.
- Specifying a string method name that doesn't match up with the name of a Method object.
- Specifying a method name that has the wrong type signature for its intended use.

Pedigree

```
java.lang.Object
   ⇨ java.lang.Throwable
      ⇨ java.lang.Exception
         ⇨ java.beans.IntrospectionException
```

Constructors

There's only one way to construct an IntrospectionException!

IntrospectionException(String)

This constructor is short and sweet; all it requires is a message so that the cause of an exception can be propagated back up through the Java code to the user.

Signature:

```
public IntrospectionException(String mess)
```

mess is a message explaining exactly what went wrong to cause the exception.

Example:

```
IntrospectionException aNoIndexedReadException =
    new IntrospectionException( Couldn t get the indexed
    read method because it doesn t exist. );
```

Methods

No methods are associated with the IntrospectionException class.

Introspector

An application builder can use the Introspector class to analyze a bean. When you invoke a getBeanInfo() method on Introspector, getBeanInfo() first looks for explicitly defined information — that is, it searches the search path for an implementation of the BeanInfo class associated with the specified bean. If getBeanInfo() doesn't find any explicitly defined information, it constructs all the information that it can, based on some standard design patterns (that is, it uses reflection). For more information about design patterns and introspection, check out Chapter 2.

Pedigree

```
java.lang.Object
    ⇨ java.beans.Introspector
```

Constructors

No public constructors are associated with the Introspector class. Not to worry, though — an instance of Introspector is created automatically when you invoke either of the getBeanInfo() methods.

Don't give me any of your static!

A *static* method (also known as a *class* method) is a special kind of method that relates not to one instance of a class, but to *all* instances of a class. Suppose that you have a class called `Person` and a billion instances of the class, including one called `Marcia`. A static method called `sing()` would cause all the people in the world to sing; a regular old instance method `sing()` would cause just one person to sing. Take a look at the code below and you see what I mean:

```
// static method
Person.sing() // everybody
   sings!
Person Marcia = new
   Person( Marcia Sampson );
// instance method
Marcia.sing() // only Marcia
   sings this time
```

Notice the difference in how these two types of methods are called? Because a static method doesn't have anything to do with any one particular instance, you call it using the name of the class, like so:

```
Person.sing()
```

On the other hand, instance methods can be called only on an instance of a class, so before you can call an instance method, you need to create an instance, like this:

```
Person Marcia = new
   Person( Marcia Sampson );
Marcia.sing() // only Marcia
   sings this time
```

Methods

The really significant methods associated with `Introspector` are the `getBeanInfo()` methods. A few convenient utility methods are also available.

decapitalize(String)

This utility method accepts a string and converts it to normal Java-variable-name capitalization, which involves converting the first character from uppercase to lowercase. If both the first and second characters are uppercase, however, the string is returned intact. This exception to the rule exists so you can create names like URL, IRS, and so on, which would look pretty funny if they were converted to uRL and iRS!

Signature:

```
public static String decapitalize(String name)
```

Example:

```
String correctJavaName =
  Introspector.decapitalize( PropertyName );
```

getBeanInfo(Class)

This method returns the implementation of the BeanInfo interface associated with a bean. See the section devoted to BeanInfo later in this chapter for details.

Signature:

```
public static BeanInfo getBeanInfo(Class beanClass)
  throws IntrospectionException
```

beanClass is the Class object associated with the bean that you want to get information about.

Example:

```
Introspector.getBeanInfo(anObject.getClass());
```

getBeanInfo(Class, Class)

This method returns the implementation of the BeanInfo interface associated with a specified class. By accepting a value representing a stopClass, this method purportedly allows you to choose a section of a hierarchy to report on.

Signature:

```
public static BeanInfo getBeanInfo(Class beanClass,
                  Class stopClass)
  throws IntrospectionException
```

In the preceding syntax:

- ✔ beanClass is the Class object associated with the bean that you want to analyze.
- ✔ stopClass is the class at which you want to stop the analysis. No bean information associated with the stopClass or with any of the stopClass's parent classes is returned.

Example:

```
Introspector.getBeanInfo(
          java.beans.IntrospectionException,
          java.lang.Throwable);
```

getBeanInfoSearchPath()

This method returns the array of package names that will be searched to find BeanInfo classes. The return value is initially set to java.beans.infos, but you can modify it with the setBeanInfoSearchPath() method (see setBeanIfoSearchPath() for details).

Signature:

```
public static String[] getBeanInfoSearchPath()
```

Example:

```
Introspector.getBeanInfoSearchPath();
```

setBeanInfoSearchPath(String[])

Use this method to change the list of package names to be used to find BeanInfo classes (refer to getBeanInfoSearchPath() earlier in this chapter).

Signature:

```
public static void setBeanInfoSearchPath(String path[])
```

Example:

```
Introspector.setBeanInfoSearchPath(listOfPackages);
```

MethodDescriptor

A MethodDescriptor can be associated with any publicly accessible method (that is, any method declared with the public keyword) that a bean supports.

Pedigree

```
java.lang.Object
    ⇨ java.beans.FeatureDescriptor
        ⇨ java.beans.MethodDescriptor
```

Constructors

The `MethodDescriptor` class defines two constructors for your constructing convenience.

MethodDescriptor(Method)

Use this constructor to create a `MethodDescriptor` given a `Method` object. The constructor constructs a `MethodDescriptor` by making educated guesses, based on what the `Method` object looks like.

Signature:

```
public MethodDescriptor(Method method)
```

Example:

```
MethodDescriptor anMD = new MethodDescriptor(someMethod);
```

MethodDescriptor(Method, ParameterDescriptor[])

If you've got `ParameterDescriptor` objects defined for a method's parameters, you can pass them in to this constructor. The result is an exhaustive description of the specified method.

Signature:

```
public MethodDescriptor(Method method,
        ParameterDescriptor parameterDescriptors[])
```

In the preceding syntax:

- ✔ method is the `Method` object that you want to associate the `MethodDescriptor` with.
- ✔ parameterDescriptors[] is an array of `ParameterDescriptor` objects, each of which contains descriptive information about one of the method's parameters.

Example:

```
MethodDescriptor anMD = new MethodDescriptor(someMethod,
        someArrayOfParameterDescriptors);
```

Methods

Only two methods are associated with the `MethodDescriptor` object. One method returns the associated `Method`, and the other returns the associated `Method`'s parameter descriptions. You set these values by using the constructors described in the preceding section.

getMethod()

This method returns the `Method` object associated with a `MethodDescriptor`.

Signature:

```
public Method getMethod()
```

Example:

```
someMethodDescriptor.getMethod();
```

getParameterDescriptors()

This method returns an array of `ParameterDescriptor` objects associated with a `MethodDescriptor`. If no associated `ParameterDescriptor`s exist, this method returns `null`.

Signature:

```
public ParameterDescriptor[] getParameterDescriptors()
```

Example:

```
someMethodDescriptor.getParameterDescriptors();
```

ParameterDescriptor

The `ParameterDescriptor` class describes (you guessed it) method parameters. Like many of the other descriptor classes — `MethodDescriptor`, `EventSetDescriptor`, and `PropertyDescriptor` — this class inherits directly from `FeatureDescriptor`.

Pedigree

```
java.lang.Object
    ⇨ java.beans.FeatureDescriptor
        ⇨ java.beans.ParameterDescriptor
```

Constructors

The `ParameterDescriptor` class contains just one constructor.

ParameterDescriptor()

This bare-bones constructor accepts no arguments.

Signature:

```
public ParameterDescriptor()
```

Example:

```
ParameterDescriptor aPD = new ParameterDescriptor();
```

Methods

No methods are associated directly with the `ParameterDescriptor` class. This class inherits all of its behavior from its parent, `FeatureDescriptor`. (Refer to the description of `FeatureDescriptor` earlier in this chapter for details.)

PropertyDescriptor

Use the `PropertyDescriptor` class to provide detailed information about each (or just some) of a bean's properties.

Pedigree

```
java.lang.Object
   ⇨ java.beans.FeatureDescriptor
      ⇨ java.beans.PropertyDescriptor
```

Constructors

Three constructors are associated with the `PropertyDescriptor` class.

PropertyDescriptor(String, Class)

This constructor creates a `PropertyDescriptor` object, given a class and the name of a property. To accomplish this task, this constructor assumes that the accessor methods for this property are named `getPropertyName()` and `setPropertyName()`. If the names are different, for some reason, use one of the other `PropertyDescriptor` constructors explained in the following sections.

Signature:

```
public PropertyDescriptor(String propertyName,
            Class beanClass)
    throws IntrospectionException
```

In the preceding syntax:

- ✔ propertyName is the programmatic name of the property.

- ✔ beanClass is the Class object of the bean that contains the property described by propertyName.

Example:

```
PropertyDescriptor aPD = new
    PropertyDescriptor( lastName , my.package.myBean);
```

PropertyDescriptor(String, Class, String, String)

If the standard Java naming conventions for get and set accessor methods just won't cut it, use this constructor, which allows you to specify the accessor method names yourself.

Signature:

```
public PropertyDescriptor(String propertyName,
            Class beanClass,
            String getterName,
            String setterName)
    throws IntrospectionException
```

In the preceding syntax:

- ✔ propertyName is the programmatic name of the property.

- ✔ beanClass is the Class object of the bean that contains the property described by propertyName.

- ✔ getterName is the name of the read accessor method associated with this property. The value should be null if the property is write-only.

- ✔ setterName is the name of the write accessor method associated with this property. The value should be null if the property is read-only.

Example:

```
PropertyDescriptor aPD = new
  PropertyDescriptor( lastName , my.package.myBean,
  mySpecialGetMethod , mySpecialSetMethod );
```

PropertyDescriptor(String, Method, Method)

This constructor is similar to the preceding one. The only difference is that this constructor accepts Method objects for the get and set accessors instead of accepting method names represented by strings.

Signature:

```
public PropertyDescriptor(String propertyName,
            Method getter,
            Method setter)
  throws IntrospectionException
```

In the preceding syntax:

- propertyName is the programmatic name of the property.
- getter is the Method object corresponding to the read accessor method for this property. The value should be null if the property is write-only.
- setter is the Method object corresponding to the write accessor method for this property. The value should be null if the property is read-only.

Example:

```
PropertyDescriptor aPD = new
  PropertyDescriptor( lastName , my.package.myBean,
  mySpecialGetMethod, mySpecialSetMethod);
```

Methods

Nine instance methods are associated with the java.beans.PropertyDescriptor class.

getPropertyEditorClass()

This method returns the PropertyEditor class associated with a PropertyDescriptor.

Normally, this method returns null, because the PropertyEditorManager (defined later in this chapter) takes care of finding the correct PropertyEditor based on standard Java naming conventions. This method is really useful only if you're providing a custom PropertyEditor class.

Signature:

```
public Class getPropertyEditorClass()
```

Example:

```
somePropertyDescriptor.getPropertyEditorClass();
```

getPropertyType()

This method returns the Class associated with a property described by a PropertyDescriptor. The return value represents the class of the property, not the class of the bean that contains the property.

Signature:

```
public Class getPropertyType()
```

Example:

```
somePropertyDescriptor.getPropertyType();
```

getReadMethod()

This method returns the read (or get) accessor method for a property. This method returns null if no associated read accessor method exists.

Signature:

```
public Method getReadMethod()
```

Example:

```
somePropertyDescriptor.getReadMethod();
```

getWriteMethod()

This method returns the write (also called set) accessor method associated with a property. This method returns null if no associated write accessor method exists.

Signature:

```
public Method getWriteMethod()
```

Example:

```
somePropertyDescriptor.getWriteMethod();
```

isBound()

This method returns `true` if the `PropertyDescriptor` indicates that a property is bound; otherwise, returns `false`. You set this value via the `setBound()` method (described later in this chapter).

For an overview of bound properties, refer to Chapter 3.

Signature:

```
public boolean isBound()
```

Example:

```
somePropertyDescriptor.isBound();
```

isConstrained()

This method returns `true` if the `PropertyDescriptor` indicates that a property is constrained; otherwise, returns `false`. You set this value via the `setConstrained()` method (described later in this chapter).

Constrained properties are discussed in detail in Chapter 3.

Signature:

```
public boolean isConstrained()
```

Example:

```
somePropertyDescriptor.isConstrained();
```

setBound(boolean)

Use this method to flag a property as bound. You can retrieve this value via the `getBound()` method (described earlier in this chapter).

For a description of what bound properties are and how they work, check out Chapter 3.

Signature:

```
public void setBound(boolean bound)
```

Example:

```
somePropertyDescriptor.setBound(true);
```

setConstrained(boolean)

Use this method to mark a property as constrained. You can retrieve this value via the `getConstrained()` method (described earlier in this chapter).

For a description of what constrained properties are and how they work, refer to Chapter 3.

Signature:

```
public void setConstrained(boolean constrained)
```

Example:

```
somePropertyDescriptor.setConstrained(true);
```

setPropertyEditorClass(Class)

Use this method to associate a `PropertyEditor` class with a property. `getPropertyEditorClass()` (described earlier in this chapter) retrieves the value set via `setPropertyEditorClass()`.

Most properties are edited by a standard property editor designed specifically for that type of property. The only reason to use this method is if you want to override the standard approach and to provide a specially named `PropertyEditor` for a property type.

Signature:

```
public void setPropertyEditorClass(Class
                  propertyEditorClass)
```

Bean and BeanInfo, sittin' in a tree...

It's no accident that the information in BeanInfo is implemented as a separate class. Because BeanInfo is useful only at design time, it has nothing to gain by hanging around at runtime, taking up space, doing nothing — and because it's implemented separately, it doesn't have to!

Here's how a bean and its associated BeanInfo are related: When an application developer calls Introspector.getBeanInfo(someBean), the association is made right there, on the spot. Cool, huh?

Example:

```
aPropertyDescriptor.setPropertyEditorClass(someSpecialPEC);
```

SimpleBeanInfo

SimpleBeanInfo implements the BeanInfo interface, which is described in the "Interfaces" section later in this chapter. SimpleBeanInfo is a good example of how to go about implementing the BeanInfo interface. SimpleBeanInfo is also useful in its own right, because you can inherit from it and override just the methods that are appropriate for your application.

Pedigree

```
java.lang.Object
    ⇨ java.beans.SimpleBeanInfo
```

Constructors

Only one constructor is associated with SimpleBeanInfo.

SimpleBeanInfo()
This constructor accepts no parameters. What could be simpler?

Signature:

```
public SimpleBeanInfo()
```

Example:

```
SimpleBeanInfo mySBI = new SimpleBeanInfo();
```

Methods

All the methods in the `BeanInfo` interface are implemented in the `SimpleBeanInfo` class, but all of them return `null`. Why? So that you can derive from `SimpleBeanInfo` and override just the methods you want to override. You could instead create your own class that implements the `BeanInfo` interface, if you like, but deriving from `SimpleBeanInfo` is quicker and easier than starting from scratch.

getAdditionalBeanInfo()

This method can be overridden to return an array of `BeanInfo` objects associated with a bean. By default, the method returns none.

Signature:

```
public BeanInfo[] getAdditionalBeanInfo()
```

Example:

```
someSimpleBeanInfo.getAdditionalBeanInfo();
```

getBeanDescriptor()

You can override this method to return a bean's `BeanDescriptor`. By default, the method returns none.

Signature:

```
public BeanDescriptor getBeanDescriptor()
```

Example:

```
someSimpleBeanInfo.getBeanDescriptor();
```

getDefaultEventIndex()

Override this method to return a bean's associated default event index. By default, the method returns `null`.

Signature:

```
public int getDefaultEventIndex()
```

Example:

```
someSimpleBeanInfo.getDefaultEventIndex();
```

getDefaultPropertyIndex()

Override this method to return a bean's associated default property index. By default, the method returns `null`.

Signature:

```
public int getDefaultPropertyIndex()
```

Example:

```
someSimpleBeanInfo.getDefaultPropertyIndex();
```

getEventSetDescriptors()

Override this method to return an array of `EventSetDescriptor` objects associated with a bean. By default, the method returns `null`.

Signature:

```
public EventSetDescriptor[] getEventSetDescriptors()
```

Example:

```
someSimpleBeanInfo.getEventSetDescriptors();
```

getIcon(int)

Override this method to return an icon image associated with a bean, given an integer describing the kind of icon that you want to get. By default, the method returns `null`.

Signature:

```
public Image getIcon(int iconKind)
```

Example:

```
someSimpleBeanInfo.getIcon(BeanInfo.ICON_COLOR_32x32);
```

getMethodDescriptors()

Override this method to return an array of `MethodDescriptor` objects associated with a bean. By default, the method returns `null`.

Signature:

```
public MethodDescriptor[] getMethodDescriptors()
```

Example:

```
someSimpleBeanInfo.getMethodDescriptors();
```

getPropertyDescriptors()

Override this method to return an array of `PropertyDescriptor` objects associated with a bean. By default, the method returns `null`.

Signature:

```
public PropertyDescriptor[] getPropertyDescriptors()
```

Example:

```
someSimpleBeanInfo.getPropertyDescriptors();
```

loadImage(String)

This utility method accepts a string representing the name of an image file. If the method is successful in its attempt to load the named image, it returns the loaded `Image` object; otherwise, it returns `null`.

Signature:

```
public Image loadImage(String resourceName)
```

resourceName is a path name relative to the base directory of the current class loader.

Example:

```
public java.awt.Image getIcon(int iconKind) {
    if (iconKind == BeanInfo.ICON_COLOR_16x16) {
        java.awt.Image img = loadImage( JugglerIcon.gif );
        return img;
    }
    return null;
}
```

Interfaces

An interface is an *abstract class*, which is a class that contains only abstract methods. (An *abstract method* is a method that has no body defined for it — just a signature.) Think of an interface as being a template that you have to fill in with concrete information before you can use it. You need to define a class that implements the interface's abstract methods and *then* use that class.

Only one interface is associated with bean introspection: `BeanInfo`.

BeanInfo

`BeanInfo` is the Big Cheese when it comes to introspection. The methods of the `Introspector` class (defined earlier in this chapter) look for an implementation of `BeanInfo` immediately, and if they find one, they use all the methods that the `BeanInfo` implementation has defined to get the scoop on a particular bean.

`BeanInfo` isn't an all-or-nothing proposition; you can be as detailed as you want in your bean description. Want to supply accessor method descriptions but nothing else? No problem! Want to go whole-hog and describe every single element of a bean? That's fine, too; it's all up to you.

For a quick-and-dirty implementation of the `BeanInfo` interface, refer to the `SimpleBeanInfo` class, described earlier in this chapter.

Methods

This section lists all the methods that you can implement as part of the `BeanInfo` interface. You can implement as many methods as you like, as long as you implement at least one. Because these methods belong to an interface, not a class, no concrete examples can be given; instead, check out `SimpleBeanInfo` to see examples of any of the `BeanInfo` methods.

getAdditionalBeanInfo()

Implement this method to return an array of `BeanInfo` objects that represent additional information related to a bean. If any conflicts exist between the information in the initial `BeanInfo` and any of the `BeanInfo` objects in the returned array, the initial `BeanInfo` wins the toss.

Signature:

```
public abstract BeanInfo[] getAdditionalBeanInfo()
```

`getBeanDescriptor()`

Implement this method to return a `BeanDescriptor` object.
(`BeanDescriptor`s provide overall information about a bean; refer to the
section on `BeanDescriptor` earlier in this chapter.) If no `BeanDescriptor`
is associated with a bean, this method returns `null`.

Signature:

```
public abstract BeanDescriptor getBeanDescriptor()
```

`getDefaultEventIndex()`

Implement this method to return the index of the default event, if any, that's
associated with a bean. (Default events are set for a bean by means of the
`setInDefaultEventSet()` method of the `EventSetDescriptor` class, both
of which are described earlier in this chapter.) If no default event is associated with a bean, this method returns a value of -1.

Signature:

```
public abstract int getDefaultEventIndex()
```

`getDefaultPropertyIndex()`

Implement this method to return the index of the default property, if any,
that's associated with a bean. (A default property is the property that's
voted most likely to be updated by someone who is customizing the bean;
see the `PropertyDescriptor` class in this chapter for details.) If no default
property is associated with a bean, this method should return the value -1.

Signature:

```
public abstract int getDefaultPropertyIndex()
```

`getEventSetDescriptors()`

Implement this method to return an array of `EventSetDescriptor` objects
associated with a bean. (For more information on the `EventSetDescriptor`
class, which is used to describe the events that a bean can fire, refer to the
"EventSetDescriptor" section earlier in this chapter.) This method returns
`null` if no `EventSetDescriptor`s are associated with a bean.

Signature:

```
public abstract EventSetDescriptor[]
  getEventSetDescriptors()
```

getIcon(int)

Implement this method to return an image object (an icon) that can be used to represent the bean in application-development tools (toolboxes, toolbars — that kind of thing). Currently, icon images must be .GIF files, but in the future, support for other image formats may be provided. This method should return a value of `null` if no icon image is associated with a bean.

Signature:

```
public abstract Image getIcon(int iconKind)
```

The `int` parameter passed to `getIcon()` must be one of the following four choices, all of which are integers defined as constant values in `BeanInfo`:

- ✔ ICON_COLOR_16x16
- ✔ ICON_COLOR_32x32
- ✔ ICON_MONO_16x16
- ✔ ICON_MONO_32x32

getMethodDescriptors()

Implement this method to return an array of `MethodDescriptor` objects associated with a bean. (The `MethodDescriptor` class, detailed earlier in this chapter, describes the externally accessible, or *public*, methods supported by a bean.) This method should return a value of `null` if no `MethodDescriptor`s are associated with a bean.

Signature:

```
public abstract MethodDescriptor[] getMethodDescriptors()
```

getPropertyDescriptors()

Implement this method to return an array of `PropertyDescriptor` objects associated with a bean. (The `PropertyDescriptor` class, detailed earlier in this chapter, describes the editable properties associated with a bean.) This method should return a value of `null` if no `PropertyDescriptor`s are associated with a bean.

Signature:

```
public abstract PropertyDescriptor[]
  getPropertyDescriptors()
```

Chapter 12

Handle with Care

• •

In This Chapter

▶ Creating events

▶ Using predefined events

▶ Designating beans as event sources and targets

• •

*B*ecause event handling isn't a bean-specific issue, support for it is
implemented in the Java package `java.util`. Only two classes and
one interface in the `java.util` package are directly related to event handling, so getting familiar with the API is a snap. What's a little more challeng-
ing is understanding the steps associated with event implementation, so this
chapter covers all that, too — along with a couple of advanced event
features for exploring when you're feeling frisky.

The Least You Need to Know about Event Handling

The bean-event-handling process has three conceptual participants:

> ✔ **The event source.** As soon as this bean detects an event, it fires off an
> announcement (okay, a method) to any other bean that's interested.
>
> ✔ **The event target.** Beans that are interested in hearing about the event
> when it occurs call a method on the event source to register their
> interest. (Event targets must implement the `java.util.Event`
> `Listener` interface, described later in this chapter.)
>
> ✔ **The event itself.** An event can be any significant happening that a
> developer wants to define. Some familiar examples include a change in
> a property value and a click of a button. (Events must derive from the
> `java.util.EventObject` class, which is described later in this
> chapter.)

Classes

This section organizes alphabetically all of the classes related to event handling. As I do in all of the chapters in this part, for each class I provide a description, a pedigree (a list of the class's parent, grandparent, and so on), and a list of the class's methods.

Only two classes relate directly to event handling: the event itself (Event Object) and a special kind of exception, called TooManyListeners, that you can use to restrict an event to one listener. (Check out the section on unicast event delivery later in this chapter for more information on TooManyListeners.)

EventObject

java.util.EventObject is an abstract event (and no, I don't know why they didn't just call it Event!) and you use it when you want to create a new kind of event that beans can recognize. Because the event is abstract, you can't use it directly — that is, you can't create an instance of EventObject.

What you *can* do, though, is derive your own class of event from Event Object and then create instances of that derived class. Listing 12-1 shows how the folks who put together the BDK did exactly this (that is, derived a new class of event from EventObject) when they created the Property ChangeEvent. PropertyChangeEvent inherits directly from Event Object and calls EventObject's constructor from its own (a common inheritance trick).

Listing 12-1	EventObject

See how this class extends EventObject? —

First call is to — Property-Change-Event's parent's constructor

```
...
public class PropertyChangeEvent
    extends java.util.EventObject {
    public PropertyChangeEvent(Object source,
                String propertyName,
                Object oldValue,
                Object newValue) {

        // call EventObject's constructor
        super(source);
        this.propertyName = propertyName;
        this.newValue = newValue;
    }
    ...
```

TIP

The `VetoableChange` class, also available as part of the BDK, is another example of an `EventObject` implementation.

Pedigree

```
java.lang.Object
   ⇨ java.util.EventObject
```

Constructors

Only one constructor is associated with the `EventObject` class.

EventObject(Object)

This constructor requires just one parameter: a value representing the event source (in other words, the bean responsible for detecting the event and notifying other beans of the event).

Signature:

```
public EventObject(Object source)
```

Because you can't instantiate `EventObject` directly, you never see `new EventObject(source)`. Instead, you have to call this constructor from within the constructor of a derived class, like this:

```
public class PropertyChangeEvent
   extends java.util.EventObject {

   public PropertyChangeEvent(Object source,
               String propertyName,
               Object oldValue,
               Object newValue) {

      // call EventObject's constructor
      super(source);
      ...
      }
```

Here's the call to Event-Object's constructor

Methods

The abstract `EventObject` class has two associated methods: `getSource()` and `toString()`. Just because you inherit from `EventObject` doesn't mean that you *have* to implement these methods, but I recommend that you do; they're useful to have around.

getSource()

This method returns the source bean associated with an `EventObject`.

Signature:

```
public Object getSource()
```

Example:

```
someEventObject.getSource();
```

toString()

This method returns a string representation of an `EventObject`.

Signature:

```
public String toString()
```

Example:

```
someEventObject.toString();
```

TooManyListenersException

Use this exception class to limit the number of beans that can receive an event to one. (See the section "A Cast of Thousands," later in this chapter for the complete scoop on using `java..util.TooManyListeners Exception` to create a unicast event.)

Pedigree

```
java.lang.Object
    ⇨ java.lang.Throwable
        ⇨ java.lang.Exception
            ⇨ java.util.TooManyListenersException
```

Constructors

You can construct a `TooManyListenersException` in two ways. One method requires no parameters; the other method accepts a parameter representing a detailed message.

TooManyListenersException()

Use this constructor to create a plain-vanilla `TooManyListenersException` exception.

Signature:

```
public TooManyListenersException()
```

Example:

```
TooManyListenersException aTMLE =
  new TooManyListenersException();
```

TooManyListenersException(String)

Use this constructor to create a TooManyListenersException with a specified detail message.

Signature:

```
public TooManyListenersException(String s)
```

s is a string that describes this particular exception.

Example:

```
String aMessage = Sorry, only one bean is allowed to reg-
              ister itself as a listener for this event.

TooManyListenersException aTMLE =
  new TooManyListenersException(aMessage);
```

Methods

No methods are associated with the TooManyListenersException class.

Interfaces

Only one interface is directly related to event handling: java.util.Event Listener.

EventListener

If you want to create a target bean (that is, a bean that can listen for events), you must do two things:

- ✔ Create a new type of interface that extends the EventListener interface
- ✔ Have your target bean implement the new interface, either directly or via an adapter

The EventListener interface is a little different from some of the other Java interfaces that you may have run across in that it has no associated methods. Now, it's true that the whole point of an interface normally is to declare some methods. In this case, though, the interface keyword is used more as an organizing mechanism — a way of associating a bean with the role of a listener. Look at the real-life example of creating a new interface based on EventListener shown in Listing 12-2.

Listing 12-2	The EventListener Interface

```
public interface PropertyChangeListener
   extends java.util.EventListener {
   void propertyChange(PropertyChangeEvent evt);
}
```

As you can see in the preceding code, the only method that has to be defined for an event listener is the one that the event source calls (in this case, propertyChange()).

Methods

No methods are associated with the EventListener interface.

Event Handling 101

Because implementing events involves several source files, the process can be a little confusing until you're used to it. To help you hit the ground running, here's a blow-by-blow description of an event that you've probably seen before (the PropertyChangeEvent), along with an example showing you how to hook it up to both source and target beans.

When you understand what event handling is and how it works conceptually (Chapter 3 contains a nice overview), all you really need to know are the answers to these questions:

✔ What classes and methods do I need to write to implement an event, and what source files do the classes and methods need to go in?

✔ How do these classes and methods work together to implement an event?

The following sections provide detailed answers to these questions.

The play

The classes and methods defined in the following sections represent the complete event implementation. The following list explains how the pieces fit together at runtime. (You can flip back to the code listings to verify your understanding; just match up the following numbers below with the numbers in the listings.)

1. A user changes the `debug` property of `OurButton` by invoking `setDebug()`.

2. `setDebug()` calls `changes.firePropertyChange()`. (`changes` is an instance of `PropertyChangeSupport`.)

3. `firePropertyChange()` does two things:

   A. Creates a new instance of `PropertyChangeEvent`

   B. For each registered listener, calls `propertyChange()`

4. `DemoChangeReporter` is a registered listener, so

   A. its `propertyChange()` method is called, which in turn calls

   B. `reporter.reportChange()`. (`reporter` is an instance of the `ChangeReporter` class.)

5. The `reporter.reportChange()` method does all the work necessary to display the changed property's name and new value on-screen.

The players

A complete event implementation involves five distinct chunks of functions:

- **An event.** First, you need to define an event (in this example, the event is named `PropertyChangeEvent`, as shown in Listing 12-3 later in this chapter) that describes the type of event you're implementing.

- **A new type of listener.** The listener in this example is `Property ChangeListener`, as you see in Listing 12-4 later in this chapter.

- **A support class.** As shown in Listing 12-5 later in this chapter, the `PropertyChangeSupport` class (a utility class) is used to define a pair of registration/deregistration methods and a broadcast method.

- **A pair of registration/deregistration wrapper methods and a call to the broadcast method.** The source bean (`OurButton`, as you see in Listing 12-6 later in this chapter) needs to define a pair of registration/deregistration wrapper methods. The source bean also needs to contain a call to the broadcast method defined in the support class.

That's quite an event!

Event handling is absurdly easy on the surface, but it gets a little stickier when you start thinking about complex bean interaction. How am I (an application developer) supposed to know what you (a bean developer) mean by `CiaoBabyEvent`, `LeftHanded DoubleClickEvent`, and so on? Unless a master handbook somewhere tells me, I have to rely on your abundant and accurate documentation. (Go ahead, indulge yourself; I'll wait until the laughter subsides.)

Now, for basic user-interface issues, event semantics aren't a big deal. Most developers can quickly figure out what a `ButtonClick`, a `PropertyChangeEvent`, or even an `ActionEvent` is. But what about events that are conceptual — that are tied to the internal logic of your bean? If I buy an accounting bean from you, for example, how the heck am I supposed to know what to do with the events that your bean generates if I know absolutely nothing about accounting?

The solutions generally fall into one of two categories:

✔ I look up the name of each of your bean's events in a huge dictionary that contains all the standard events that developers can use. (Believe it or not, this approach is actually used for at least one event model that I know of.)

✔ I drop your bean into an application-building tool, and the tool displays a nice little description of the events that your bean supports. I point and click, attaching events to the methods of other beans as appropriate for my application. The tool takes care of all the grunt work — in fact, adapters were devised for just this reason.

Adapters are a little clunky when you code them by hand, but they allow a tool to connect beans without having any advance knowledge of them. Even so, I still have to have enough domain knowledge — of accounting in general, of your bean in particular, and of the application that I'm trying to create — to be able to use your bean intelligently.

I've said it before, but it's worth saying again: The bottom line is that somebody somewhere *has* to know what's going on. Constructing nontrivial (read *valuable*) component software won't be viable, in the near or distant future, unless you have access to all of the following:

✔ Standards (formal, de facto, or both)

✔ Really good development tools

✔ Last, but certainly not least, a clue!

Nobody would consider putting a car together with nonstandard parts, second-rate tools, and no idea of what the finished car should look like or how it should perform! Software, in some respects, is no different.

✔ **An adapter and a call to the registration method.** In the example shown in Listing 12-7, later in this chapter, the target bean is `DemoChangeReporter`, the adapter is an implementation of the `PropertyChangeListener`, and the call to the registration method is located in `OurButton`.

After you read the listings in the following sections, read "The play" for an analysis of each listing.

The code in the following listings can be a little overwhelming at first, if for no other reason than there's so much of it! It would be nice if you could implement an event by writing only three little code statements — one each for the source, the target, and the event. Unfortunately (or fortunately; see the sidebar "That's quite an event!"), there's more to implementing events than three simple code statements. I suggest that you glance through the listings and then read the blow-by-blow description in "The play" to reinforce your understanding of how all the source code ties together.

PropertyChangeEvent

The PropertyChangeEvent class definition shown in Listing 12-3 contains a constructor and a few accessor methods.

PropertyChange-Event inherits from the EventObject. —

Listing 12-3	**PropertyChangeEvent.java**

```
public class PropertyChangeEvent extends
   java.util.EventObject {
   public PropertyChangeEvent(Object source,
                String propertyName,
                Object oldValue,
                Object newValue) {
     super(source);
     this.propertyName = propertyName;
     this.newValue = newValue;
   }

   /**
    * Returns the programmatic name of the
    * property that was changed.
    */
   public String getPropertyName() {
     return propertyName;
   }

   /**
    * Returns the new value for the property.
    */
   public Object getNewValue() {
     return newValue;
   }
```

(continued)

Listing 12-3 *(continued)*

```
/**
 * Returns the old value for the property.
 */
public Object getOldValue() {
  return oldValue;
}

…
private String propertyName;
private Object newValue;
private Object oldValue;
…
}
```

PropertyChangeListener

The `PropertyChangeListener` class definition, shown in Listing 12-4, is short and to the point.

Listing 12-4   `PropertyChangeListener.java`

```
package java.beans;

/**
 * A PropertyChangeEvent gets fired whenever a bean
 * changes a bound property.
 */

public interface PropertyChangeListener
  extends java.util.EventListener {
  /**
   * This method gets called when a bound property is
   * changed.
   */

  void propertyChange(PropertyChangeEvent evt);
}
```

Property-
Change-
Listener
extends
plain old ———
EventListener.

Called by the
source bean
when an
event
occurs. ———

PropertyChangeSupport

The `PropertyChangeSupport` class, shown in Listing 12-5, implements all the methods related to registering and firing this type of event.

Listing 12-5   PropertyChangeSupport.java

```
package java.beans;

/**
 * This is a utility class that can be used by beans
 * that support bound
 * properties.
 */
…
public class PropertyChangeSupport implements
  java.io.Serializable {

  /**
   * Constructor
   */

  public PropertyChangeSupport(Object sourceBean) {
    source = sourceBean;
  }

  /**
   * Add a PropertyChangeListener to the listener list.
   */

  public synchronized void addPropertyChangeListener(
          PropertyChangeListener listener) {
    if (listeners == null) {
      listeners = new java.util.Vector();
    }
    listeners.addElement(listener);
  }

  /**
   * Remove a PropertyChangeListener from the
   * list of listeners.
   */

  public synchronized void
    removePropertyChangeListener(
          PropertyChangeListener listener) {
    if (listeners == null) {
      return;
```

Here's the implementation of the registration method. ———

Here's the implementation of the deregistration method. ———

(continued)

Listing 12-5 *(continued)*

```
    }
    listeners.removeElement(listener);
  }


  /**
   * Report a bound property update to any
   * registered listeners.
   *
   * propertyName is the programmatic name of
   * the property that was changed.
   * oldValue is he old value of the property.
   * newValue is the new value of the property.
   */
```

Refer to #3 in "The play" section —————

```
  public void firePropertyChange(String propertyName,
                    Object oldValue,
                    Object newValue) {
java.util.Vector targets;
    synchronized (this) {
      if (listeners == null) {
        return;
      }
```

Refer to #3a in "The play" section —————

```
      targets = (java.util.Vector) listeners.clone();
    }
    PropertyChangeEvent evt = new
        PropertyChangeEvent(source,
                  propertyName,
                  oldValue,
                  newValue);
```

Refer to #3b in "The play" section —————

```
    for (int i = 0; i < targets.size(); i++) {
      PropertyChangeListener target =
      (PropertyChangeListener)targets.elementAt(i);
      target.propertyChange(evt);
    }
  }


  private java.util.Vector listeners;
  private Object source;
}
```

TIP

Synchin' up

You may be wondering about the `synchro- nized` keyword that appears so frequently in the preceding code, as in the following example:

```
public synchronized void
  addPropertyChangeListener(
        PropertyChangeListener
  listener) {
```

Synchronous delivery means sending something and then putting everything else aside and waiting for a reply (as opposed to asynchronous delivery, which means sending something and then going on about your business until a reply taps you on the shoulder).

Event registration and deregistration methods typically are declared as synchronous to lessen the possibility that these calls will be short-circuited before they have a chance to finish.

OurButton

Listing 12-6 pulls the whole event handling process together! It shows the source code for `OurButton`, the source bean.

Listing 12-6	OurButton.java

```java
package sun.demo.buttons;

import java.awt.*;
import java.awt.event.*;
import java.beans.*;
import java.io.Serializable;
import java.util.Vector;

/**
 * A simple Java Bean button.
 */
public class OurButton extends Canvas
  implements Serializable {

  /**
   * Constructs a Button with the default label.
   */
  public OurButton() {
    this( press );
  }
```

(continued)

Listing 12-6 *(continued)*

OurButton's
registration
method
immediately
calls the one
defined in the —
support class

OurButton's
deregistration —
method also
calls the
one defined
in the
support
class

Refer to #1 —
in "The
play"
section

Refer to #2 —
in "The
play"
section

The ————
changes
property is
an instance
of Property-
Change-
Support

```
...
// Methods for registering/de-registering
// event listeners

public void addPropertyChangeListener(
        PropertyChangeListener listener) {
  changes.addPropertyChangeListener(listener);
}

public void removePropertyChangeListener(
        PropertyChangeListener listener) {
  changes.removePropertyChangeListener(listener);
}

/**
 * Enable debugging output. This is a bound property.
 */
public void setDebug(boolean x) {
  boolean old = debug;
  debug = x;
  changes.firePropertyChange("debug",
              new Boolean(old),
              new Boolean(x));
}

private boolean debug;
private PropertyChangeSupport changes =
  new PropertyChangeSupport(this);
...
}
```

DemoChangeReporter

In Listing 12-7, DemoChangeReporter listens for PropertyChangeEvents.
When DemoChangeReporter receives those events, it displays information
about the changed properties.

Listing 12-7	DemoChangeReporter
	(Described in ChangeReporter.java**)**

```
import sun.demo.buttons.OurButton;
import sun.demo.misc.ChangeReporter;
import java.awt.*;
import java.beans.*;

public class DemoChangeReporter {
  OurButton button = new OurButton();
  ChangeReporter reporter = new ChangeReporter();
  PropertyChangeAdapter adapter = new
    PropertyChangeAdapter();
  DemoChangeReporter() { // constructor
   button.addPropertyChangeListener(adapter);
   button.setLabel("Report This");

   Frame f = new Frame("Demo Change Reporter");
   ...
   f.add(button);
   f.add(reporter);
   ...
  }

  class PropertyChangeAdapter
      implements PropertyChangeListener {
    public void propertyChange(
        PropertyChangeEvent e){
      reporter.reportChange(e);
    }
  }
  public static void main(String[] argv) {
    new DemoChangeReporter();
  }
}
```

An adapter instance is created here

The adapter registers its interest in hearing about any properties about to change

Refer to #4a, "The play" section

The buck starts here: A new DemoChange-Reporter is born

ChangeReporter

In Listing 12-8, ChangeReporter takes action when it receives its event notification.

Listing 12-8	ChangeReporter.java

Refer to #4b in
"The play"
section

```
public class ChangeReporter extends TextField
  implements Serializable {
  ...

  public void reportChange(PropertyChangeEvent evt) {
    String text = evt.getPropertyName()
          + " := "
          + evt.getNewValue();

    int width = size().width - 10;
    Font f = getFont();
    if (f != null) {
    // Trim the text to fit.
     FontMetrics fm = getFontMetrics(f);
     while (fm.stringWidth(text) > width) {
      text = text.substring(0, text.length()-1);
     }
    }

    setText(text);
  }
}
```

Adapting to Change

An *adapter* is nothing more than a utility class that implements one or more
listener interfaces. You saw an example of an adapter in Listing 12-7 earlier
in this chapter. To keep you from having to flip back, I repeat that listing here:

```
class PropertyChangeAdapter
  implements PropertyChangeListener {
  public void propertyChange(
      PropertyChangeEvent e){
    reporter.reportChange(e);
  }
}
```

When a handful of beans exists, it's up to the application developer to match up event sources and the targets. (Who else would know what events are significant to that particular application?) Because the application developer is the one who needs to make the event connections, it's typically the job of the application developer (or the application-building tool) to create any necessary adapters.

This adapter is relatively basic. All that the adapter does is insert itself between the bean source and the target by mapping the `propertyChange()` method to the `reportChange()` method — handy if the names of the two methods don't match exactly. In real life, method names rarely do match. One bean defines an event, and three months later, someone in a different country creates a bean that needs to receive an event notification from the first bean.

Adapters can be much more sophisticated than the example shown at the beginning of this section, though; they provide the perfect opportunity to add any extra function that you decide is appropriate. You may want to analyze the event that's passed in and invoke one of a few methods on the target bean, depending on some criterion.

A Cast of Thousands

By default, events support *multicast notification,* which means that the number of beans that can register their interest in an event is virtually unlimited. If, for some reason, you want to restrict the number of beans that can receive an event notification to just one, you can do so by forcing an event to support *unicast* notification. Here's how:

```
public void addPropertyChangeListener(
        PropertyChangeListener listener)
  throws java.util.TooManyListenersException;
```

It's that simple! Now, when the second (and any subsequent) bean tries to register interest by calling the `addPropertyChangeListener()` method, `addPropertyChangeListener()` throws a `TooManyListenersException`. (In developer terms, throwing an exception is sometimes referred to as *barfing.*)

You can find implementation details for the `TooManyListenersException` class earlier in this chapter.

Real-time issues

Imagine that an event occurs and that the source bean starts sending out a bunch of notifications, just as it always does. Now imagine that in the middle of this process, before all the notifications have been sent and received, one of the listeners deregisters its interest — or, conversely, that some other bean registers its interest, or that both conditions occur. Yikes! What do you suppose would happen?

Well, your guess is as good as anybody's, because there *is* no one correct answer; what happens all depends on your implementation.

You can approach this potentially confusing situation in a couple of ways:

- ✔ Right before you send each notification, you can check the current list of target beans again and adjust the notifications accordingly.

- ✔ You can copy the list of target beans at the instant when the event occurs and then deliver the notification to those events and only those events, no matter what else happens.

Chapter 13

Persistence of Vision

· ·

In This Chapter

▶ Understanding the importance of persistence

▶ Exploring the options for making your beans persistent

▶ Using Java APIs to make your beans persistent

· ·

*P*ersistence (per-sis´-tence), adj. 1. As applied to Java Beans, *persistence* refers to a bean's capability to save its data to disk.

Almost every bean you create — okay, I'll go out on a limb and make it *every* bean you create — should be persistent. After all, what good is making sure your beans are customizable if none of the custom combinations other developers dream up for your bean can ever be saved persistently?

Conceptually, you can store your beans' data persistently in two ways:

  ✔ Object serialization, via `java.io.Serializable` and a `java.io.FileOutputStream`

  ✔ Externalization (for do-it-yourselfers), via `java.io.Externalizable` and `java.io.FileOutputStream`)

In this chapter, you become familiar with the most commonly used APIs that support bean serialization and externalization. You also get a peek at some real-life examples of putting each persistence-related API to work.

A third way to store your beans' data persistently is to tuck it away in a relational database via the JDBC. Exploiting the JDBC is a much more sophisticated approach than plain old serialization and externalization, though, so it's usually discussed separately. Refer to Chapter 10 if you're interested in learning how to store bean data in a relational database.

Beans across time and space

In theory, serialization enables the transportation of beans across both time and space — across time, because you can save a bean's contents to a file and then retrieve, or *reconstitute*, the bean a week later; and across space, because serialization is used within the RMI API to implement distribution via remote method invocation.

Beans rarely stand alone, though; as you know, their usefulness lies in their participation in bean-based applications. Fortunately, as you see in the following sections, serialization provides built-in support for saving these groups of related beans (called *graphs*) as well as individual beans.

The Least You Have to Know about Persistence

You may be able to dream up a bean that doesn't need to support introspection, customization, or event handling, but it's hard to imagine a bean worth its salt that doesn't need to be persistent. Fortunately, making your beans persistent isn't hard to master.

This chapter describes many classes and methods, all of which are useful (otherwise, I wouldn't have included them!). But for the lowest-rent, barest-bone overview of persistence, all you really need to know can be summed up in the following couple of paragraphs. The rest of the chapter expands on this overview information and gives you all the specific implementation details that you need to make your persistent dreams come true.

You can make beans persistent through serialization (the default, easy way) or through externalization (the harder way, but you have more control).

Here's how you make beans persistent through serialization:

1. **Make sure that your class implements the** `java.io.Serializable` **interface, which I discuss in detail in the "Interfaces" section later in this chapter.**

    In the following line of code, `myPersistentBean` is implementing the `java.io.Serializable` interface:

    ```
    public class myPersistentBean implements Serializable {
    ```

2. **Decide when you want your bean to save its data. (Generally, you want to give other developers a "Save this bean!" option they can select when they finish configuring your bean. Take a look at Figure 8-1 in Chapter 8 to see what I mean.)**

At whatever point you want your bean to be savable, create an `ObjectOutputStream` with an associated file and invoke `ObjectOutputStream`'s `writeObject()` method, passing your bean as an argument. (You see an example of this approach in action in the "ObjectOutputStream" section further along in this chapter.)

`defaultWriteObject()` and `defaultReadObject()` are called automatically when your bean is stored and reconstituted, respectively (that is, when the `writeObject()` and `readObject()` methods are invoked and your bean is passed to them as an argument). If the function that these two default methods provide isn't sufficient, you can implement `readObject()` and `writeObject()` methods for your class; otherwise, you don't have to do anything special.

And here's how you make beans persistent through externalization:

1. **Make sure that your class implements the `java.io.Externalizable` interface.**

   The example below shows `myPersistentBean` implementing the `java.io.Externalizable` interface:

   ```
   public class myPersistentBean implements Externalizable {
   ```

2. **Override the `writeExternal()` and `readExternal()` methods.**

   Overriding these methods means you're completely on your own with respect to the format that you use to save your bean's data, how you write it out, and how you read it back in.

3. **Decide when you want your bean to save its data.**

   Typically, you want to give other developers a "Save this bean!" option they can select when they finish configuring your bean — but the choice is completely up to you.

   At whatever point you want your bean to be savable, call your class's `writeExternal()` method, passing as an argument a class that implements the `ObjectOutput` interface.

4. **When you want your bean to reconstitute its data (for example, in response to a "Load this bean!" option), call `readExternal()`, passing as an argument a class that implements the `ObjectInput` interface.**

Safe and secure

If all that you have to do to make a class persistent is add two little words to the class definition (`implements Serializable`), why not just make every class implement the `Serializable` interface? After all, it couldn't do any harm, right? Well, yes, actually, it *could* do some harm. When you serialize a bean's contents, you save those contents to disk. Because no inherent encryption is implemented in any of the persistence-related classes, any sensitive data that your bean contains is at risk when it's serialized, hanging out there like that in a readable file where anyone can get hold of it.

You can approach the persistence of sensitive data in three ways:

✔ **Don't save it.**

No law says that you have to implement a bean as serializable. And even if you do, you can mark individual fields with the `transient` keyword, so that their values aren't saved to disk along with the rest of the bean's contents.

✔ **Save it, but provide your own encryption/ decryption schemes.**

If you implement a bean by using the `Externalizable` interface, you must provide your own `writeExternal()` and `readExternal()` methods. You're in complete control; no default behavior exists, as it does for the `Serializable` interface. If you want, you can encrypt any sensitive data that your bean contains in `writeExternal()` and then decrypt it on the way back in, in `readExternal()`.

✔ **Save it, but provide a checking mechanism.**

Before a bean is reconstituted, implement some code to ensure that sensitive data hasn't been tampered with since it was saved. How you do this is up to you. You may check the time stamp of the saved file, check the size of the file, or use any other scheme that makes sense for your application.

Classes

In this section you find a few representative Java classes that provide persistence support. This section should look familiar to you if you've scanned any of the other chapters in this part; as always, for each class I provide a description, a pedigree (a list of the class's parent class, grandparent class, etc.) and a list of the class's methods. I list each class's constructors separately (even though technically, they're methods, too) so you can spot them easily.

The `java.io` package implements scads of classes that you can use to serialize your bean-based applications and then deserialize (or *reconstitute*) them again. In fact, `java.io` implements so many of these classes that a complete list would make this book twice as long as it already is! For that reason, I include just a smattering of the most common classes, along with the ones that are most representative of the others. Because almost all the classes contained in `java.io` are similar conceptually, you can easily apply the information in this section to the classes that I left out.

You can find documentation covering the entire `java.io` package at

```
http://www.javasoft.com/products/JDK/1.1/docs/api/Package-
          java.io.html
```

Basically, the classes presented in this section fall into two categories: classes that are useful for serializing objects, and classes that are useful for serializing primitive data types (things like integers, characters, and Boolean values). All the rest is gravy.

DataInputStream

Use the `DataInputStream` class, which implements the `DataInput` interface, when you want to read primitive Java data types from a stream. For details on writing Java primitives, see the description of the `DataOutputStream` class later in this chapter.

Pedigree

```
java.lang.Object
    ⇨ java.io.InputStream
        ⇨ java.io.FilterInputStream
            ⇨ java.io.DataInputStream
```

Constructors

Only one constructor is associated with the `DataInputStream` class.

DataInputStream(InputStream)

This constructor accepts one input argument: an `InputStream` object.

Signature:

```
public DataInputStream(InputStream in)
```

Row, row, row your boat . . . gently down the `OutputStream`

When you use serialization, you're dealing primarily with streams, so it's a good idea to understand exactly what they are.

A *stream* represents a sequential flow of data, either to somewhere (when you write data to an output stream, for example) or from somewhere (when you read data from an input stream). Different types of streams are used for different types of operations. You can read primitive data type information from a `DataInputStream`, but to write bean-based (object-based) information, you need to use an `ObjectOutputStream`. If you want to read from and write to a file saved on a disk to make your bean persistent, you use (you guessed it!) `FileInputStream` and `FileOutputStream`.

Streams are your friends; they shield you from having to know the nitty-gritty implementation details of the thing that you're ultimately streaming information to or from (such as a file on a disk).

Example:

The constructor in action

```
DataInputStream aDataInStream = null;
 try {
   InputStream aFileInStream =
     new FileInStream(someFileNameString);
     if (aFileInStream != null) {
        aDataInStream = new DataInStream(aFileInStream);
   }
 }
```

Methods

As the following methods attest, you can read from a data input stream in many ways.

read(byte[])

This method reads bytes from the `DataInputStream` into the byte array passed in as an argument. The method returns the number of bytes read, unless it hits the end of the stream before it finishes filling the array. If the method does hit the end of the stream prematurely, it returns the value −1.

Signature:

```
public final int read(byte b[]) throws IOException
```

Example:

```
numberBytesRead = aDataInputStream.read(aByteArray);
```

read(byte[], int, int)

This method reads data from a DataInputStream into a specified byte array based on a specified offset and number of bytes to read. This method returns the number of bytes that it has read unless it tried to read past the end of the stream; in that case, it returns the value −1.

Signature:

```
public final int read(byte b[],
          int off,
          int len) throws IOException
```

In the preceding syntax

- ✔ b is the byte array that you want the data to be read into.
- ✔ off is the number of bytes to skip before starting to read. This value is called the *offset*.
- ✔ len is the number of bytes read.

Example:

```
numberBytesRead = aDataInputStream.read(aByteArray,
                  offset,
                  bytesToRead);
```

readBoolean()

This method reads and returns a boolean value from a DataInputStream.

Signature:

```
public final boolean readBoolean() throws IOException
```

Example:

```
aBooleanVariable = aDataInputStream.readBoolean();
```

And that's final!

You may have noticed (and wondered) about an unusual keyword in the method signatures in this chapter: the final keyword. When applied to a method, the final keyword means that the method can't be overridden. If you were to subclass DataInputStream, for example, and create a class called MyDataInputStream, you wouldn't be able to override and reimplement any method (read(), readBoolean(), and so on) that was originally declared in DataInputStream with the final identifier.

Methods are declared as final for a couple of reasons. One reason is for clarity.

someDataInputStream.readBoolean(), for example, is fairly cut-and-dried; it reads a boolean value, and a programmer has no reason to redefine it. ("Hey, guys, check this out! I've reimplemented readBoolean(). Instead of reading a boolean value, it makes a really loud oinking sound instead!")

Another reason methods are declared as final is for enhanced performance. The Java compiler knows that a final method can't be overridden, so it can make some assumptions as it goes about its job. The result is faster-performing code.

readByte()
This method reads and returns one 8-bit byte value.

Signature:

```
public final byte readByte() throws IOException
```

Example:

```
aByteVariable = aDataInputStream.readByte();
```

readChar()
This method reads and returns one 16-bit char (character) value.

Signature:

```
public final char readChar() throws IOException
```

Example:

```
aCharVariable = aDataInputStream.readChar();
```

readDouble()

This method reads and returns one 64-bit double value.

Signature:

```
public final double readDouble() throws IOException
```

Example:

```
aDoubleVariable = aDataInputStream.readDouble();
```

readFloat()

This method reads and returns one 32-bit float value.

Signature:

```
public final float readFloat() throws IOException
```

Example:

```
aFloatVariable = aDataInputStream.readFloat();
```

readFully(byte[])

This method reads bytes from a DataInputStream into a specified byte array. If, for any reason, not all the data in the input data stream can be read, this method throws an exception.

Signature:

```
public final void readFully(byte b[]) throws IOException
```

b is the byte array that you want the data to be read into.

Example:

```
aDataInputStream.readFully(aByteArray);
```

readFully(byte[], int, int)

This method reads bytes from a DataInputStream into a specified byte array based on a specified offset and number of bytes to read. If the specified number of bytes can't be read, for some reason, this method throws an exception.

Signature:

```
public final void readFully(byte b[],
            int off,
            int len) throws IOException
```

In the preceding syntax:

- ✔ b is the byte array that you want the data to be read into.
- ✔ off is the number of bytes to skip before starting to read.
- ✔ len is the number of bytes to read.

Example:

```
aDataInputStream.readFully(aByteArray,
            offset,
            bytesToRead);
```

readInt()

This method reads and returns a 32-bit int (integer) value from a
DataInputStream.

Signature:

```
public final int readInt() throws IOException
```

Example:

```
anIntVariable = aDataInputStream.readInt();
```

readLine()

This method reads and returns a copy of a line. A line is a string that has
been terminated by one of these end-of-line characters: \n, \r, \r\n, and EOF.

At this writing, this method contains a teensy-tiny bug that causes it to
behave unpredictably when the moon's full. Until the bug is fixed (with any
luck, in the next version of the JDK), you may want to check out
BufferedReader.readLine() for your line-of-text-reading needs.

Signature:

```
public final String readLine() throws IOException
```

Example:

```
aStringVariable = aDataInputStream.readLine();
```

readLong()
This method reads and returns a 64-bit long value.

Signature:

```
public final long readLong() throws IOException
```

Example:

```
aLongVariable = aDataInputStream.readLong();
```

readShort()
This method reads and returns a 16-bit short value.

Signature:

```
public final short readShort() throws IOException
```

Example:

```
aShortVariable = aDataInputStream.readShort();
```

readUnsignedByte()
This method reads and returns an 8-bit unsigned byte value.

Signature:

```
public final int readUnsignedByte() throws IOException
```

Example:

```
anIntVariable = aDataInputStream.readUnsignedByte();
```

readUnsignedShort()
This method reads and returns a 16-bit unsigned short value.

Signature:

```
public final int readUnsignedShort() throws IOException
```

Example:

```
anIntVariable = aDataInputStream.readUnsignedShort();
```

DataOutputStream

DataOutputStream is the flip side of the DataInputStream class, which I describe previously in this chapter. Instead of reading in primitive Java data types, as you can with DataInputStream, you can *write* primitive Java data types to a DataOutputStream.

Pedigree

```
java.lang.Object
   ➪ java.io.OutputStream
      ➪ java.io.FilterOutputStream
         ➪ java.io.DataOutputStream
```

Constructors

Only one constructor is associated with the DataOutputStream class.

DataOutputStream(OutputStream)

Use this constructor to create a DataOutputStream, given a plain old OutputStream.

Signature:

```
public DataOutputStream(OutputStream out)
```

Example:

Here's the ——
constructor

```
DataOutputStream aDataOutStream = null;
  try {
    OutputStream aFileOutStream =
    new FileOutStream(someFileNameString);
    if (aFileOutStream != null) {
      aDataOutStream = new DataOutStream(aFileOutStream);
    }
  }
```

Methods

As you'd expect, the DataOutputStream class's methods are all about writing output to the stream. Each of the write() methods has a corresponding read() method, courtesy of DataInputStream (DataInputStream is described earlier in this chapter.)

flush()

When you use one of the methods in this section to write data to a DataOutputStream, the computer (in its infinite wisdom) sometimes defers writing the data until a more convenient time. This delay is called *buffering* data.

The flush() method flushes the stream, which causes any buffered data that's hanging around to be written to the DataOutputStream immediately.

Signature:

```
public void flush() throws IOException
```

Example:

```
aDataOutputStream.flush();
```

size()

This method returns the number of bytes written to a DataOutputStream so far.

Signature:

```
public final int size()
```

Example:

```
sizeOfDataOutputStream = aDataOutputStream.size();
```

write(byte[], int, int)

This method writes data from a specified byte array to a DataOutputStream based on specified offset and length values.

Signature:

```
public synchronized void write(byte b[],
                int off,
                int len)
   throws IOException
```

In the preceding syntax

- ✔ b is the byte array that you want the data to be written from.
- ✔ off is the number of bytes in the array to skip before starting to write the data.
- ✔ len is the number of bytes to write.

Example:

```
aDataOutputStream.write(aByteArray,
              offset,
              bytesToWrite);
```

write(int)

This method writes a single int (integer) to a DataOutputStream.

Signature:

```
public synchronized void write(int b) throws IOException
```

Example:

```
aDataOutputStream.write(anInt);
```

writeBoolean(boolean)

This method writes a boolean value to a DataOutputStream.

Signature:

```
public final void writeBoolean(boolean v)
  throws IOException
```

Example:

```
aDataOutputStream.writeBoolean(true);
```

writeByte(byte)

This method writes an 8-bit byte value to a DataOutputStream.

Signature:

```
public final void writeByte(byte v) throws IOException
```

Example:

```
aDataOutputStream.writeByte(aByte);
```

writeBytes(String)

This method writes a specified String value to a DataOutputStream as a sequence of bytes.

Signature:

```
public final void writeBytes(String s) throws IOException
```

Example:

```
aDataOutputStream.writeBytes(aStringVariable);
```

writeChar(int)

This method writes a 16-bit char value to a DataOutputStream.

Signature:

```
public final void writeChar(int v) throws IOException
```

Example:

```
aDataOutputStream.writeChar( a );
```

writeChars(String)

This method writes a specified String value to a DataOutputStream as a sequence of characters.

Signature:

```
public final void writeChars(String s) throws IOException
```

Example:

```
aDataOutputStream.writeChars( Salamanders Rule );
```

writeDouble(double)

This method writes a 64-bit double value to a DataOutputStream.

Signature:

```
public final void writeDouble(double v)
    throws IOException
```

Example:

```
aDataOutputStream.writeDouble(aDoubleVariable);
```

writeFloat(float)
This method writes a 32-bit float value to a DataOutputStream.

Signature:

```
public final void writeFloat(float v) throws IOException
```

Example:

```
aDataOutputStream.writeFloat(aFloatVariable);
```

writeInt(int)
This method writes a 32-bit int value to a DataOutputStream.

Signature:

```
public final void writeInt(int v) throws IOException
```

Example:

```
aDataOutputStream.writeInt(anIntVariable);
```

writeLong(long)
This method writes a 64-bit long value to a DataOutputStream.

Signature:

```
public final void writeLong(long v) throws IOException
```

Example:

```
aDataOutputStream.writeLong(aLongVariable);
```

writeShort(int)
This method writes a 16-bit short value to a DataOutputStream.

Signature:

```
public final void writeShort(int v) throws IOException
```

Example:

```
aDataOutputStream.writeShort(aShortVariable);
```

FileInputStream

A FileInputStream is a plain old input stream with one big difference: It flows from a file. You specify a filename when you construct a FileInputStream, as you see in "Constructors" later in this chapter.

Pedigree

```
java.lang.Object
    ⇨ java.io.InputStream
        ⇨ java.io.FileInputStream
```

Constructors

As you see in this section, you can construct a FileInputStream in a couple of ways.

FileInputStream(File)

This constructor creates a FileInputStream, given a File object.

Signature:

```
public FileInputStream(File file)
  throws FileNotFoundException
```

Example:

```
java.io.FileInputStream aFileInputStream =
  new java.io.FileInputStream(aFile);
```

FileInputStream(String)

This constructor creates a FileInputStream based on the specified system-dependent filename.

Signature:

```
public FileInputStream(String name)
  throws FileNotFoundException
```

Example:

```
java.io.FileInputStream aFileInputStream =
    new java.io.FileInputStream( c:\myInput.txt );
```

Methods

A blue million methods are associated with the FileInputStream. Rather than list them all, I include only the methods of FileInputStream that you're most likely to use.

For complete documentation on all the methods of this class, see

```
http://java.sun.com/products/JDK/1.1/docs/api/
                java.io.FileInputStream.html
```

close()

This method closes the FileInputStream and releases the file so that someone else can access it.

Signature:

```
public void close() throws IOException
```

Example:

```
aFileInputStream.close();
```

read()

This method reads and returns 1 byte of data from a FileInputStream.

Signature:

```
public int read() throws IOException
```

Example:

```
aByte = aFileInputStream.read();
```

read(byte[])

This method reads data from a FileInputStream into a specified byte array and returns one of two values: the number of bytes read or −1 (if the end of the file was reached before the array was filled).

Signature:

```
public int read(byte b[]) throws IOException
```

Why so negative?

You may have noticed that some of the methods in this chapter return a value of −1 if the end of a stream is reached during a read or write operation. This negative return value makes it easy for you to tell whether the operation succeeded.

Suppose that you want to read 10 bytes from a file, but only 8 bytes exist in the file. If a negative value is returned, you know that the file didn't contain enough data to satisfy your request. (After all, the method couldn't have read in a negative number of bytes!) All that you have to do is check the return code, like this:

```
if
  (aFileInputStream.read(aByteArray,
                  offset,
                  10) > 0) {
  // A positive value means all
  systems go
}
else {
  // Oops   there wasn t enough
  data!
}
```

Example:

```
aFileInputStream.read(aByteArray);
```

read(byte[], int, int)

This method reads data from a `FileInputStream` into an array of bytes based on a specified offset and number of bytes to read. This method returns one of two values: the number of bytes read or −1 (if the end of the file is reached before the read operation finishes).

Signature:

```
public int read(byte b[],
         int off,
         int len) throws IOException
```

In the preceding syntax

- ✔ b is the byte array that you want the data to be written into.

- ✔ off is the number of bytes to skip before starting to read the data.

- ✔ len is the number of bytes to read.

Example:

```
aFileInputStream.read(aByteArray,
          offset,
          bytesToRead);
```

FileOutputStream

Use a `FileOutputStream` when you want to save your bean data to a file on disk.

Pedigree

```
java.lang.Object
   ⇨ java.io.OutputStream
      ⇨ java.io.FileOutputStream
```

Constructors

The constructors for the `FileOutputStream` class are similar to those for the corresponding `FileInputStream`, as you see in this section.

FileOutputStream(File)

This constructor creates a `FileOutputStream` based on a given `File` object.

Signature:

```
public FileOutputStream(File file) throws IOException
```

Example:

```
java.io.FileOutputStream aFileOutStream =
  new java.io.FileOutputStream(someFile);
```

FileOutputStream(String)

This constructor creates a `FileOutputStream` based on a specified system-dependent filename.

Signature:

```
public FileOutputStream(String name) throws IOException
```

Example:

```
java.io.FileOutputStream aFileOutStream =
  new java.io.FileOutputStream( c:\someFile.txt );
```

FileOutputStream(String, boolean)

Like the preceding constructor, this constructor creates a
FileOutputStream based on a specified system-dependent filename. But
unlike the preceding constructor, which opens a brand-new file each time
it's invoked (meaning that it overwrites the old file, if one exists), this
constructor allows you to add (or *append*) written data to an existing file.

Signature:

```
public FileOutputStream(String name,
          boolean append)
  throws IOException
```

In the preceding syntax

  ✔ name is a String representing the name of the output file.

  ✔ append is a boolean value denoting whether the file should be ap-
    pended to rather than overwritten.

Example:

```
java.io.FileOutputStream aFileOutStream =
    new java.io.FileOutputStream( c:\someFile.txt ,
                                  true);
```

Methods

This section represents only a subset of the total FileOutputStream
methods — the ones that you're most likely to need.

For complete documentation on all the methods of this class, see

```
http://java.sun.com/products/JDK/1.1/docs/api/
            java.io.FileOutputStream.html
```

close()

This method closes the FileOutputStream and releases the file so that
someone else can access it.

Signature:

```
public void close() throws IOException
```

Example:

```
aFileOutputStream.close();
```

write(byte[])

This method writes a specified array of bytes to a `FileOutputStream`.

Signature:

```
public void write(byte b[]) throws IOException
```

Example:

```
aFileOutputStream.write(aByteArray);
```

write(byte[], int, int)

This method writes a piece of a byte array to a `FileOutputStream` based on a given array, offset, and number of bytes to write.

Signature:

```
public void write(byte b[],
          int off,
          int len) throws IOException
```

In the preceding syntax

- ✔ b is the byte array that you want the data to be written from.
- ✔ off is the number of bytes to skip from the beginning of the byte array before starting to write the data.
- ✔ len is the total number of bytes to write.

Example:

```
aFileOutputStream.write(aByteArray,
          offset,
          bytesToRead);
```

write(int)

This method writes a single byte of data to a `FileOutputStream`.

Signature:

```
public void write(byte b) throws IOException
```

Example:

```
aFileOutputStream.write(aByte);
```

IOException

IOException is just one of the exceptions that persistence-related methods can throw. Due to space considerations, I left the other exceptions out of this chapter, but all of them work pretty much the same way.

All the persistence-related exceptions are detailed at the following site:

```
http://java.sun.com/products/JDK/1.1/docs/api/Package-
java.io.html
```

Pedigree

```
java.lang.Object
    ⇨ java.lang.Throwable
        ⇨ java.lang.Exception
            ⇨ java.io.IOException
```

Constructors

Two constructors are associated with the IOException class.

IOException()

Use this constructor to create a plain-vanilla IOException (one with no detail message).

Signature:

```
public IOException()
```

Example:

```
java.io.IOException anIOException =
  new java.io.IOException();
```

IOException(String)

This constructor accepts a `String` argument representing a specific detailed message to associate with the newly created `IOException`.

Signature:

```
public IOException(String s)
```

Example:

```
java.io.IOException anIOException =
  new java.io.IOException(someMessageString);
```

Methods

No methods are associated with the `IOException` class.

ObjectInputStream

Often, you don't want to work with bytes of data, but with objects. In short, you want to work with entire beans and bean-based applications. The `ObjectInputStream` and `ObjectOutputStream` classes enable you to do just that.

Pedigree

```
java.lang.Object
   ⇨ java.io.InputStream
      ⇨ java.io.ObjectInputStream
```

Constructors

You can use only one constructor to create an `ObjectInputStream`.

ObjectInputStream(InputStream)

This constructor creates an `ObjectInputStream` that reads from the specified `InputStream`.

Signature:

```
public ObjectInputStream(InputStream in)
   throws IOException, StreamCorruptedException
```

Example:

```
FileInputStream aFileIn
  = new FileInputStream("tempFile.txt");

ObjectInputStream aNewObjectInputStream
  = new ObjectInputStream(aFileIn);
```

Methods

As you can see from its pedigree, ObjectInputStream shares a parent class (java.io.InputStream) with FileInputStream. Therefore, these two classes share many methods: close(), read(), readBoolean(), and so on. In the interest of keeping this book's weight down to a level that won't give you a hernia when you pick it up, this chapter lists only the really unique methods of ObjectInputStream.

If you want to look at the complete API documentation for ObjectInputStream, all you need to do is load the following URL:

```
http://java.sun.com/products/JDK/1.1/docs/api/
             java.io.ObjectInputStream.html
```

defaultReadObject()

This method reads the nonstatic and nontransient fields of the current class from an ObjectInputStream.

You can call this method only from inside the readObject() method, so it's useful to you only if you intend to reimplement readObject() (which you need to do if you want to override the default implementation of readObject() described in the following section). If you try to invoke defaultReadObject() from anywhere but readObject(), you get a NotActiveException for your trouble.

Signature:

```
public final void defaultReadObject()
   throws IOException,
       ClassNotFoundException,
       NotActiveException
```

Example:

defaultRead
Object()
being called —

```
private void readObject(ObjectInputStream anObjectIn)
    throws ClassNotFoundException, IOException {
    anObjectIn.defaultReadObject();
    …
  }
```

readObject()

This method reads an object from the `ObjectInputStream`; specifically, reads the class of the object, the signature of the class, and the values of the nontransient and nonstatic fields of the class and all that class's superclasses.

Any objects referenced by the read-in object are read-in, too (along with the objects that *they* reference, and so on, and so on. . .), so that a complete graph of objects is reconstructed.

Signature:

```
public final Object readObject()
    throws OptionalDataException,
        ClassNotFoundException,
        IOException
```

Example:

The ————
readObject()
method being
called

```
java.io.FileInputStream aFileIn
    = new java.io.FileInputStream( beanbox.clipboard );

java.io.ObjectInput anObjectIn
    = new java.io.ObjectInputStream(aFileIn);
Component c = (Component) anObjectIn.readObject();
```

ObjectOutputStream

`ObjectOutputStream` is `ObjectInputStream`'s alter ego. Whereas `ObjectInputStream` allows you to read objects from a stream, `ObjectOutputStream` allows you to *write* objects (and collections of related objects) to a stream. The cool thing about `ObjectOutputStream` is that it enables you to write out data in cohesive, object-size chunks instead of piecemeal, 1 byte or 1 character at a time.

Pedigree

```
java.lang.Object
    ⇨ java.io.OutputStream
        ⇨ java.io.ObjectOutputStream
```

Constructors

`ObjectOutputStream` has just one constructor.

ObjectOutputStream(OutputStream)

This constructor creates an `ObjectOutputStream` that writes to the specified `OutputStream`.

Signature:

```
public ObjectOutputStream(OutputStream out)
  throws IOException
```

Example:

```
// Need a FileOutStream to construct an
// ObjectOutputStream
FileOutputStream aFileOutStream
  = new FileOutputStream( temp.txt );

ObjectOutputStream anObjectOutStream
  = new ObjectOutputStream(aFileOutStream);
```

Methods

`ObjectOutputStream` shares a parent class (`java.io.OutputStream`) with `FileOutputStream`, which I discuss earlier in this chapter. These two classes share many methods: `close()`, `write()`, `writeByte()`, `writeChar()`, and so on. Because these shared methods are practically identical, this section includes only methods that are unique to `ObjectOutputStream`.

To view the complete API documentation for `ObjectOutputStream`, check out this Web site:

```
http://java.sun.com/products/JDK/1.1/docs/api/
java.io.ObjectInputStream.html
```

defaultWriteObject()

This method writes the nonstatic and nontransient fields of the current class to this stream.

You can call this method only from inside the `writeObject()` method, so it's of use to you only if you intend to reimplement `writeObject()` (which you do if you want to override the default implementation of `writeObject()` described in the following section). If you try to invoke `defaultWriteObject()` from anywhere but `writeObject()`, you get a `NotActiveException`.

Signature:

```
public final void defaultWriteObject() throws IOException
```

Example:

The call to
defaultWrite
Object()

```
private void writeObject(ObjectOutputStream
    anObjectOutStream) throws IOException {
  anObjectOutStream.defaultWriteObject();
  // Some more processing
}
```

writeObject(Object)

This method writes the specified object to the `ObjectOutputStream`; specifically, writes the class of the object, the signature of the class, and the values of the nontransient and nonstatic fields of the class and all the class's superclasses.

Any serializable objects referenced by the specified object are written out, too (along with the serializable objects that *they* reference, and so on, and so on . . .), so that a complete graph of objects can be read in via `readObject()` and fully reconstructed.

Signature:

```
public final void writeObject(Object obj)
  throws IOException
```

Example:

```
Component focus = BeanBoxFrame.getCurrentFocus();
...
java.io.FileOutputStream aFileOutStream
  = new java.io.FileOutputStream("beanbox.clipboard");

java.io.ObjectOutput anObjectOut
  = new java.io.ObjectOutputStream(aFileOutStream);

anObjectOut.writeObject(focus);
```

writeObject()
is called

A FAQ (a list of answers to the most *frequently asked questions*) is devoted exclusively to the topic of object serialization. Check it out at

```
http://chatsubo.javasoft.com/current/faq.html#whyserial
```

Interfaces

The two Java interfaces that provide basic support for persistence are
Externalizable and Serializable.

Externalizable

Implementing the Externalizable interface allows you the freedom to
assume complete control of the contents and format of an object's serialized
form. The down side is that you have to do more work! Unlike the
Serializable interface, which provides default readObject() and
writeObject() methods (you *can* override them but you don't have to),
you *must* implement the writeExternal() and readExternal() methods
to implement the Externalizable interface.

Methods

You must override two methods when you implement the Externalizable
interface: readExternal() and writeExternal().

readExternal(ObjectInput)

Override this method to specify custom logic for restoring the contents of a
specified input object. You can implement the ObjectInput interface to
read in primitive types, objects, strings, and arrays. ObjectInputStream is
a good example of an implementation of the ObjectInput interface.

The readExternal() method must read in the object's values in the same
sequence and with the same types that were written by writeExternal().

Signature:

```
public abstract void readExternal(ObjectInput in)
   throws IOException, ClassNotFoundException
```

writeExternal(ObjectOutput)

Override this method to specify custom logic for saving the contents of a
specified output object. You can implement the ObjectOutput interface to
write out primitive types, objects, strings, and arrays. ObjectOutputStream
is a good example of an implementation of the ObjectOutput interface.

Signature:

```
public abstract void writeExternal(ObjectOutput out)
   throws IOException
```

Serializable

Implementing the `Serializable` interface allows the default object-serialization mechanism to save and restore the entire state of an object via the `ObjectInputStream.readObject()` and `ObjectOutputStream.writeObject()` methods, explained earlier in this chapter. The default mechanism is relatively flexible; it allows classes to evolve somewhat between the time when the stream is written and the time when the stream is read. (The exception to this rule is when a class evolves so much that it doesn't resemble the old version closely enough for the data to be restorable. For example, if the new version of a class no longer contains half the properties it once did, the object would no longer be restorable.)

What's more, serialization automatically traverses references between objects so that you can save and then restore entire graphs of related objects in one fell swoop.

Methods

No methods are associated with the `Serializable` interface. The `readObject()` and `writeObject()` methods that you override (if you want to override them) are methods of the `InputObjectStream` and `OutputObjectStream` classes, respectively.

Chapter 14

Building Your ABS (Application Builder Support) Through Customization

In This Chapter

▶ Providing property-level customization support for a bean with property editors

▶ Providing bean-level customization support for a bean with property sheets and customizers

• •

Keeping in mind that the whole point of creating a Java bean (as opposed to creating a Java applet or application) is that beans can be reused in different applications, it won't come as any surprise that the easier a bean is for developers to customize, the more useful it is.

This chapter describes the APIs that you can use to provide customization support for all your beans, from the simplest to the most sophisticated.

The Least You Need to Know about Customization

Customization is primarily relevant at design time to folks who are building bean-based applications inside some kind of application-development tool. Suppose that you're interested in stringing together several beans to create a cool Web application that's really going to wow 'em back at the office. Perhaps you purchased these beans; perhaps your friend Sid gave them to you; maybe you even created them yourself. No matter how you came by them, odds are that these beans are not exactly perfect in every respect for the application that you have in mind.

No problem; all you need to do is *customize* the beans — that is, modify the beans' property values to suit your needs. How? You use the customization tools (property editors, customizers, or a combination of both) that were so thoughtfully provided by whoever created the beans.

Each property type should have an associated property editor. (A *property type* can be anything from a string to a number to some custom class that you define yourself.) The Java `Boolean` type, for example, comes with a corresponding class called `BoolEditor`; the `Color` type comes with a class called `ColorEditor`. (For a peek at `ColorEditor`'s insides, see Listing 14-1 later in this chapter.)

All the property editors that you need to edit a bean's properties can be grouped into one bean-customizing class called a property sheet. But wait — there's more. If plain old property editors won't make the grade, you have a second option: implementing the `Customizer` interface.

Classes

Only one class is directly involved with customization: the `java.beans.PropertyEditorManager` class.

PropertyEditorManager

The `PropertyEditorManager` class provides methods that you can use to do either of the following things:

- ✔ Associate a `PropertyEditor` with a certain type of property.
- ✔ Look for a `PropertyEditor`, given a certain property type.

Associating a property type with a property editor is fairly straightforward; all you do is use the `register()` method, as you see in the upcoming "Methods" section. Trying to find a property editor, though, is a little trickier. The `PropertyEditorManager` has three techniques at its disposal to help it track down a wily `PropertyEditor`:

- ✔ It checks to see whether someone previously associated a `PropertyEditor` with a property type by invoking the `PropertyEditorManager`'s `registerEditor()` method. If the `registerEditor()` method doesn't return a `PropertyEditor`, the `PropertyEditorManager` keeps looking.

✔ It checks the package that implements a property's class to see whether someone cleverly provided an editor called `PropertyTypeEditor` and placed it in the same package. If the complete (fully qualified) name of the property is `myapp.web.download.Filename`, for example, `PropertyEditorManager` looks for `myapp.web.download.FilenameEditor`. If `PropertyEditorManager` doesn't find a file called `FilenameEditor`, it keeps looking.

✔ It checks *every* package in its search path for an editor called `PropertyTypeEditor`. To continue the preceding example, `PropertyEditorManager` looks for an editor called `FilenameEditor` in every directory listed in its search path. If `PropertyEditorManager` doesn't find a `PropertyEditor` this time, it gives up.

Pedigree

```
java.lang.Object
   ⇨ java.beans.PropertyEditorManager
```

Constructor

All of `PropertyEditorManager`'s methods are static, meaning that you don't have to construct an instance of `PropertyEditorManager` to use them. In fact, chances are that you'll never have occasion to use the constructor described in the following sections; I simply include it for completeness.

PropertyEditorManager()

As you can see, this constructor takes no arguments.

Signature:

```
public PropertyEditorManager()
```

Example:

```
PropertyEditorManager aPEM = new PropertyEditorManager();
```

Methods

`PropertyEditorManager` defines the following handful of useful methods:

findEditor(Class)

This method returns a property editor based on a specified property type.

Signature:

```
public static PropertyEditor findEditor(Class targetType)
```

Example:

```
Class type = properties[i].getPropertyType();
PropertyEditor editor
  = PropertyEditorManager.findEditor(type);
```

getEditorSearchPath()

Returns the array of package names to be searched for property editors. The initial value returned by this method is `java.beans.editors`, but the value this method returns can be modified by means of the `setEditorSearchPath()` method, described later in this section.

Signature:

```
public static String[] getEditorSearchPath()
```

Example:

```
arrayOfStrings
  = PropertyEditorManager.getEditorSearchPath();
```

registerEditor(Class, Class)

This method registers (or *associates*) a specified property-editor class with a specified property type.

Signature:

```
public static void registerEditor(Class targetType,
          Class editorClass)
```

In the preceding syntax:

- ✔ `targetType` is the property type that you want to associate with `editorClass`.
- ✔ `editorClass` is the editor class that you want to associate with `targetType`.

Example:

```
PropertyEditorManager.registerEditor(somePropertyType,
          someEditorType);
```

`setEditorSearchPath(String[])`

Use this method to modify the list of package names to be used to find property editors. You can retrieve the value set by this method via the `getEditorSearchPath()` method.

Signature:

```
public static void setEditorSearchPath(String path[])
```

Example:

```
PropertyEditorManager.setEditorSearchPath(aListOfPackages);
```

Interfaces

Two interfaces provide customization support for beans: `java.beans.Customizer` and `java.beans.PropertyEditor`. A property editor works fine for simple property types, but if you want to enable developers to customize a bean in one fell swoop, you need to create a customizer.

Customizer

An implementation of the `Customizer` interface should inherit from the `java.awt.Component` class, so that it can be embedded inside an AWT dialog box or panel (which, more than likely, is how an application-building tool will present it).

A customizer is responsible for providing a custom-built GUI (graphical user interface) that is capable of gathering customization information for all of a bean's properties. A customizer can use property editors as part of its display (but doesn't have to).

If you implement your own customizer class, you also need to implement your own `BeanInfo` class (always a good idea), so that developers can access the customizer by calling the implemented `someBeanInfo.getCustomerClass()` method.

Methods

Few methods are associated with the `Customizer` interface, but you need to provide an implementation of each of them to implement a customizer. You can implement all the additional methods that you want.

`addPropertyChangeListener(PropertyChangeListener)`

The purpose of this method is to register a specified listener's interest in hearing about any `PropertyChangeEvent` tied to the bean that is being customized.

Customizers, by definition, need to contain `set` accessor methods that allow users to change property values. Therefore, like any other objects that can change a property's value, customizers should fire a `PropertyChangeEvent` on all registered `PropertyChangeListeners`. (Refer to Chapter 12 for details on event handling.)

Signature:

```
public abstract void
    addPropertyChangeListener(PropertyChangeListener
        listener)
```

`removePropertyChangeListener(PropertyChangeListener)`

This method deregisters a specified listener's interest in hearing about the `PropertyChangeEvent`.

Signature:

```
public abstract void
    removePropertyChangeListener(PropertyChangeListener
        listener)
```

`setObject(Object)`

Implement this method to specify the object to be customized and to set up its graphical display.

You should call this method only one time, before you add the customizer to any parent AWT container.

Signature:

```
public abstract void setObject(Object bean)
```

PropertyEditor

Implementing the `PropertyEditor` interface allows you to provide application developers an easy, graphical way to change the value of a new type of property. You have to provide `PropertyEditors` only for properties that you create. `PropertyEditors` for all the built-in Java types are the responsibility of the folks at JavaSoft and eventually will be delivered as part of the JDK.

Suppose that in the course of your development efforts, you come up with a new property type and decide to call it `EmailAddress`. You can (and should) provide a corresponding implementation of the `PropertyEditor` interface to allow application developers to view and change instances of `EmailAddress` easily.

Because the naming convention for property editors is `PropertyTypeEditor`, if the name of your property is `EmailAddress`, you should name the corresponding property editor `EmailAddressEditor`. This practice ensures that the `PropertyEditorManager` can access the property editor when it needs to.

Methods

When you define a class that implements the `PropertyEditor` interface, you don't have to implement all these methods — just the ones that are appropriate for the property type for which you're providing editing access.

addPropertyChangeListener(PropertyChangeListener)

This method registers a specified listener's interest in hearing about the `PropertyChangeEvent`.

Property editors, by definition, need to contain at least one `set` accessor method to allow users to change property values. Therefore, like any other objects that can change a property's value, property editors should fire a `PropertyChangeEvent` on all registered `PropertyChangeListeners`. (Refer to Chapter 12 for details on event handling.)

The property editor's mission statement

Every property editor must provide the following:

✔ Support for at least one of the following display styles:

`isPaintable()` // (must return `true`)

`getTags()` // (must return a non-null array of `String`s)

`getAsText()` // (must return a non-null `String`)

✔ An implementation of `setValue()`

✔ A custom editor (or an implementation of `setAsText()`)

✔ A constructor that requires no arguments (also called a *null constructor*)

Signature:

```
public abstract void
  addPropertyChangeListener(PropertyChangeListener
  listener)
```

getAsText()

This method returns the property value as a human-editable string, if possible; otherwise, this method returns `null`. If `getAsText()` is implemented, `setAsText()` should be, too. (`setAsText()` is described later in this chapter.)

Signature:

```
public abstract String getAsText()
```

getCustomEditor()

This method returns a full-blown GUI custom implementation of `PropertyEditor` (derived from `java.awt.Component`), if one exists; otherwise, this method returns `null`.

The calling code can embed the returned custom property editor in a property sheet or a dialog box, or present it directly to the developer.

Signature:

```
public abstract Component getCustomEditor()
```

getJavaInitializationString()

Useful to developers who are interested in generating Java code, this method should return a fragment of Java code that describes the current property value in variable-initialization terms.

If the value of an edited `int` property is 69, for example, this property-editor method should return `69`. If the value of an edited `Color` property is green, this method should return `Color.green`.

Signature:

```
public abstract String getJavaInitializationString()
```

getTags()

If the property value must be part of a set of known tagged values — for example, enumerated (or `enum`) values, which are described in the "One potato, two potato" sidebar in this chapter — this method should return an array of the tags; otherwise, it should return `null`. To set a tagged value, implement `setAsText()` with tag values.

One potato, two potato: Enumerated types in Java

An *enumeration* is a special kind of data type. In most other programming languages, the enumerated data type is nothing more than a plain old integer dressed up in fancy clothes. For example, here's how you might create and use an enumerated variable called color (based on an enumerated data type called rainbow) in C:

```
enum rainbow {red, orange,
    yellow, green, blue, violet};

enum rainbow color;

color = blue;

// isn t this easier to under-
    stand than  color = 4 ?
```

Behind the scenes, of course, red is really 0, orange is 1, yellow is 2, green is 3, blue is 4, and violet is 5; the labels red, orange, yellow, and so on are for the benefit of humans, who are generally more comfortable with descriptive words than with numbers.

Java's support for enumerated types is a little different. Any class (not just Integer) can participate in an enumeration just by implementing the java.util.Enumeration interface, like so:

```
public class rainbow implements
    Enumeration {
```

Signature:

```
public abstract String[] getTags()
```

getValue()

This method returns the value of a property. Built-in primitive types should be returned wrapped in their corresponding Java object type. An int value, for example, should be returned as java.lang.Integer. Refer to Chapter 3 for more details on primitive types and wrapper classes.

Signature:

```
public abstract Object getValue()
```

isPaintable()

This method returns a boolean value denoting whether a property editor implemented the paintValue() method described later in this section. isPaintable() returns true if a property editor did implement the method; otherwise, it returns false.

Signature:

```
public abstract boolean isPaintable()
```

`paintValue(Graphics, Rectangle)`

This method paints a representation of a property value in a given area of screen real estate, based on a specified `Graphics` object and `Rectangle`. If the property editor doesn't honor paint requests (that is, if `isPaintable()` returns `false`), this method should discreetly do nothing.

Signature:

```
public abstract void paintValue(Graphics gfx,
                  Rectangle box)
```

In the preceding syntax

- ✔ `gfx` is the graphics object to be painted into.
- ✔ `box` is the rectangle within the graphics object to be painted into.

Kids, don't try programming graphics at home without a reference that's devoted exclusively to the Java AWT! (Programming graphics in any language, Java included, is a Big Deal. In my experience, Swahili is easy to learn by comparison.) One mighty nice reference work that you may want to check out is *Graphic Java*, by David M. Geary and Alan L. McClellan (published by the folks at SunSoft).

`removePropertyChangeListener(PropertyChangeListener)`

This method deregisters a specified listener's interest in hearing about the `PropertyChangeEvent`.

Signature:

```
public abstract void
   removePropertyChangeListener(PropertyChangeListener
      listener)
```

`setAsText(String)`

Implement this method to set a property value to a specified string. You can retrieve the value that you set with `setAsText()` via the `getAsText()` method (described earlier in this chapter).

Signature:

```
public abstract void setAsText(String text)
   throws IllegalArgumentException
```

`setValue(Object)`

Implement this method to set or change the value of a property. Built-in primitive types should be wrapped in their corresponding Java object type. A `char` value, for example, should be passed as `java.lang.Character`. Refer to Chapter 3 for details on primitive types and wrapper classes.

Signature:

```
public abstract void setValue(Object value)
```

`supportsCustomEditor()`

This method returns `true` if an implementation of `PropertyEditor` can provide a custom editor (that is, if `getCustomEditor()` returns a custom editor). Otherwise, this method returns `false`.

Signature:

```
public abstract boolean supportsCustomEditor()
```

Customization 101

There's nothing like an example to help you understand how everything fits together. The following sections show you what a property editor, a property sheet, and a customizer look like; then, for each of these items, it reveals the corresponding Java source code that made it all happen.

All the examples are included in the BDK which you can find on the CD that came with this book. To see the full listings, check out `ColorEditor.java` (Listing 14-1), `PropertySheet.java` (Listing 14-2), and `BridgeTesterCustomizer.java` (Listing 14-3).

To start, take a look at Figure 14-1. This figure shows what the property editor for the `Color` property looks like in the `BeanBox`. As you know if you've had a chance to experiment with the `BeanBox` (tips for doing just that can be found in Chapter 4), this property editor pops up when you select the color property displayed in the `JellyBean`'s property sheet.

A lot's going on in Figure 14-1, so it won't surprise you that the code responsible for Figure 14-1, which is shown in Listing 14-1, is a little lengthy. The program is not all that complicated, though, if you step through it a line at a time. Best of all, Listing 14-1 contains a lot of the methods described earlier in this chapter, so you get to see them used in a real-life, working situation.

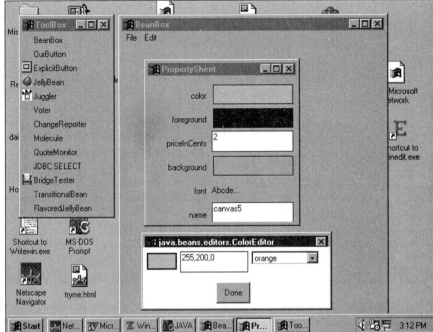

Figure 14-1:
The property editor for Color.

Listing 14-1 ColorEditor.java

```
package sun.beans.editors;

import java.awt.*;
import java.beans.*;

public class ColorEditor extends Panel
  implements PropertyEditor {
  public ColorEditor() {
    // lots of graphical display calls

    ...
  }

  public void setValue(Object o) {
    color = (Color)o;
    changeColor(color);
  }
  ...
  public void setAsText(String s) throws
    java.lang.IllegalArgumentException {
    ...
```

See how ColorEditor inherits from PropertyEditor?

A null-argument constructor is a must

This method changes the color value based on a color object

```
        Color c = new Color(r,g,b);
        changeColor(c);
        …
    }

    public String getJavaInitializationString() {
        return "new java.awt.Color(" + getAsText() + ")";
    }

    private void changeColor(Color c) {
        …
        support.firePropertyChange("", null, null);
    }

    public Object getValue() {
        return color;
    }

    public boolean isPaintable() {
        return true;
    }

    public void paintValue(java.awt.Graphics gfx,
                java.awt.Rectangle box) {
        Color oldColor = gfx.getColor();
        gfx.setColor(Color.black);
        gfx.drawRect(box.x, box.y, box.width-3, box.height-3);
        gfx.setColor(color);
        gfx.fillRect(box.x+1, box.y+1, box.width-4,
                box.height-4);
        gfx.setColor(oldColor);
    }

    public String getAsText() {
        return text.getText();
    }

    public String[] getTags() {
        return null;
    }

    public java.awt.Component getCustomEditor() {
        return this;
    }
```

While this method changes the color value based on a string

Changing the color is an event that gets distributed to all interested listeners

The body of this method shows what I mean about graphics being a challenge!

(continued)

Listing 14-1 (continued)

Of course this method returns true; getCustomEditor() is defined right above it!

```java
public boolean supportsCustomEditor() {
    return true;
        }

public void addPropertyChangeListener
            (PropertyChangeListener l) {
    support.addPropertyChangeListener(l);
}

public void removePropertyChangeListener
            (PropertyChangeListener l) {
    support.removePropertyChangeListener(l);
}

...

private PropertyChangeSupport support
    = new PropertyChangeSupport(this);
}
```

The registration method for listeners

The deregistration method for listeners

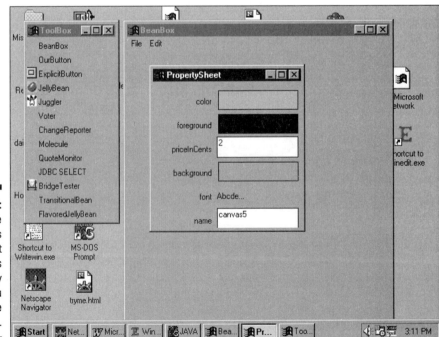

Figure 14-2:
The JellyBean's property sheet appears automatically when you click the JellyBean.

You saw what a single property editor looks like in Figure 14-1. Now, take a look at Figure 14-2 to get familiar with a property sheet.

Listing 14-2 shows the code responsible for implementing the property sheet shown in Figure 14-2.

Listing 14-2	PropertySheet.java

```
package sun.beanbox;

import java.beans.*;
import java.awt.*;
...


public class PropertySheet extends Frame {
  ...
    synchronized void setTarget(Object targ) {
      target = targ;
      ...
      BeanInfo bi =
          Introspector.getBeanInfo(target.getClass());
      properties = bi.getPropertyDescriptors();
      ...

      // Create an array to hold the property editors
      editors = new PropertyEditor[properties.length];
      ...



      for (int i = 0; i < properties.length; i++) {
        ...

          Class type = properties[i].getPropertyType();
          PropertyEditor editor =
            PropertyEditorManager.findEditor(type);
          editors[i] = editor;
          // set the property value associated
          // with the editor
          editor.setValue(value);

          // register a listener
          editor.addPropertyChangeListener(adaptor);

          // Determine how to display the editor
          if (editor.isPaintable() &&
```

Getting an instance of BeanInfo for a bean

Getting a list of the bean's properties

For each property in the list . . .

Find a PropertyEditor

Add this property editor to the list

(continued)

Listing 14-2 *(continued)*

Determine how to display the editor in the property sheet

```
        editor.supportsCustomEditor()) {
    view = new PropertyCanvas(this, editor);
  } else if (editor.getTags() != null) {
    view = new PropertySelector(editor);
  } else if (editor.getAsText() != null) {
    String init = editor.getAsText();
    view = new PropertyText(editor);
  }
      ...
  }
```

Now that you've seen an example of a property editor and a property sheet, it's time to see a customizer in action. Check out Figure 14-3 to see what a customizer looks like in the BeanBox.

The code fragment shown in Listing 14-3 implements what you see in Figure 14-3; that is, a customizer for the `BridgeTester` bean.

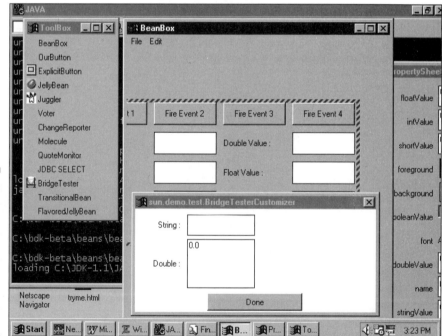

Figure 14-3:
To view the
BridgeTester
customizer,
choose
Edit⇨
Customization
from the
BeanBox
menu.

Listing 14-3   `BridgeTesterCustomizer.java`

This class extends an AWT component (Panel) and implements Customizer

setObject() is one of the required methods

This method and the following one are both required to be implemented, too

```java
// Notice how this class extends an AWT component (Panel)
// and implements Customizer?
public class BridgeTesterCustomizer extends Panel
  implements Customizer {
  // A null constructor is required.
  public BridgeTesterCustomizer() {
    setLayout(null);
  }

  public void setObject(Object obj) {
  // lots of graphic calls
  }

  // If a user clicks the label field, set a
  // string value; if a user clicks the double
  // field, set a double value. Either way,
  // fire a PropertyChangeEvent.
  public boolean handleEvent(Event evt) {
    if (evt.id == Event.KEY_RELEASE && evt.target == labelField) {
      String txt = labelField.getText();
      target.setStringValue(txt);
      support.firePropertyChange("", null, null);
    }
    if (evt.id == Event.KEY_RELEASE && evt.target == doubleField) {
      String txt = doubleField.getText();
      target.setDoubleValue((new
        Double(txt)).doubleValue());
      }
      support.firePropertyChange("", null, null);
    }
    ...
  }

  public void
  addPropertyChangeListener(PropertyChangeListener l) {
    support.addPropertyChangeListener(l);
  }

  public void
  removePropertyChangeListener(PropertyChangeListener l) {
    support.removePropertyChangeListener(l);
  }
  ...
}
```

Chapter 15

Leftovers: A Delicious Assortment of Useful (If Unclassifiable) Bean APIs

In This Chapter

▶ Instantiating serialized beans

▶ Creating invisible beans

*T*he java.beans package implements a couple of items that don't fit easily into the categories of introspection, event handling, persistence, and application-builder support, which are discussed in the preceding chapters of this part. But although they may not be easy to categorize, the leftovers in this chapter are just too good to throw away. Read on to get up-close and personal with

✔ The java.beans.Beans class

✔ The java.beans.Visibility interface

Classes

Only one class is highlighted in this chapter: the Beans class. Because the Beans class enables you to work with existing beans (instantiate them, query them, and so forth), this class is useful if you're creating a bean-based application development tool (As you'd expect, the BeanBox bean included in the BDK makes liberal use of this class's methods.)

`Beans` is a freebie; that is, you don't have to create an instance of the `Beans` class before you can call `Beans` methods. Why? Because all of the `Beans` methods are *static*. (I've included more information on static methods in the "Constructors" section later in this chapter.) In this section, you find a description of `Beans`, a pedigree (a list of the class's parent, grandparent, and so on) and a list of `Beans` methods.

Beans

All beans "belong" to the `Beans` class. `Beans` is kind of a den mother, if you will.

Thinking of the `Beans` class as the `BeanEnvironment` class helps make its purpose a little clearer.

Pedigree

```
java.lang.Object
    ⇨ java.beans.Beans
```

Constructors

All the `java.beans.Beans` methods are *static*, which means that you don't have to construct an instance of the Beans class to call them. In fact, you *can't* call these methods on an instance of the `Beans` class — only on the class itself, as you see in the following sections. The `Beans` class does have a constructor, though.

Beans()

Because all the methods in this section are static methods, you really have no reason to create an instance of the `Beans` class at all. I include this constructor just for the sake of completeness.

Signature:

```
public Beans()
```

Example:

```
Beans aNewBeanEnvironment = new Beans();
```

Sure, it's small, but it's got a great view

In the world of software-application development, a *view* is a special way of looking at something. Database managers, for example, often create several views of a database based on how different people want to look at, or view, the data.

Imagine the existence of a database that's devoted to cataloging your physical characteristics, qualities, and accomplishments. Based on the many roles that you play, different people may want to view you differently, as in the following list:

✔ **Prospective employers** may be interested only in the data pertaining to your employment background, level of education, and extracurricular activities.

✔ **Your insurance company** may be interested only in seeing your medical information — things like height, weight, blood pressure, and the date of your last checkup.

✔ **Your bank** may be interested in viewing only your financial information.

Conceptually, views are applicable to beans, too, although version 1.0 of the BDK has no support for multiple views at the time of this writing. You may want to create one bean but allow different developers (who have different agendas) to view and use the bean from different angles — in which case, you want to implement different interfaces, one per view. (Where beans are concerned, you can think of a view as being the same thing as an interface implementation.)

Methods

Each of the following static methods applies to the overall bean environment — not to any particular bean, but to *all* beans. If you're unfamiliar with the way that static methods work, pay particularly close attention to the examples of each method.

getInstanceOf(Object, Class)

This method returns an object representing the specified view (implemented interface) of a specified bean. If the designated view isn't implemented for the bean, this method just returns the bean.

Because in the current JavaBeans implementation one bean is always represented by one corresponding Java object, you won't have much use for this method right now. The method always returns the bean that you pass to it, no matter what type of view you specify. In the future, though, this situation is expected to change, making this method useful for those of you who want to develop multiple-view beans.

Signature:

```
public static Object getInstanceOf(Object bean,
                    Class targetType)
```

In this example:

- ✔ `bean` is the bean for which you want to get a particular `targetType` view.

- ✔ `targetType` is the type of view you want to see if `bean` supports (that is, the type of view you want to determine is associated with `bean` or not).

Example:

```
Beans.getInstanceOf(someBean, someView);
```

`instantiate(ClassLoader, String)`

This method creates and returns an instance of a specified `my.dir.beanName` in either of two ways, given an (optional) class loader:

- ✔ `instantiate()` first looks for a serialized bean that matches `beanName`. In the example later in this section, it tries to read a serialized bean from the file `my/dir/mySerializedBean.ser`.

- ✔ If that attempt fails, `instantiate()` tries to load the class `/my/dir/mySerializedBean` and to create (and return) an instance of that class.

Signature:

```
public static Object instantiate(ClassLoader cls,
                  String beanName)
   throws IOException, ClassNotFoundException
```

In this example:

- ✔ `cls` is the class loader to use to fetch the serialized object. Pass `null` for this value, and the method uses the default system class loader.

- ✔ `beanName` is the fully qualified package name of the serialized object to fetch (without the `.ser` suffix).

Example:

```
ClassLoader aCL = this.getClass().getClassLoader();
DownloadBean myDL = (DownloadBean) Beans.instantiate(aCL,
    "my.dir.mySerializedBean");
```

isDesignTime()

This method returns `true` if all instantiated beans are running in an application-construction environment; otherwise, this method returns `false`. You set the returned value via the `setDesignTime()` method, described later in this chapter.

Signature:

```
public static boolean isDesignTime()
```

Example:

```
if (Beans.isDesignTime()) {
   // All beans are in application building mode

   ...
}
```

isGuiAvailable()

`isGuiAvailable()` returns `true` if all instantiated beans can assume that an interactive GUI is available to them (so they can do things like display dialog boxes). Otherwise, this method returns `false`. You can use `setGuiAvailable()`, described later in this chapter, to set the value that this method returns.

This method typically should return `true` in a windowing environment such as Windows 95/NT or the Macintosh OS and `false` in a server environment (or if beans are running as part of a batch job in which no human intervention is expected).

Signature:

```
public static boolean isGuiAvailable()
```

Example:

```
if (Beans.isGuiAvailable()) {
   // There's a GUI available, so we must be in
   // a windowing environment

   ...
}
```

isInstanceOf(Object, Class)

This method returns `true` if a specified view is associated with a specified bean; otherwise, it returns `false`.

This method is closely related to `getInstanceOf()`; but whereas `getInstanceOf()` returns a view object associated with a bean, this method just returns `true` or `false`. Yes, the specified view is valid for the specified bean, or no, it's not.

Signature:

```
public static boolean isInstanceOf(Object bean,
                    Class targetType)
```

In this example:

- bean is any bean.
- targetType is the type of view that you want to see if bean supports (that is, the type of view you want to determine is associated with bean or not).

Example:

```
if (Beans.isInstanceOf(someBean, someView)) {
  // someBean implements someView

   ...

}
```

setDesignTime(boolean)

Use this method to indicate whether instantiated beans are running in an application-builder environment. You can return the `set` value via the `isDesignTime()` method, described earlier in this chapter.

Signature:

```
public static void setDesignTime(boolean isDesignTime)
   throws SecurityException
```

Example:

```
Beans.setDesignTime(true);
```

setGuiAvailable(boolean)

Use this method to indicate whether instantiated beans have access to GUI interaction. (Unless the beans are meant to run in a nonwindowing environment, the value should be set to `true`.) You can retrieve the `set` value (which must be `true` or `false`) via the `isGuiAvailable()` method, described earlier in this chapter.

Signature:

```
public static void setGuiAvailable(boolean
    isGuiAvailable) throws SecurityException
```

Example:

```
Beans.setGuiAvailable(true);
```

Interfaces

One interface, called `Visibility`, provides support for invisible beans.

Visibility

Visibility refers to the graphical representation of a bean at runtime. All beans need to have some sort of visual representation at design time, so that developers can display a property sheet or customizer and configure the way that the bean behaves. Depending on your application, though, you may not need to display the bean at runtime.

The `OurButton` and `JellyBean` beans packed into the BDK, for example, are visual components. These beans appear in the `BeanBox` palette so that you can customize them inside the `BeanBox` container bean at design time, but they also display at runtime. (Runtime for these beans, as you may remember if you've had a chance to read Chapter 5, consists of a user's clicking the `button` bean to change the color of the `JellyBean` bean.)

Other beans, though, may be designed to hang out on a server (where GUI services aren't even an option) and to take care of their business without the need for any human intervention at runtime. The `Visibility` interface was designed to support just such invisible beans.

The BeanBox enables you to hide and show invisible beans at will. Try dropping an instance of the (invisible) TickTock bean on the BeanBox and then selecting View⇨Hide Invisible Beans from the BeanBox menu. Poof! TickTock disappears. To bring it back, select View⇨Show Invisible Beans from the BeanBox menu.

Methods

As you see in the following sections, only a few methods are associated with the Visibility interface.

No, it's not your imagination — the methods described in the following sections don't follow the standard method-naming conventions for accessors. You won't find a getPropertyName() or setPropertyName() anywhere. The reason for this apparent lack of consistency? The bean architects recognized the fact that although invisible beans have a useful role to play, they probably won't be implemented often in proportion to visible beans. The architects wanted to keep beginning bean developers from assuming that they had to implement the Visibility interface to make their beans visible, and they figured that naming these methods something unconventional would do the trick.

avoidingGui()

This method should return true if the bean is currently avoiding using a GUI, indicating that the bean is still out of sight — that is, if the method dontUseGui() (described later in this chapter) was previously invoked; otherwise, avoidingGui() should return false. Here's an example of the syntax for this method:

```
public abstract boolean avoidingGui()
```

dontUseGui()

This method tells a bean that it should not attempt to use the GUI, thereby rendering it invisible. Here's the correct syntax for dontUseGui():

```
public abstract void dontUseGui()
```

needsGui()

This method should return true if the bean absolutely, positively needs a GUI to get its work done; otherwise, it should return false. The syntax for this method, as you see below, is fairly straightforward:

```
public abstract boolean needsGui()
```

okToUseGui()

The following syntax describes the okToUseGui() method, which notifies the caller that it's okay to use the GUI to interact with the bean.

```
public abstract void okToUseGui()
```

Part V
The Part of Tens

The 5th Wave   By Rich Tennant

In this part . . .

This book contains an awful lot of information — so much that you might find yourself a little over-whelmed at times, especially if you're brand new to Java and object-oriented programming. In order to help you pick out and reinforce the really essential bits of bean lore, I've pulled together a couple of chapters that emphasize these essentials. One chapter describes the ten characteristics all world-class beans should possess, and one lists the ten most confusing misconceptions folks tend to struggle with as they march up the JavaBeans learning curve.

Finally, I've included a chapter devoted to online re-sources you can use to complement the information you find in *JavaBeans For Dummies* to keep up-to-date with the newest developments in the world of JavaBeans. Enjoy!

Chapter 16

The Top Ten (Or So) Characteristics of Highly Effective Beans

• •

In This Chapter

▶ Understanding what makes some beans better than others — and why

▶ Finding out how to incorporate the most important characteristics into your beans

• •

*T*he JavaBeans architecture provides you with all the services you need (packaged as APIs) to create reusable Java components. That's all the architecture does, however; how you use these services to design and implement your beans is strictly up to you. Flexible? Absolutely. Foolproof? Hardly!

Designing software components is much different than designing ordinary applications because of one very important fact: Unlike with traditional applications, you must design components with integration in mind from the start. Much like well-trained dogs, solid, reusable beans are no accident: They are both the result of careful planning, considerable effort, and practice!

This chapter describes the elements that contribute to robust, reusable components and offers practical advice that you can use to apply these elements to each and every bean that you develop.

 The characteristics you find in this chapter are ideals; in general, adhering to these characteristics yields the best results. Make sure, however, that you keep in mind that each of these suggestions is meant to improve your life by making application development with JavaBeans easier and faster. If you find yourself going crazy trying to make your bean implementation fit one of these recommendations, stop! Component software really is an iterative process, and you always find room for improvement. No law says that you can't modify your bean six weeks from now!

Simple Is As Simple Does

A bean, like any other software component, should do just one thing — and do that one thing well so that you can rely on that bean to perform its task perfectly, over and over again. The programmers in the audience should immediately recognize the following popular non-bean components:

- Lists
- Arrays
- Push buttons

These tried-and-true components, available in just about every programming language known to humankind, are ubiquitous not only because they're useful (how's that for a preview of the next characteristic?) but because they're simple.

Take the humble *list* as an example. You can do anything that you can possibly think of with a list — as long as what you think of is legitimately list-related: You can create a new list, add items to the list, delete items from the list, display the list, delete the entire list, and so on — but that's pretty much all you can do. A list can't help you calculate the value of pi or figure out how many payments you still need to make on your Yugo. A list's job is simply to be a list — and this simplicity, this singularity of purpose is what makes lists (like all effective components) so valuable to so many application scenarios in so many disparate development environments.

If you catch yourself creating dozens of constructors for a bean and using a great deal of If statements in your bean methods (For example, "If it's a red bean, do this; otherwise, if it's a blue bean, do that; otherwise …"), you may be trying to make one bean do double-duty. If the thing you're trying to model is really two (or more) conceptual entities, consider breaking up the function into multiple beans.

A Bean of Substance

Because the whole point of creating JavaBeans is to reuse the beans in different applications, make sure that the beans that you create fill some practical need that's not already satisfied by some other means (such as a bean that's delivered with the BDK).

Okay, I can hear what you're saying to yourself right about now: "Really. No kidding? Wow, I'd never have thought on my own to create a *useful* bean!

Knowing that's worth the price of the book!" Well, of course the concept's obvious — but one look at the number of calculator components hanging out on the Internet proves that the statement bears repeating! Until you get the hang of it (and especially if you're used to developing traditional applications), developing component software is a challenge. Why go to all the trouble of developing a bean if you don't expect your effort to pay off in spades?

Looking for examples of the kinds of software components that are so good that the components purportedly make buckets o'cash for the folks who developed them? Then check out one of the following component warehouse sites, where you find several such examples:

```
http://www.partbank.com/
```

```
http://www.earthweb.net/activex/
```

```
http://www.microsoft.com/activex/gallery/
```

Versatility Is the Key

Generally speaking, the more useful a bean is in a wide variety of applications, the better. Some of the most enduring components (charting components, multimedia components, and translation components to name a few) are in demand precisely because just about everyone can use these components; they're discipline- and application-neutral.

Which comes first — the bean or the application?

Good components typically aren't designed in a vacuum. I'm not saying that you can't possibly create a useful bean if you have no clue how someone may use that bean, but I certainly don't recommend such an approach! Software components, after all, are abstractions of real-world components. Can you imagine manufacturing a wheel if you had no idea what vehicle you were making the wheel to fit? For starters, how could you know how big to make that particular wheel? (You'll find quite a difference between a scooter wheel and a dump truck wheel!)

In software, as in life, necessity is often the mother of invention. After the fourth time you spend all day coding a connection between one of your company's mainframe applications and the cool Intranet Web page you're designing, for example, you probably stop and think to yourself, "Hey! I just did this last week, and I know I'm going to need to do the same thing again a week from now. Hmmm . . . How can I turn this code into a mainframe-connection bean and just keep reusing the thing?" Voilà! A useful, reusable component is born.

People — in their myriad and ever changing roles — are at the heart of pretty much every software application, whether as a customer, student, employee, or something more specific (departmental manager, scientist, game player — you get the idea). If your job is creating human resource applications for your company's Intranet, you may see people in terms of full-time Acme employees, so creating an employee bean to keep track of such employee information as names, home addresses, dates of hire, salaries, and so on, may be just what the doctor ordered.

Now, *employee* is a pretty versatile construct, and if all you ever expect to develop are human-resource applications, an employee bean is probably sufficient for your needs. But what about abstracting *employee* a bit more — stepping back just a little and creating a "person" bean that encompasses all of the characteristics of "employee" and adds a few more besides? If you did that, you could reuse the same "person" bean in accounting applications, online education sites — you name it!

How versatile you need to make your beans really depends on what you want to do with them. If you're a developer trying to create beans that have the broadest applicability possible to increase your market, you want to focus on creating the most flexible beans you can. If you're creating beans for your own consumption, versatility may not be as significant a concern as making the darn thing work right.

A Bean for All Occasions

You can use the best beans in many different types of applications. Why? Because they're ultra-generic. Imagine, for example, a 3-D button bean. Conceivably, all kinds of applications can make use of a really neat 3-D push button, as long as the button's *generic* — that is, as long as it doesn't make any assumptions (or, to be a little less anthropomorphic, as long as the bean doesn't contain any hard-coded properties).

A 3-D button bean should leave the following kinds of decisions to whomever's using that bean to create an application:

- The size of the button
- The color of the button
- What label appears on the button
- What the button does after someone presses it

Leaving such decisions to the application developer increases the flexibility of the bean and thus the number of potential application scenarios to which that bean can adapt itself.

Generic beans, by definition, are highly customizable, and the way that you customize beans is by setting their properties. A good rule of thumb is that, for every descriptive adjective you can think of for a bean (`size`, `color`, and `label`, for example, are adjectives describing the 3-D bean in the preceding example), you should implement one property and two corresponding accessor methods (that is, one method to set the property value and one to retrieve the value).

Self-Sufficiency: A Worthy Bean Goal

One of the hallmarks of good object-oriented design is something called *encapsulation*, which basically translates into English as the following concept: "An object should contain all the knowledge it needs to do its job — but not one scrap more."

A real-life parakeet object, for example, "knows" how to eat, sing, fly, and whatever else that it is parakeets do in their spare time. The bird does not, however, know how to change the oil on a pickup truck or bake a rhubarb crisp. (And with good reason; potholders just don't come in a size small enough for parakeets to use comfortably!)

Read on for specific examples of how encapsulation applies to beans.

Keep all your bean stuff in one place

You need to implement all the data and behavior relevant to a bean (with two exceptions, which I explain in the following list) in the bean's class as properties and methods. In other words, if you ship your friend Marlis a bean across the Internet, she should have no problem dropping the bean into her application-building tool and running with it. She shouldn't need to call you on the phone an hour later and say, "Hey, I tried compiling your bean and I got a compile error saying that I need two more files, lickety.class and split.exe. What's the deal?"

The exceptions to the you-must-implement-everything-bean-related-in-the-bean-class rule are as follows:

> ✔ **Data and behavior related to design-time customization and intro-spection.** You want to keep these properties and methods separate and implement them in instances of `PropertyEditor`, `Customizer`, and `BeanInfo`, as appropriate. (See Chapters 11 and 14 for all the scoop on customization and introspection.)

✔ **External resources.** If you have a GIF file containing an icon (or some other resource file) that you want folks to associate with your bean, keep that file separate.

Make sure that you package both customization classes and external resources, if any, together with the beans with which those items belong by poking all of these files in the same JAR file. (See Chapter 4 for more information on JAR files.)

Respect your beans' right to privacy

Another important self-containment rule to remember is to declare all your beans' private properties; you should never enable any other bean to get or set your beans' property values without using an accessor method (which you declare as public).

In addition, you should declare all your beans' behavior (methods) as private — unless you have a darn good reason to do otherwise. Whether you declare your beans' methods private depends on whether other software (other beans, application development tools, and so on) legitimately needs the capability to call your beans' methods. You obviously need to declare customization methods and accessor methods public; the entire point of these methods is to provide a way for others to interact with your beans. On the other hand, if you define some methods that you call internally (from inside your bean) but that just don't make sense to expose to the outside world, you want to declare those methods private.

A Bean of Letters

In essence, *documentation* is nothing more than telling others exactly how your bean appears — and why. Documentation is a good thing, especially if you expect other folks to use your bean extensively.

You have several different ways to document your bean, as the following sections describe, and these methods aren't mutually exclusive. In fact, I suggest that you use all three!

Describing bean properties and methods with BeanInfo

One good idea is to define your bean's innards explicitly by implementing the BeanInfo interface. That way, if an application builder uses introspection to figure out what methods your bean supports, he doesn't have to use guesswork. (Flip to Chapter 11 for a primer on introspection.)

Providing free-style comments with javadoc

As Chapter 4 discusses, you can use the `javadoc` tool to generate really nifty hypertext-linked HTML files that describe your classes and methods. In addition to the class and method names and relationships, however, the `javadoc` tool also includes in the automatically generated HTML output any comments that you care to specify in your source — as long as you surround the comments with the special `javadoc` commenting symbols, as shown in the following example:

```
/** This comment appears automatically in all documentation
you generate by using the javadoc utility. */
```

You can add plain old Java-style comments to your bean code, too. (Check out Chapter 4 if you need a refresher on the two different kinds of Java comments available to you.) These non-`javadoc` comments don't appear in the HTML files that the `javadoc` tool generates, but the comments are available to anybody (yourself included!) hunting through the source code six months from now, trying to decipher a particularly elegant solution.

Specifying JAR file details with a manifest

As you know after you glance through Chapter 4, after you develop a bean, you don't just pass the bean around to other developers stark naked (the bean that is); instead, after you compile your bean, you tuck it safely away inside a JAR file — and pass that JAR file on to other developers.

You can attach special text files called *manifests* to JAR files to explain the JAR file contents — details such as when you created the JAR file, who created the file, the version of the JAR file, which of the files in the JAR file are beans and which are bean-related resources, and so on.

At the time of this writing, folks from Sun and Netscape are still in the process of hammering out the manifest specification. To keep up with the latest developments, keep an eye on the following URL:

```
http://java.sun.com/products/JDK/1.1/designspecs/jar/
manifest.html
```

Putting Your Bean to the Test

At the time most folks first hear about component software, their initial reaction is usually something along the lines of "That's *so cool!*" Their second reaction (especially if they're involved in the software industry, whether as a producer or as a consumer) is usually "Oh, wait a minute. . . . Does this thing mean that if you build an application from 10 separate components, you then have 10 different components that may crash and 10 different companies to call for technical support? Yikes!" Component software's very nature poses some interesting challenges in terms of reliability and quality. In this section, you discover how to increase your odds for producing bulletproof beans and bean-based applications.

The challenge

Hardware components are pretty well licked. (Rare is the telephone cord that doesn't fit the wall jack on one end and the phone on the other.) Unfortunately, however, you can't say the same of software components. Even software developers admit that a quality problem exists in the software industry! The primary cause of this problem is that software developers, unlike hardware manufacturers, don't consistently build components to precise, standard specifications.

To be fair, software standards weren't a pressing issue until component software came along. If you're building a traditional monolithic program, standards don't have much of a role to play; all you need to do is to make sure that your application works on the platform you're targeting.

As you begin to assemble components (especially cross-platform components), however, standards become essential. Remember the old adage "A chain is only as strong as its weakest link?" Well, a component-based application is only as robust as its least-reliable component.

Fortunately, help is on the way in the form of standards and standards-based certification programs!

Certification programs

As with any other software, you need to test beans within an inch of their lives before you pronounce them finished; that goes without saying. Beyond testing, however, you need to make sure that your beans follow certain standards so that other developers can depend on your beans to behave in an expected fashion.

To this end, certification programs are springing up throughout the industry. The announcement for the latest Java-based certification program, the 100 Percent Pure Java Initiative, came out at roughly the same time the first JavaBeans beta release hit the streets. By the time you read this, details of this initiative's education and testing programs (which developers can use to verify that their beans meet all the standard requirements of beanhood) should be available.

The good folks at CILabs also have a certification program in place. Their focus is on component-software validation, and although their current emphasis is on CORBA-based component models, they're expected to incorporate the JavaBeans architecture as it matures.

For more information on the 100 Percent Pure Java Initiative and CILabs' Live Objects component certification program, visit the following Web sites:

```
http://www.javasoft.com/100percent/index.html
```

```
http://www.cilabs.org/LiveObjects/
```

Teaching Your Beans Good Manners

As you know, the JavaBeans architecture provides guidelines for your bean-building efforts; whether you follow the guidelines (and how closely) is strictly up to you, the bean developer. When component-validation suites become commonplace (see the preceding section for details) and people start affixing the "Certified, Card-Carrying, 100 Percent Guaranteed Great All-Around Bean" sticker to every bean advertisement in sight, developers should feel more comfortable about using each others' beans in their own application-development efforts. Until then, however, bean developers must discipline themselves to create components that "play by the rules."

The following techniques, for example, are among those in which bean developers should *not* indulge, no matter how tempting:

- ✔ Including calls to platform-specific code
- ✔ Refusing to follow the method-naming conventions that the BDK outlines
- ✔ Forgetting to provide customization classes and property editors for new property types

✔ Implementing common methods in uncommon ways (providing a
`save()` method that prints a bean instead of saving it, for example)

The bottom line is that software components offer an unprecedented level of
programming efficiency, but this efficiency isn't automatic; it results only
from careful adherence to standards.

Chapter 17

The Ten Most Common Misconceptions about JavaBeans

• •

In This Chapter

▶ Exploding silly bean myths

▶ Sifting the truth from bean rumors

• •

*B*ecause JavaBeans is still fairly new, even in Net years (where three person-months is roughly equal to about one Net year) lots of confusing, even contradictory claims are circulating with regard to the role this component model is best suited to play in Internet application development.

Although the rumors in this chapter may not seem quite as amusing as some of the more well-known urban myths (and none quite measures up to my personal favorite, "Lady dries out toy poodle in the microwave"), they're still worth considering. The more that you know what beans *aren't*, the more you can appreciate and take advantage of beans for what they are!

Beans Are Nothing More Than Document Controls

In the press, beans are often cast in the role of widget: combo boxes, scroll bars, sliders — that type of thing. Widgets are great (in fact, some of my best friends are widgets), and beans *can* fill that role handily. Beans aren't limited to the role of GUI control, however, by any stretch of the imagination. In fact, as the JavaBeans implementation continues to mature, beans can far more easily show their true colors — specifically, their capability to act as miniapplication building blocks that only their developers' imaginations can limit in function.

Beans Can Talk Only to Other Beans

One of the great debates regarding any component software strategy is the Compatibility Question. IT department heads around the world realize that committing to one component model is risky in a business as volatile as the software industry. "We must keep our options open" is an oft-repeated mantra. "Beans sound great — but most of our legacy systems are in relational databases and mainframe applications."

Fortunately, "compatibility" is JavaBeans' middle name. After the implementation is complete, beans will not only be able to interface with any other Java program on any Java-supporting platform, but also with relational databases and CORBA-compliant ORBS via IIOP, OpenDoc components, Netscape plug-ins, and ActiveX components. (Chapters 9 and 10 contain explanations of each of these interoperability options.)

End Users Can Assemble Beans into Complex Applications

If you're familiar at all with the concept of component software, you've no doubt been treated to glowing visions of a future world in which end users snap components together and create their own software applications.

This state of affairs is definitely a worthy goal, but in terms of attainability, it ranks somewhere between world peace and tasty low-fat cookies. For the foreseeable future, the only "end users" who snap beans together are developers, and the primary reason for this situation can't be overemphasized: No matter how easily the parts fit together, *somebody somewhere must possess intimate knowledge of the entire application.* The following list describes a couple more reasons why my mom isn't going to be building her own bean-based application any time soon:

  ✔ **End users aren't developers.** The majority of end users hold down jobs that have nothing whatsoever to do with the art of programming. These users are experts at their particular fields of endeavor, whether parenting, accounting, retail sales, or social work. Such users aren't (and shouldn't need to be) familiar with software construction; expecting such a level of familiarity is like expecting pizza delivery drivers to assemble their own cars.

> 🗸 **The technology hasn't yet reached the mass production stage.**
> Assuming that end users ever show any interest in developing their
> own applications from components (and if history repeats itself, a small
> percentage of curious folks may), they are sure to need robust, easy-to-
> use tools that make construction productive and relatively painless.
> They also need scads of beans to use as raw material. As I write this
> book, neither of these requirements has yet materialized (although
> both are on their way).

Expecting end users to seize the reins, so to speak, is a combination of
logical extrapolation and wishful thinking that you can boil down to one
mistaken assumption:

> 🗸 **Assumption:** Users can purchase only the components they want,
> saving them time, disk space, and the perennial hassle and expense of
> upgrading to the latest version of a software package, of which they use
> only about 8 percent on a good day.

> 🗸 **Reality:** According to this model, users are responsible for hunting
> down components and making those components work together. The
> last time anyone checked, folks who do this sort of thing had a specific
> name — "obscenely high-paid consultant." Assembling components
> into useful applications is just not that easy!

Beans Can Live Only inside the BeanBox

Developers just becoming acquainted with the BDK frequently assume that
the BeanBox is an integral, necessary part of any bean development effort.
This assumption, although perfectly logical, is incorrect.

At the time of this writing, the BeanBox *is* the best and easiest way to
become comfortable with the JavaBeans APIs, both as a reference implementation (as in "Okay, *now* I see how they did that!") and as a testing utility for
your first bean attempts. The utility's not meant to replace a full-blown
development environment, however; that's the job of the IDEs I discuss in
Chapter 6. In fact, the BeanBox imposes some arbitrary restrictions on
beans (for example, that beans must inherit from AWT classes), which aren't
limits of the JavaBeans architecture at all. So in its present incarnation, the
BeanBox is not something you'd do well to rely on exclusively. (Of course,
the BeanBox, as is true of the rest of the JavaBeans implementation, is still
evolving rapidly. Most experts expect the utility to adapt and become more
full-featured in the coming months.)

Whenever you encounter a situation in which the JavaBeans documentation disagrees with the way the BeanBox implements (and you're sure to do so), rely on the documentation.

Beans Are Just a Fad

At the risk of joining in infamy that nameless editor who gave the thumbs-up to the "Dewey Defeats Truman" headline, I'm going out on a limb here and predicting that JavaBeans are to represent a significant development alternative in the coming years. The following list describes the observations that persuade me — a woman so conservative that I make gray pinstriped suits look trendy — that such an assessment is realistic:

- **The component model is proven.** The question has never been whether components make product construction easier or more efficient; the Industrial Revolution laid that one to rest. The only question now is how best to manage component *software*. Taking a page from the success of computer hardware, the software industry is beginning to focus on nonproprietary, openly available standards, such as the 100 Percent Pure Java Initiative — the first step toward recognizing that you can approach software construction as both a practical applied science *and* an art.

- **JavaBeans is different from any other software component model.** Sure, other component models are available, and I have no reason to believe that some of these models aren't going to continue as viable alternatives for special-case development. JavaBeans, however, is poised for much wider adoption. Why? Because . . .

  - **JavaBeans is Internet-exploitive.** JavaBeans is the only component software model around that was designed from the ground up for Internet application development — and if the recent past is any indication, the number of Internet applications is going to continue to mushroom uncontrollably for quite some time.

  - **JavaBeans is relatively easy to use.** If you're familiar with other component models, you may be surprised at how easy beans are to implement in comparison to those models. Beyond the simplicity of the API and the beans architecture, however, the tremendous collection of Java-supportive IDEs (at last count, 50!) suggests that developing beans can only become easier as time goes by.

- **The Internet changed the rules.** Much of the resistance folks had to component software in the past was completely valid. "Why," they wondered, "should we break up applications that work perfectly fine into these newfangled components?" The answer is that they shouldn't! Rewriting code isn't something sane people do for fun: They do so only for a compelling reason, such as their business changing so that the current application is no longer sufficient — or technology changes and presents a brand new opportunity to communicate and conduct their business even better than before.

This kind of radical change is exactly what's fueling the explosive growth of interest in programming for the Internet. The Internet offers unprecedented possibilities for creating *new* applications — the Net's a whole new model, and traditional applications just don't fit the model. Of course, you can — and should — retain *parts* of old legacy applications; no use throwing the baby out with the bathwater. Even in these cases, however, someone needs (at the very least) to develop and graft new user interfaces (beans!) onto the old mainframe workhorse applications.

Beans Have Nothing to Do with Java

In my opinion, the marketing folks at JavaSoft responsible for coining the term "JavaBeans" were really onto something. Face it — the name's cute! (Hey, the opportunity for puns alone is worth the price of admission; see the sidebar for a few you may not have come across yet.)

The truth, however, is that beans are inseparable from Java. Beans *are* Java — specifically, Java components. (Some say that a distinct possibility exists for the name "JavaBeans" to be dropped eventually, after folks become comfortable with what components are and how they work; at that point, people may start referring to beans as plain old Java components.)

Very punny

Question: What do you call a bean in the alpha release stage?

Answer: A green bean.

Question: What do you call a fix that you need to distribute for your bean?

Answer: A bean patch.

Question: What are you doing if you surf the Web for beans?

Answer: Picking beans.

Beans and ActiveX Components Are Virtually the Same Thing

JavaBeans and ActiveX are constantly compared in the press as an "either/or" proposition. True, both are component models, but that's where the similarity ends. The biggest difference? JavaBeans are first and foremost Internet-optimized components; ActiveX components' claim to fame lies in the desktop component arena. Sure, some overlap exists; the JavaBeans/ActiveX bridge, for example, enables components that you implement in the two separate models to communicate. Right now, however, if you're considering picking one over the other, think carefully about how you expect people to use your application.

The bottom line? If you're developing an Internet or Intranet application you really need to investigate JavaBeans. If, on the other hand, you know for a fact that the application you have in mind is never going to see the light of the Internet, consider instead ActiveX (for Windows platforms) or OpenDoc (for Macintosh, Windows, or OS/2).

All Beans Must Derive from the Same Class

Some folks mistakenly think that, because beans are Java components, beans must extend from the Java class `java.awt.component`. Technically, a bean doesn't need to inherit from *any* other class. The characteristic that makes a bean a bean is simply that a bean supports the JavaBeans component model. In other words, a bean contains methods that implement persistence, interface publishing and discovery, and event handling, as appropriate.

Having said that mouthful, I need to add that, in many cases, deriving beans from AWT classes makes sense; after all, what bean wouldn't benefit from the graphical services that the AWT provides? If you notice, most of the beans in the 1.0 release of the BDK derive, in fact, from AWT components — and the BeanBox expects them to. Convenient? Sure! But, as is also the case with the visibility constraint you see later in this chapter, this limitation is based on the current level of the BeanBox implementation, not on any hard-and-fast bean rule.

Some component models provide a *base* component; the OpenDoc class library, for example, contains a class called `ODPart` from which developers can inherit to get a head start on any noncontainer component they're building. JavaBeans has no such base component.

The Beans Architecture Is Complete

To listen to some marketing folks, you'd think that NASA was implementing mission-critical applications in JavaBeans as we speak! If you had the chance to browse through just about any of the other chapters in this book, however, you know better. The JavaBeans initial specification and first implementation is complete — but a smidge more work remains to be done before missile-guiding systems (or any production-ready system, for that matter) can rely entirely on JavaBeans.

Beans Must Be Visible

Theoretically, beans can be completely invisible. This concept isn't as strange as it may sound at first if you keep in mind that the entire point of a bean is to perform some useful, reusable function.

What if you want to connect a bean-based GUI, for example, to a mainframe application via a communication bean? The odds are good that you wouldn't want a visible communication bean. After all, end users don't want to see the communication bean any more than they'd want to listen to data streaming from their machine to the mainframe. In fact, only one person wants to see the communication bean — the developer using that bean to construct the bean-based application for the end user. And that developer is working with the bean at design time — not at runtime.

The answer? A separate (visible) GUI for customization. (Now you can see how smart those bean architects were to separate the design-time classes from the runtime classes! If they hadn't, you couldn't create invisible beans.) Flip to Chapter 14 for an in-depth look at customization.

Chapter 18

Ten (Or So) Essential JavaBeans Resources

• •

In This Chapter

▶ Communicating with other bean aficionados via newsgroups and mailing lists

▶ Taking advantage of online bean-related magazines and documentation

▶ Finding cool beans on the Web

• •

*J*avaBeans is officially classified as an *emerging technology*, which is geek-speak for "this puppy's firming up faster than Jello in the freezer."
Keeping up with the unbelievable development pace of Internet technologies is hard for traditional print media (including this tome), but fortunately, the Internet itself helps out. From Web sites to Usenet user groups to mailing lists, up-to-the-nanosecond Java resources (examples, documentation — you name it) abound. This chapter introduces you to some of the most indispensable.

LISTSERV Mailing Lists

LISTSERV was the mass-communication mechanism of choice before the appearance on the scene of Usenet user groups, and although more sophisticated alternatives now exist, many people still use LISTSERV quite a bit.

Here's how LISTSERV works: You sign up for, or *subscribe to,* a particular list by sending an e-mail message to the list owner. Then whenever anyone (the list owner or any of the other list participants) posts a message to the list, a copy of the message automatically goes out to your e-mail address. The following sections describe actual examples of subscribing to two very useful bean-related mailing lists.

Electronic mailing lists are just like the traditional "snail-mail" kind. They're essential if you're just finding out about something and are eager for any related information you can get your hands on, and are amusing if you're bored — but such lists can turn just plain annoying as the "junk" messages start to pour in by the dozens. I personally find both lists in the following sections of great help, and I hope that you do, too; just prepare yourself for a swamped inbox every once in awhile!

If anything changes, they tell you

Sun maintains a generic bean-information list called *beans-info*. This is a relatively low-volume list; its purpose is to tell subscribers whenever something "big" happens — for example, if Sun issues a JavaBeans-related press release or makes publicly available a new version of the BDK.

Let me on!

To subscribe to the beans-info list, send an e-mail message to the following address:

```
beans-info-request@wombat.eng.sun.com
```

In the body of the message, type something similar to the following line. (The wording doesn't need to be exactly the same as this example, because a real, live person reads your message, but the gist of the text should remain pretty close to these words.)

```
Please add me to the beans-info list.
```

That's all you do! Within a couple days or so, you begin to receive exciting bean messages. You also receive a regular electronic newsletter, the *JavaBeans Advisor* (see Figure 18-1), that offers the latest news, technical tips, and release-specific hints.

Let me off!

Should you decide at some point that you'd like to stop your subscription to beans-info, all you need to do is send an e-mail message to the same address you contacted to subscribe, this time including a request that Sun drop you from the mailing list. Contact the URL listed below with the following message:

```
beans-info-request@wombat.eng.sun.com
```

```
Please remove me from the beans-info list.
```

Unless you're one of a select group of folks at Sun, you don't have the authority to contribute messages to this mailing list.

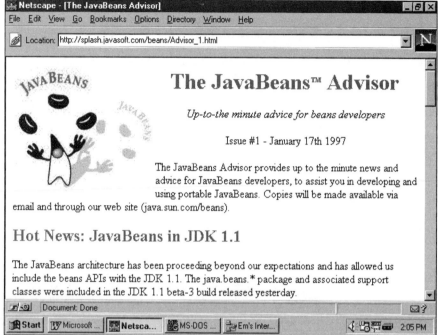

Figure 18-1:
You can
view the
JavaBeans
Advisor
Web page
at your
leisure or
have the
page sent
directly
to your
e-mailbox
(at no extra
charge).

The bean scene

The *beans-users* list is an interactive forum boasting an ever-expanding group of bean developers, from gurus to wanna-bes and everything in between. This forum is a great place to get clarification, advice, examples, and emotional support on virtually every aspect of bean development.

This mailing list gets a lot of traffic. If you subscribe and find yourself totally overwhelmed by the avalanche of messages peppering your in-box, you can always de-subscribe and check out the archived version from time to time, at your leisure, at the following URL:

```
http://splash.javasoft.com/beans/beans-users/
```

Let me on!

To subscribe to the beans-users list, send an e-mail message to the following address:

```
listserv@javasoft.com
```

In the body of the message, type the following line exactly (except for the name, of course; you need to substitute your own name for the one shown in the example):

```
SUBSCRIBE BEANS-USERS Lucretia J. Smirnoff
```

Let me off!

To unsubscribe from the beans-users mailing list, send another e-mail message to the same address:

```
listserv@javasoft.com
```

include the following line in the body of the message:

```
SIGNOFF BEANS-USERS
```

How to give others the benefit of your insight and wisdom

Posting your own questions and answering others' are tons of fun — and easy, too! To send a message to all the folks who subscribe to the bean-users list, all at once, all you need to do is send one e-mail message to the following address:

```
beans-users@javasoft.com
```

Specifying a clear, succinct subject line increases your chances of getting a quick response from fellow bean enthusiasts.

User groups

Java-related Usenet user groups (also called *news groups*) are the next best thing to having a brother-in-law who knows Java inside out. If you can't figure something out after going through the documentation, browse through one of the user groups described in the following sections.

If you scan through the existing messages and still don't see an answer to your question, feel free to post a message.

In addition to the newsgroups that I list in the following sections, the powers that be are considering at this very time a new series of as-yet-unnamed, bean-specific newsgroups. Look for these groups soon in a mail browser near you.

comp.lang.java.api

Get information about any Java API — how the API works, how to use it, that kind of thing — from this newsgroup.

comp.lang.java.programmer

Peruse this high-traffic newsgroup for Java language-related information that isn't specific to any single API.

comp.lang.java.tech

Keep your finger on the pulse of nonprogramming Java technical issues by browsing periodically through this newsgroup. Visit comp.lang.java.tech to find a wealth of information on great stuff such as virtual machines, performance and optimization, porting, and integrating Java with other languages.

Bean-Flavored Web Sites

This section lists the Web sites you want to browse through regularly. Here you find the latest bean-related announcements, toolkits, and gossip — from the horse's mouth, so to speak.

JavaBeans home page

If you're serious about bean development, you want to bookmark the JavaBeans home page at the following URL. This page contains links to the BDK, white papers, bean-based development tools — and much more.

```
http://splash.javasoft.com/beans/
```

Sun's Java home page

Visit Sun's Java home page for news about Java-based products, events, and success stories at the following Web address:

```
http://java.sun.com/
```

Java-related newsgroup FAQ

The `comp.lang.java` *FAQ* (Frequently Asked Question list) is more than just an etiquette guide for folks considering posting to one of the `comp.lang.java` newsgroups; this FAQ list is also a mini-Java manual, with sections covering everything from common installation problems to security issues. You can find the FAQ for the newsgroup at the following URL:

```
http://sunsite.unc.edu/javafaq/javafaq.html
```

Component Warehouses (Or, Where's the Bean?)

Because the JavaBeans implementation is still wet behind the ears, the component repositories on the Web aren't exactly overflowing with beans just yet. By the time you read this book, however, the chances are good that you can find a potload of beans! The following sections describe some cool sites to check out that I can practically guarantee are going to host beans as soon as the components roll off the various developer presses.

Gamelan

Gamelan is the "official" directory for all things Java — and that includes beans! Visit its Web site at the following URL:

```
http://www-b.gamelan.com/index.shtml
```

JARS

The *JARS* Web site (*JARS* stands for *Java Applet Rating Service*) contains lots of Java and Java-related resource listings rated for coolness by a panel of independent judges. The JavaBeans resource URL is as follows:

```
http://www.jars.com/listing-JavaBeans.shtml
```

components.software.net

`components.software.net` claims to have the largest, most diverse collection of component software available anywhere. Check out these claims at the following address:

```
http://www.software.net/components/index.htm
```

Online Documentation

As a wise old programmer I knew once said, "If all else fails, consult the documentation." The following sections give you plenty of choices for all your documentation needs, covering everything from the core Java API to distributed beans and database connectivity.

The mother of all Java documentation: JDK 1.1

The *JDK 1.1* online documentation contains complete API and tool specifications, a list of known bugs, and even a way to contact JavaSoft directly with your technical questions. You find this documentation at the following URL:

```
http://java.sun.com/products/JDK/1.1/docs/index.html
```

RMI and serialization

From the good folks at JavaSoft's Distributed Systems Group comes in-depth documentation relating to the RMI and serialization, at the following Web site:

```
http://chatsubo.javasoft.com/current/
```

The JDBC

You can find everything you could possibly want to know about JDBC (other than what you find in Chapter 10, that is!) at the following URL:

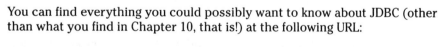

```
http://splash.javasoft.com/jdbc/index.html
```

Java IDL

Interested in the Java IDL and connecting beans to the ORB du jour? If so, after you scope out Chapter 10, take a look at the following site:

```
http://splash.javasoft.com/JavaIDL-alpha2.0/pages/
                    index.html
```

The Java Magazine Rack

For those times that you want a little light reading before you fall asleep, check out one of the Java-related publications that I describe in the following sections. Pleasant dreams guaranteed!

JavaWorld

JavaWorld is a monthly electronic magazine devoted to the Java developer in all of us. *JavaWorld* contains tutorials, reviews, and trends — and, best of all, it's online! (Save a tree.) Contact the magazine at the following URL:

```
http://www.javaworld.com/
```

The Java Report

The *Java Report* is a relatively new magazine in the tradition of the *C++ Report* and the *Smalltalk Report*. *Java Report* is a hard-copy publication, but you can find plenty of neat stuff on the online version's home page, including a Java "community center" and a free trial subscription to the paper version at the following address:

```
http://www.sigs.com/jro/
```

Internet and Java Advisor

Internet and Java Advisor focuses on the technical aspects of developing Internet, Intranet, Web, Java, and ActiveX solutions. Find out how to subscribe by visiting the magazine's Web site at the following URL:

```
http://www.advisor.com/ia.htm
```

Part VI
Appendixes

In this part . . .

Ah, dessert! In this final part, you find three appendixes. The first appendix spells out all the nitty-gritty details you need to successfully install the toolkits and IDEs provided on the companion CD-ROM. The second appendix gives you a rundown on all the JavaBeans jargon you need to know.

To inspire you as you begin your own bean development efforts, the third appendix contains an in-depth look at a handful of real-life beans and bean utilities culled from the Web. I've included plenty of actual code so that you can see exactly how and why each bean works as it does; and although the beans you find in this appendix are implemented in a slightly more sophisticated manner than some of the other beans you explore in this book, each of the real-life beans you find here follows the JavaBeans guidelines for introspection, event handling, and persistence. In other words, you find no "smoke and mirrors" in this appendix — just cool beans. Enjoy!

Appendix A

About the CD

This appendix describes all the goodies you can find on the *JavaBeans For Dummies* CD-ROM, including how to install them. You'll find

✔ Both the JDK version 1.1 and the BDK version 1.0

✔ Java authoring tools for non-programmers

✔ Full-fledged Java development environments designed for Java experts

✔ Some miscellaneous programming-type utilities

CD-ROM and software compilation copyright © 1997 IDG Books Worldwide, Inc. All rights reserved. Individual programs are copyrighted by their respective owners and may require separate licensing. This CD-ROM may not be redistributed without prior written permission from the publisher. The right to redistribute the individual programs on the disc depends on each program's license. Consult each program for details.

System Requirements

Make sure that your computer meets the following system requirements for using this CD:

✔ A CD-ROM drive — double-speed (2x) or faster

✔ A modem with a speed of 14,400 bps or faster, along with a working Internet connection

✔ Microsoft Windows 95, Windows NT 3.5.1, or Windows NT 4.0

✔ If you're running Windows 95 or Windows NT: a 486 or faster processor with *at least* 16MB of total RAM

✔ A copy of a Java-enabled Web browser, such as Microsoft's Internet Explorer 3.0 or Netscape Navigator 3.0

✔ At least 105MB of hard drive space available to install all the software from this CD. (You'll need less space if you don't install every program.)

If you need more information on PC or Windows basics, check out *PCs For Dummies,* 4th Edition, by Dan Gookin, or *Windows 95 For Dummies,* by Andy Rathbone (both published by IDG Books Worldwide, Inc.).

Installing Support Software

The JavaBeans Development Kit contains a tutorial saved in *Portable Document Format,* a cool file technology that keeps the graphics and formatting of the original published document. To read the tutorial, you must install Adobe Acrobat Reader. You also might want to check out the URLs that follow so you can download a copy of the make utility (nmake.exe for Windows 95/NT and gnumake.exe for Solaris).

To install Adobe Acrobat Reader 3.0 for Windows 95, follow these steps:

1. **Insert the CD into your computer's CD-ROM drive and close the drive door.**

2. **Click the Start button and click Run.**

3. **In the dialog box that appears, type** c:\utils\ar32e30.exe.

4. **Click OK.**

After you've installed the BDK, start Acrobat Reader and view the tutorial. The tutorial is in the BDK\DOC folder. You can also use Acrobat Reader to print out a copy.

The nmake make utility comes bundled with many popular Windows-based compilers, so if you're a developer, you may already have a copy on your system. If you don't, no problem; you can download a copy of nmake from the following site:

```
http://www.serve.com/ballen/nmake.htm
```

If you're running Solaris, the make utility you need is called gnumake. If you don't already have a copy of gnumake on your system, you can find a freely downloadable version at

```
http://www.ifctr.mi.cnr.it/News/gnumake.html
```

What You'll Find

Here is a summary of the all software on this CD. Follow the instructions for each program to install the software.

Java Developers Kit 1.1, from JavaSoft

The Java Developers Kit, or JDK, contains everything you need to develop Java programs. You can get online instructions for installing the JDK on Solaris systems, as well as up-to-the-minute updates, at

```
http://www.javasoft.com/products/jdk/1.1/
```

To install the JDK 1.1 on a Windows 95 or Windows NT system:

1. **Open the Tools folder and double-click on the Jdk11 icon; then follow the instructions the installation program displays, specifying** c:/jdk1.1 **as the install directory.**

2. **Still in the Tools folder, click on the Jdkdocs icon and again, follow the instructions that appear. (This program installs documentation you find helpful as you work with the JDK.)**

   After installing the software, update your path and environment variables.

3. **Start a text editor by selecting Start⇨Programs⇨Accessories and then choosing either WordPad or NotePad.**

4. **Select File⇨Open and type** c:\autoexec.bat **when prompted for the filename.**

5. **Look for the** PATH **statement. Notice that the** PATH **statement is a series of directories separated by semicolons (;). Windows looks for executable programs in the** PATH **directories in order, from left to right, so put the Java directory at the end of the path statement, as follows:**

```
PATH
C:\WINDOWS;C:\WINDOWS\COMMAND;C:\;C:\DOS;C:\JDK1.1\BIN
```

If you are running Windows NT, make the following environment variable changes in the Control Panel. Start the Control Panel, select System, and then edit the environment variables PATH and CLASSPATH.

Finally, set the CLASSPATH environment variable.

6. **Edit the** autoexec.bat **file (as in Steps 3 and 4) and add a statement to set the** CLASSPATH **environment variable to the current directory (the current directory is represented by a period, like this.)** *and* **the directory containing the Java core class library file (CLASSES.ZIP). Separate the two directories with a semicolon as shown:**

```
SET CLASSPATH=.;C:\JDK1.1\LIB\CLASSES.ZIP
```

7. **Reboot your machine.**

After completing the changes to autoexec.bat described in Steps 3 through 6, save the file and reboot your computer to force the changes to take effect.

JavaBeans Development Kit 1.0, also from JavaSoft

The JavaBeans Development Kit, or BDK, contains bean-specific documentation and over a dozen example beans.

To install the BDK on a Windows 95 or Windows NT system:

1. **Open the Tools folder and double-click on the Bdk297 icon.**

2. **Follow the instructions the installation program displays, specifying** c:/bdk **as the install directory.**

An introduction to the release is available in the beans/README.html file.

AppletAuthor from IBM

AppletAuthor, a Java authoring tool designed for use by nonprogrammers, lets you create Web pages that include customized JavaBeans about as easily as you can create fancy documents with a word processing application.

To install a 30-day trial version of AppletAuthor, open the Ides folder on the CD. Then open the Appauth folder and double-click on the Setup program icon.

Visit the AppletAuthor homepage to keep up with the latest on this tool:

```
http://www.ibm.com/java/appletauthor/html/
    appletauthor_home.html
```

Jamba from Aimtech Corporation

Jamba is an award-winning authoring tool that lets you build Java applets to add animation, sound and navigation controls to HTML pages — without programming.

To install Jamba, open the Ides folder on the CD and then double-click on the Jambatrl program icon.

Like what you see? Then visit the Jamba home page at the following URL:

```
http://www.jamba.com
```

Java WorkShop from Sun Microsystems, Inc.

From the folks at Sun Microsystems, Inc. comes Java WorkShop, an industrial-strength Java IDE boasting a very familiar visual interface (the interface is familiar because it's based on the ever-popular Web browser interface).

To install Java WorkShop, open the Ides folder on the CD. Then open the Jws folder and double-click on the Setupws program icon.

To learn more about Java WorkShop, check out

```
http://www.sun.com/workshop/java/tnb/index.html
```

Java Workshop is copyrighted 1997 by Sun Microsystems, Inc. Sun, Sun Microsystems, the Sun Logo, Java, Java WorkShop, the Java Logo, and Duke are trademarks or registered trademarks of Sun Microsystems, Inc. in the United States and other countries.

JPadPro from ModelWorks Software

JPadPro 3.0 is a full-blown IDE including a class browser, project and package manager, custom templates for creating new Java files, and lots more.

To install JPadPro, open the Ides folder on the CD. Then open the Jpadpro folder and double-click on the Mwjpp105 icon.

To find out more about JPadPro, visit ModelWorks' home page at the following URL:

    http://www.modelworks.com/

Kawa from TEK-TOOLS Inc.

Kawa, the only shareware IDE on the CD, is getting great reviews for its intuitive interface, sophisticated online help, and fully integrated toolset.

To install Kawa, open the Ides folder on the CD. Then open the Kawa151 folder and double-click on the Kawa151 program icon.

Keep up with the latest on Kawa by visiting the following site regularly:

    http://www.fni.net/kawa/

Mojo from Penumbra Software

Mojo is actually two seamlessly integrated tools in one:

- ✔ Mojo Designer, for programmers new to Java
- ✔ Mojo Coder, for Java gurus

To install Mojo, open the Ides folder on the CD. Then open the Mojoeval folder and double-click on the Setup program icon.

For the latest Mojo-related news, keep your eye on Penumbra's Mojo site:

    http://www.penumbrasoftware.com/fresh.htm

If You've Got Problems (Of the CD Kind)

I tried my best to include programs that work on most computers with the minimum system requirements. Unfortunately, a minuscule chance exists that your computer system may differ from mine just enough to keep some of the programs on this CD from installing properly for some reason.

The two most likely causes of grief are that you don't have enough memory (RAM) for the programs you want to use, or that you have other programs running that are affecting the installation or running of the program. If you get error messages like Not enough memory or Setup cannot continue, try one or more of these methods and then try installing the software again:

- ✔ Turn off any anti-virus software that you have on your computer. Installers sometimes mimic virus activity and may make your computer incorrectly believe that it is being infected by a virus.

- ✔ Close all running programs. The more programs you're running, the less memory is available to other programs. Installers also typically update files and programs. So if you keep other programs running, installation may not work properly.

- ✔ Have your local computer store add more RAM to your computer. If you're a Windows 95 user, adding more memory can really help the speed of your computer and allow more programs to run at the same time.

If you still have trouble with installing the items from the CD, please call the IDG Books Worldwide Customer Service phone number at 800-762-2974 (outside the U.S.: 317-596-5261).

Appendix B

Glossary

● ●

ActiveX: The Microsoft *ActiveX* component model provides support for components (called ActiveX *components*) that can be used not only within the Internet Explorer Web browser, but inside Windows-based desktop applications as well.

boolean: The primitive *boolean* data type defines just two values: `true` and `false`. In addition to the primitive boolean data type, the Java language also provides a wrapper class called `java.lang.Boolean` that lets programmers work with boolean values as objects.

bridge: A *bridge* is a piece of software whose purpose is to map JavaBeans API calls to the API calls of other component models. Currently, separate development efforts are under way to produce bridges to allow collaboration between JavaBeans and OpenDoc components, JavaBeans and ActiveX components, and JavaBeans and Netscape plug-ins.

bytecode: Java source code that has been compiled into .class files but not yet interpreted (or compiled a second time via a JIT compiler) is called *bytecode*. Java is called a cross-platform language because some Java bytecode can be interpreted without change on any Java-supporting platform by platform-specific interpreters (or compiled without change by platform-specific JIT compilers).

class: A *class* is a description of a certain kind of object — `bean`, for example. Class definitions can include properties and methods. Classes that *extend* other classes inherit the original class's properties and methods.

class loader: Part of the Java virtual machine, a *class loader* fetches Java classes from wherever they are on the Internet and loads them onto the client machine to be interpreted by the Java interpreter (or compiled, if the client machine has a JIT compiler installed).

component: In broad terms, a *component* is a piece of software that has been designed (usually by adhering to the rules described in a particular component model) to work with other components. You can create components with the JavaBeans component model. (Don't confuse this generic description of a component with the Java class `java.awt.Component`, which is a specific graphical component class.)

component model: A *component model* is a conceptual structure, implemented in software, that enables developers to write software components more quickly than they could from scratch. (You can think of a component model as a mold for casting components). JavaBeans is a component model; so are OpenDoc and ActiveX.

container: A *container* is any component that has the capacity to contain, or embed, other components. The BeanBox is an example of a container.

customizer: Bean developers who want to provide a more sophisticated customization GUI than just a bunch of property editors can implement the `java.beans.Customizer` class. *Customizers* can (but don't need to) contain property editors.

event: Conceptually, an *event* is any meaningful occurrence. (An example of an event implemented in the BDK is the `PropertyChangeEvent`, which occurs whenever a property value changes.) Events are implemented in the JavaBeans model via the `java.util.EventObject` class and are passed from one or more source beans to one or more listener beans.

getter: A *getter* is a publicly declared method that gets, or retrieves, a property value. In JavaBeans, getters (also referred to as *get accessor methods*) must follow standard naming conventions in order to participate in introspection ("get" + *PropertyName*). For example, the getter for a property called `zipCode` should be named `getZipCode()`.

graph: A *graph* is a group of related bean instances. When one bean in a graph is stored persistently, the other related beans must be stored at the same time to preserve the integrity not only of the individual beans, but also of the beans' relationships to one another.

GUI: GUI stands for *graphical user interface*. Common examples of GUIs include a Web browser, the BeanBox, and most interactive development environments.

IDE: A Java IDE (*integrated development environment*) is a tool that helps developers create and test Java programs. (They're called *integrated* because they integrate Java utilities like the compiler, debugger, and so on with a text editor, graphical interface, and other goodies.) Some IDEs are pretty minimalist; some have more bells and whistles. About four dozen IDEs are available at the time of this writing.

inheritance: The capability of Java (or any object-oriented programming language, for that matter) to support the creation of an object by substantially reusing another object's characteristics is called *inheritance*. Take the Java class `PropertyDescriptor`, for example. It inherits from `FeatureDescriptor`, which means that `PropertyDescriptor` not only contains all of the methods and properties defined in the `PropertyDescriptor` class, but all of the methods and properties defined in the `FeatureDescriptor` class, too. In Java, the `extends` keyword is used to enable classes to inherit from other classes.

instance: A class describes a kind, or type, of object; an *instance* is a specific — well, instance of a class. For example, `Person` is a class; Elvis is an instance. `Car` is a class; my beat-up Nissan, license plate number 2BRNT2B, is an instance.

instantiate: Creating an instance of a class is referred to as *instantiating* that class.

interface: In Java, defining an *interface* is just like defining a class, except that only constants and abstract methods are allowed in interface definitions, and the `interface` keyword is used instead of the `class` keyword. Interfaces can inherit from other interfaces, but not from classes — and any class implementing an interface must override *all* the methods declared in the interface (as well as any parent interfaces of that interface).

Java applet: A *Java applet* is a Java program that's designed to be integrated into an HTML file (that is, a Web page). Applets can be made up of beans.

JavaBeans: *JavaBeans* is a component model implemented in Java. The JavaBeans APIs are delivered as part of the Java Developers Kit; JavaBeans tools and examples are delivered separately as part of the Beans Developers Kit.

JavaScript: A simple C-like scripting language developed by Netscape Communications, *JavaScript* makes it possible for developers to create Web pages that respond to user events and perform client-side calculations. JavaScript is implemented as an extension to HTML and is currently supported by Netscape Navigator and Microsoft Internet Explorer.

JIT compiler: A *JIT* (just-in-time) *compiler* converts bytecode to platform-native processor instructions all at once, right before execution (just in time for execution!). JIT compilers are beginning to replace the older Java interpreters because they're typically much, much faster.

method: A method, sometimes called a *member function*, is a function that is defined within a class definition. Two kinds of methods exist: *instance methods*, which operate on the data of a specific instance of a class; and *static methods*, or *class methods*, which can operate on the data of all (or none) of a class's instances.

package: The entire Java API is grouped into separate *packages* organized by function. For instance, you'll find reflection-related APIs in the `java.lang.reflect` package and bean-specific APIs in the `java.beans` package. Package names always reflect the directory in which the API .class files reside. As an example, all the .class files that implement the `java.lang.reflect` package are stored in the `java/lang/reflect` subdirectory under one of the root directories specified in the `classpath` environment variable.

platform: *Platform* refers to the specific combination of hardware and operating system that make up a computer system — for example, Windows 95 on an IBM ThinkPad 701. Compiled Java bytecode can run on any Java-supporting platform.

private: Use the `private` keyword to restrict access to class members (either properties or methods) so that only members of the same class can access them. Properties are normally declared private; their accessor methods are normally declared public.

property: A *property* is a piece of data that describes an object. For example, two of the properties belonging to the `FlavoredJellyBean` class discussed in Part II are *flavor* and *color*.

property editor: A *property editor* enables developers to change the value of a bean property through a nice visual interface. Each different property type should have a corresponding property editor implemented via the `java.beans.PropertyEditor` interface.

property sheet: A *property sheet* is the simplest way to provide customization access to your bean. Much like the fill-in forms we all know and love, a property sheet visually displays all of a bean's properties — each of which is supported by a corresponding property editor.

public: The `public` keyword is used to make a property or method accessible to any piece of code, whether that piece of code is inside the same class definition or from inside another class altogether. Accessor methods and customization methods must be declared public so that they can be used by other beans and by bean-based development tools; whether or not you declare any other methods public is up to you, the bean developer.

runtime environment: The Java *runtime environment* is the software on a machine that enables you to run (as opposed to develop) Java programs. Consisting primarily of the Java virtual machine and some class libraries, the Java runtime environment is bundled with Java-enabled Web browsers and most Java IDEs. (The Java runtime environment is also available separately as part of the JDK.)

setter: A *setter* is a publicly declared method that sets, or assigns, a value to a property. In JavaBeans, setters (also referred to as *set accessor methods*) must follow standard naming conventions in order to participate in introspection (`set` + *PropertyName*). For example, the setter for a property called `numberOfToenails` should be named

```
setNumberOfToenails()
```

static: Whenever you see the *static* keyword in front of a class member declaration, you know that you're looking at a property or method that isn't associated with any one particular instance of a class. You can think of a static member as being outside, peering in at all the instances. Take the `getBeanInfo()` method of the `Introspector` class, for example. This method is declared static because what it does isn't tied to any specific instance of `Introspector`. Static members are sometimes referred to as *class* members.

string: Conceptually, a *string* is a collection of characters treated as a single entity. Java provides two string support classes:

- `java.lang.String`
- `java.lang.StringBuffer`

virtual machine: The Java *virtual machine* is a piece of software that "pretends" to be a real hardware-and-software platform (hence the term *virtual*). There's one virtual machine per Java-supported platform; each loads, verifies, and executes Java bytecode (that is, .class files) by translating Java instructions into platform-specific instructions.

World Wide Web: The *World Wide Web*, or just plain *Web*, is a conglomeration of multimedia-rich HTML-based files called *Web pages,* along with the communication protocols, networked hardware, and software that allow users to view and interact with those pages.

Appendix C

A Preview of What Others Are Doing with JavaBeans

● ●

In This Chapter

▶ Cool beans available on the Web

▶ Utilities to help you build your own cool beans

● ●

*A*lthough the JavaBeans component model is still fairly new, some enterprising developers have already begun producing beans and making them available to others on the Web. As an extra added bonus, some of these developers have produced bare-bones bean-related utilities to help them in their efforts (necessity is, after all, the mother of invention!) and made these tools available, too.

This appendix highlights just some of the beans and bean-based utilities you can find on the Web. The items you find here are offered not by "official" companies, like the full-blown, for-sale authoring tools and integrated development environments discussed in Chapter 6, but by individual developers like yourself.

Take a look and let yourself be inspired!

Cool Beans

For each of the beans listed in this section, you find

✔ A description of the bean that focuses on any cool or unusual bean characteristics (that is, characteristics not found in the sample beans provided in the BDK)

✔ A screen-shot of the bean in action

✔ Actual code snippets showing exactly how any unique bean characteristics were implemented

Going in circles

The Circle bean demonstrates some fairly basic painting techniques: fixed sizing, dynamic resizing, and form filling. This bean also provides a great example of how to implement your very own `BeanInfo` class and property editors and display them via a standard property sheet. Figure C-1 shows what the Circle bean's property sheet looks like.

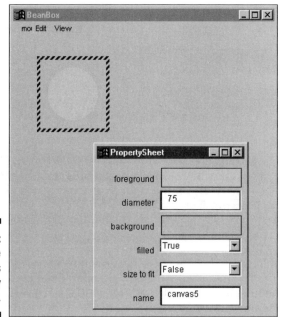

Figure C-1:
The Circle bean's property sheet.

As shown in Figure C-1, some of the properties on the Circle bean's property sheet (`color`, `foreground`, `background`, and `name`) are identical to the ones supported by the example beans delivered with the BDK. In addition to these familiar properties, however, the Circle bean's property sheet contains three additional properties: `diameter`, `filled`, and `sizeToFit`. First, take a look at the descriptions of each of these properties; then check out Figures C-2, C-3, and C-4 to see how specifying different values for each of these properties affects the appearance of the Circle bean.

- ✔ `diameter`: This numeric property describes the size (in pixels) the circle will appear when it's drawn on the screen.

- ✔ `filled`: This boolean property denotes whether or not the circle should be filled in with color, or just outlined.

✔ sizeToFit: If the value for this boolean property is set to true, the circle will automatically expand to fit the sizing boundary and the value for diameter will be calculated automatically (the sizing boundary is the hash-marked square that automatically appears around a bean when you select that bean by clicking on it). If the value for sizeToFit is set to false, the user-supplied value for the diameter property will be used to determine the size of the circle.

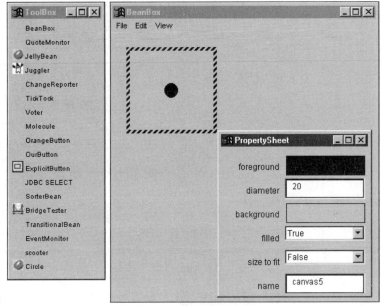

Figure C-2: The Circle bean's diameter property lets you manipulate the circle's size.

Specifying a value of 0 for the diameter property causes the Circle to disappear!

When you select true for the sizeToFit property, the appropriate value for diameter is calculated and filled in for you.

Now that you've got a good understanding of how the Circle bean looks and behaves, you're ready to dive into the code. Two classes contribute to the Circle bean: the Circle class and the CircleBeanInfo class. Listings C-1 and C-2, respectively, show you snippets of each.

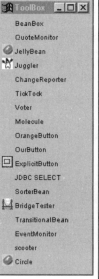
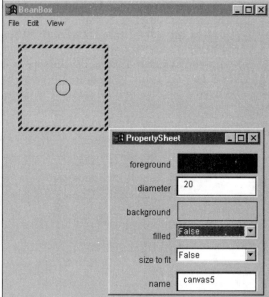

Figure C-3:
The Circle
bean's
`filled`
property
lets you
display a
circle as
either solid
or as a
hollow
outline.

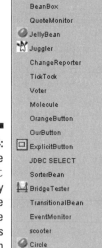
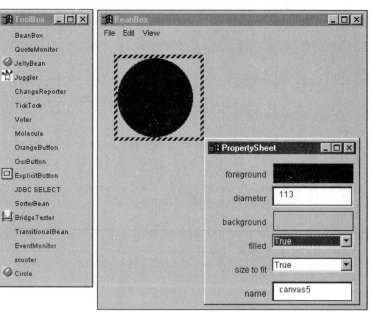

Figure C-4:
The
`sizeToFit`
property
lets the
circle
calculate its
own
diameter!

Listing C-1 `Circle.java`: **The Circle Bean Class Definition**

```
package COM.ibm.samples;

import java.awt.Canvas;
import java.awt.Dimension;
import java.awt.Graphics;
import java.beans.PropertyChangeSupport;
import java.beans.PropertyChangeListener;

public class Circle extends Canvas {
    /////////////////////////////////////////////
    // properties
    /////////////////////////////////////////////
    private int diameter;
    private boolean filled = true;
    private boolean sizeToFit = false;
    private PropertyChangeSupport pcs = new
            PropertyChangeSupport (this);

    /////////////////////////////////////////////
    // constructors
    /////////////////////////////////////////////
    public Circle (int diameter){
        this.diameter = diameter;
        setSize (diameter, diameter);
    }

    public Circle (){
        this (50);
    }

    /////////////////////////////////////////////
    // other methods
    /////////////////////////////////////////////
    ...
    public void paint (Graphics g){
        super.paint (g);

        Dimension d = getSize();
        int x;
        int y;
```

Default constructor creates a filled/ centered circle ⎯⎯

This method is respon- sible for drawing the circle ⎯⎯

(continued)

Listing C-1 (continued)

```
            if (sizeToFit){
                x = 0;
                y = 0;
                diameter =
                    (d.width < d.height) ? d.width : d.height;
            }
            else{
                x = (d.width - diameter) / 2;
                y = (d.height - diameter) / 2;
            }

            g.setColor (getForeground());
            if (filled)
                g.fillRoundRect (x, y, diameter, diameter,
                diameter, diameter);
            else
                g.drawRoundRect (x, y, diameter, diameter,
                diameter, diameter);
        }

    public void setBounds (int x, int y, int w, int h){
        super.setBounds (x, y, w, h);

        if (sizeToFit){
            int old = diameter;
            diameter = (w < h) ? w : h;
            pcs.firePropertyChange ("diameter", new Integer
            (old), new Integer (diameter));
        }
    }

    ...
    public void setDiameter (int value){
        if (sizeToFit == false){
            int old = diameter;
            diameter = value;
            pcs.firePropertyChange ("diameter", new Integer
            (old), new Integer (value));
            repaint ();
        }
```

Sets the color to the value of the foreground property — points to `g.setColor (getForeground());`

Lets listeners know that the value for diameter changed — points to `pcs.firePropertyChange ("diameter", new Integer (old), new Integer (value));`

repaint() displays the newly changed value on the screen — points to `repaint ();`

Lets listeners know that the value for filled changed ————

Lets listeners know that the value for sizeToFit changed ————

```
    }
    ...
    public void setFilled (boolean value){
        boolean old = filled;
        filled = value;
        pcs.firePropertyChange ("filled", new Boolean
                (old), new Boolean (value));
        repaint ();
    }
    ...
    public void setSizeToFit (boolean value){
        boolean old = sizeToFit;
        sizeToFit = value;
        pcs.firePropertyChange ("sizeToFit", new Boolean
                (old), new Boolean (value));
        repaint ();
    }

    public void addPropertyChangeListener
            (PropertyChangeListener l){
        pcs.addPropertyChangeListener (l);
    }

    public void removePropertyChangeListener
            (PropertyChangeListener l){
        pcs.removePropertyChangeListener (l);
    }
}
```

In Listing C-1, pay particular attention to the paint() method; that's where most of the really interesting stuff is going on. The paint() method uses the values of the diameter, filled, and sizeToFit properties to determine how the circle should be presented onscreen.

Now take a look at Listing C-2, which contains the Circle bean's BeanInfo implementation.

Listing C-2	CircleBeanInfo.java: **The CircleBeanInfo Class Definition**

```
package COM.ibm.samples;

import java.beans.*;
import java.awt.Image;
```

(continued)

CircleBeanInfo builds on SimpleBeanInfo instead of implementing the BeanInfo interface directly

Implementing the getIcon() method so that the BeanBox can call it to display an icon next to the Circle bean

Listing C-2 *(continued)*

```
public class CircleBeanInfo extends SimpleBeanInfo {
    public Image getIcon (int iconKind){
        Image image = null;

        switch (iconKind){
            case BeanInfo.ICON_COLOR_16x16:
                image = loadImage
                ( CircleIconColor16.gif );
                break;

            case BeanInfo.ICON_COLOR_32x32:
                image = loadImage
                ( CircleIconColor32.gif );
                break;

            case BeanInfo.ICON_MONO_16x16:
                image = loadImage
                ( CircleIconMono16.gif );
                break;

            case BeanInfo.ICON_MONO_32x32:
                image = loadImage
                ( CircleIconMono32.gif );
                break;
        }

        return image;
    }

    public PropertyDescriptor[] getPropertyDescriptors() {
        PropertyDescriptor pd[] =
            new PropertyDescriptor[6];
        PropertyEditorManager pem =
            new PropertyEditorManager();

        try {
            pd[0] = new PropertyDescriptor ( foreground ,
                    Circle.class);
            pd[1] = new PropertyDescriptor ( background ,
                    Circle.class);
            pd[2] = new PropertyDescriptor ( diameter ,
                    Circle.class);
```

This section creates a property descriptor for each property

This is why
the property
sheet
displays
"size to fit"
instead of
"sizeToFit" ————————

```
                    pd[3] = new PropertyDescriptor ( filled ,
                            Circle.class);
                    pd[4] = new PropertyDescriptor ( sizeToFit ,
                            Circle.class);
                    pd[5] = new PropertyDescriptor ( name ,
                            Circle.class);
            }
            catch (java.beans.IntrospectionException e) {}

            pd[4].setDisplayName ( size to fit );
            return (pd);
        }
    }
```

In Listing C-2, you see that `CircleBeanInfo` implements two methods: `getIcon()` and `getPropertyEditors()`. `getIcon()` is responsible for returning a specific icon image that the BeanBox utility — or some other tool — can then display. (When you run the BeanBox, take a look at the ToolBox window that comes up by default on the left-hand side of your screen. The images that appear to the left of each class name in the ToolBox window are displayed because the BeanBox invoked the `getIcon()` method on each of the beans' BeanInfo implementations.)

The code in `getPropertyEditors()` creates an array containing a bunch of property descriptors — one for each property — and then returns that array.

Ship-shape

The Shape bean is a fairly simple bean that displays one of several automatically resizable shapes — circle, triangle, square, heart, and so on. The really cool thing about this bean is that it provides a nice example of how to provide a custom property editor. Figure C-5 gives you an idea of what the Shape bean looks like.

Looking at Figure C-5, it's hard to see anything unusual; after all, the Shape bean's property sheet looks just like the example of the Circle bean's property sheet shown in Figure C-1 (except that the names of the properties aren't all the same). There *is* something unusual about the Shape bean, though: One of the properties (the `shape` property) has a custom property editor associated with it. Figure C-6 provides a close look at how this custom property editor appears in the BeanBox.

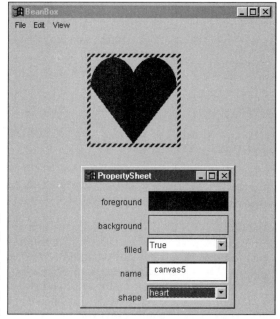

Figure C-5:
The Shape
bean's
property
sheet

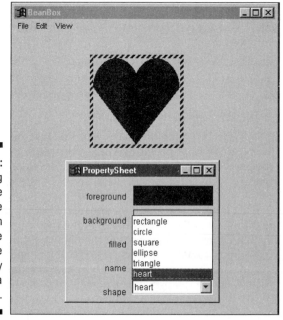

Figure C-6:
Changing
the shape
of the
Shape bean
with the
shape
property
editor is a
snap.

Three classes collaborate to produce the Shape bean: the Shape, ShapeBeanInfo, and ShapeEditor classes. You find half of the property editor-related code in Listing C-3, which contains a listing of the ShapeBeanInfo class, and half in Listing C-4, which shows the ShapeEditor class. (In Listing C-5, you can see the paint() method of the Shape class. Technically, it has nothing to do with properties or property editors whatsoever, but I think you may find it interesting!)

Listing C-3	ShapeBeanInfo.java: The ShapeBeanInfo Class Definition

```
package COM.ibm.samples;

import java.awt.Image;
import java.beans.*;

public class ShapeBeanInfo extends SimpleBeanInfo{
    ...
    public PropertyDescriptor[] getPropertyDescriptors(){
        PropertyDescriptor pd[] = new
            PropertyDescriptor[5];

        try {
            pd[0] = new PropertyDescriptor ("shape",
                    Shape.class);
            pd[1] = new PropertyDescriptor ("foreground",
                    Shape.class);
            pd[2] = new PropertyDescriptor ("background",
                    Shape.class);
            pd[3] = new PropertyDescriptor ("filled",
                    Shape.class);
            pd[4] = new PropertyDescriptor ("name",
                    Shape.class);
        }
        catch (IntrospectionException e) {}

        pd[0].setPropertyEditorClass(ShapeEditor.class);
        return (pd);
    }
}
```

This line associates the ShapeEditor class with the shape property

The first part of Listing C-3 looks very similar to Listing C-2. (Listing C-2 shows the `BeanInfo` class associated with the Circle bean.) There's one tiny difference, though: the addition of the `setPropertyEditorClass()` method near the bottom of Listing C-3. This method associates the `ShapeEditor` class with the first property descriptor in the array named `pd` — that is, with the `shape` property. Now take a look at Listing C-4, which contains the `ShapeEditor` class definition.

Listing C-4   `ShapeEditor.java`: The ShapeEditor Class Definition

```
package COM.ibm.samples;

import java.beans.PropertyEditorSupport;

public class ShapeEditor extends PropertyEditorSupport {
    /////////////////////////////////////////////
    // properties
    /////////////////////////////////////////////

    String selections[] = { rectangle , circle ,
                square , ellipse , triangle , heart };
    /////////////////////////////////////////////
    // methods
    /////////////////////////////////////////////

    public String getJavaInitializationString() {
        int value = ((Integer) getValue()).intValue();
        return (selections[value]);
    }

    public String getAsText(){
        int value = ((Integer) getValue()).intValue();
        return (selections[value]);
    }

    public void setAsText(String text) throws
                java.lang.IllegalArgumentException {
        int ctr;
        for (ctr = 0; ctr < 6; ctr ++) {
            if (text.toLowerCase().equals
            (selections[ctr])) {
                setValue (new Integer(ctr));
                break;
```

Annotations:
- ShapeEditor is deriving from the PropertyEditorSupport class
- The shape selections
- This needs to be defined so that users' values can be assigned to the shape property
- This method returns the current value of shape in the form of human-readable text
- This method sets the value of shape to the chosen (specified) string

```
            }
        }

        if (ctr == 6)
            throw(new java.lang.IllegalArgumentException
                (text));
    }

    public String[] getTags (){
        return (selections);
    }
}
```

Nothing too unusual is going on here; basically, the values for the shape property are being restricted to a list of pre-defined values ("triangle", "rectangle", "heart", and so on) and stored internally as Integer values. As shown in Listing C-4, the developer had to define only four methods in the ShapeEditor class to implement this behavior: getJavaInitializationString(), getAsText(), setAsText(), and getTags().

Listing C-5   Shape.java: The Shape Class Definition

The Graphics class is used extensively in this code snippet ———

```
package COM.ibm.samples;

import java.awt.Canvas;
import java.awt.Dimension;
import java.awt.Graphics;
...


public class Shape extends Canvas {

    ////////////////////////////////////
    // constants
    ////////////////////////////////////
    public static final int RECTANGLE = 0;
    public static final int CIRCLE    = 1;
    public static final int SQUARE    = 2;
    public static final int ELLIPSE   = 3;
    public static final int TRIANGLE  = 4;
    public static final int HEART     = 5;
    ...
```

(continued)

The paint() method is called automatically by the Java VM when it's time to display the bean

Draws a rectangle if the user selects "rectangle" from the drop-down box displayed by the shape property editor

Draws a square

Draws an ellipse

Draws a circle

Listing C-5 (continued)

```java
public void paint(Graphics g){
    int size;
    Dimension d = getSize ();
    g.setColor (getForeground ());

    switch (shape){
        case RECTANGLE:
            if (filled)
                g.fillRect (0, 0, d.width - 1, d.height
                    - 1);
            else
                g.drawRect (0, 0, d.width - 1, d.height
                    - 1);
            break;

        case SQUARE:
            size = (d.width < d.height) ? d.width - 1 :
            d.height - 1;
            if (filled)
                g.fillRect (0, 0, size, size);
            else
                g.drawRect (0, 0, size, size);
            break;

        case ELLIPSE:
            if (filled)
                g.fillRoundRect (0, 0, d.width,
                    d.height, d.width, d.height);
            else
                g.drawRoundRect (0, 0, d.width,
                    d.height, d.width, d.height);
            break;

        case CIRCLE:
            size = (d.width < d.height) ? d.width - 1 :
            d.height - 1;
            if (filled)
                g.fillRoundRect (0, 0, size, size,
                    size, size);
            else
                g.drawRoundRect (0, 0, size, size,
                    size, size);
            break;
```

Draws a triangle ——————————

```
case TRIANGLE:
    {
    int xpoints[] = { 0, d.width / 2, d.width,
    0 };
    int ypoints[] = { d.height, 0, d.height,
    d.height };

    if (filled)
        g.fillPolygon (xpoints, ypoints, 4);
    else
        g.drawPolygon (xpoints, ypoints, 4);
    break;
    }
```

Draws a ——————————
square

```
case HEART:
    {
    int midpoint = d.height / 3;
    int xpoints[] = { 0, d.width, d.width / 2,
    0 };
    int ypoints[] = { midpoint, midpoint,
    d.height, midpoint };

    if (filled){
        g.fillArc (0, 0, (d.width / 2) + 4,
        midpoint * 2, 0, 180);
        g.fillArc ((d.width / 2) - 4, 0,
        (d.width / 2) + 4, midpoint * 2, 0, 180);
        g.fillPolygon (xpoints, ypoints, 4);
    }
    else {
        g.drawArc (0, 0, d.width / 2, midpoint
* 2, 0, 180);
        g.drawArc (d.width / 2, 0, d.width / 2,
midpoint * 2, 0, 180);
        g.drawPolygon (xpoints, ypoints, 4);
    }
    break;
    }
    }
}
```

Nothing in the preceding code snippet is bean-specific, but I've included it because most beans will need to include some form of `paint()` method and this is a nice example. Right now, the most common way to implement the `paint()` method is with the `java.awt.Graphics` class, as shown in the preceding code listing.

Utilities to Help You Build Your Own Cool Beans

The tools in this section may be of use to you in two ways:

✔ They may help you create your own beans.

✔ They may inspire you to create your own bean utilities.

The JWC (Joe's Compile Window)

According to the developer (yes, his name is Joe!), this tool is "absolutely, positively the simplest IDE (to use the term *very* loosely) on the planet."

Basically, the JCW gives you the opportunity to provide

✔ An (optional) value for the `CLASSPATH` environment variable

✔ The name of the Java file you want to compile

When you click on the Compile button, the JWC displays the results in a window so that you can review them at your leisure. (Yippee, no more having to redirect the compiler output to a separate file just so that you can see what's been scrolling off your screen!) Figure C-7 shows you what the JWC looks like in action.

The Beanery

The Beanery is a Java code generation tool that you can use to create simple beans. The beans it produces can contain everything you'd expect a self-respecting bean to include: properties, event notifications — even customizers. Figure C-8 shows you what the Beanery looks like initially, when you first start it.

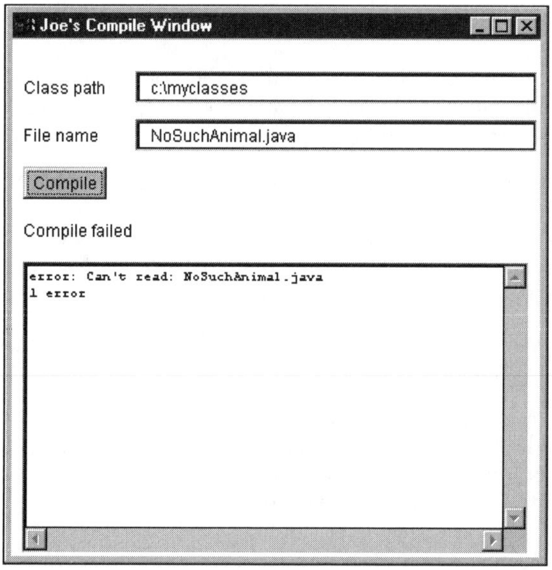

Figure C-7:
Joe's
Compile
window:
simple, yet
elegant.

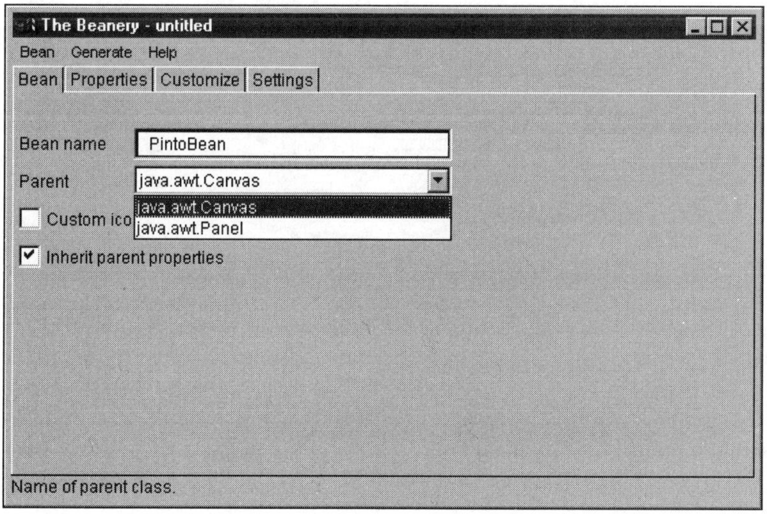

Figure C-8:
The Bean
page.

As shown in Figure C-8, the Beanery consists of four separate "notebook" pages. To create a bean, all you need to do is step through the pages by clicking on the notebook tabs (in any order), fill out any fields that are applicable to the bean you're trying to create, and then select Generate➪ Bean from the menubar.

Here are brief descriptions of the information you provide on each page:

 ✔ **Bean:** On this page, you specify the name of your bean and the parent class from which you'd like your bean to inherit. Check out Figure C-8 for an example of a filled-in Bean page.

   The Bean page displays by default when you start the Beanery, and it's as good a page as any to start your Beanery adventure. If you want a "regular," or non-container, bean, select the Canvas as your bean's parent; if you want a bean that can contain other beans (like the BeanBox bean), select the Panel instead.

 ✔ **Properties:** As Figure C-9 shows, you use this page to describe all the properties for your bean.

   Use the Properties page to describe your bean's properties in detail. Notice that whenever you click on a field in order to type in some information, a helpful message describing that field appears in the status bar at the bottom of the window.

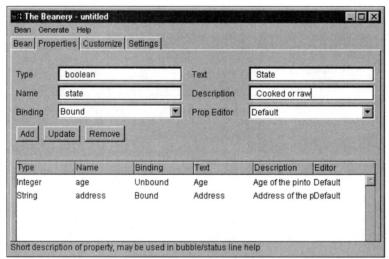

Figure C-9:
The
Properties
page of the
Beanery.

 ✔ **Customize:** This page, as shown Figure C-10, provides space for you to specify custom property editors for your bean.

   None of the information on the Beanery's Customize page is mandatory; you only have to fill in values for this page if you want to associate custom property editors with your bean.

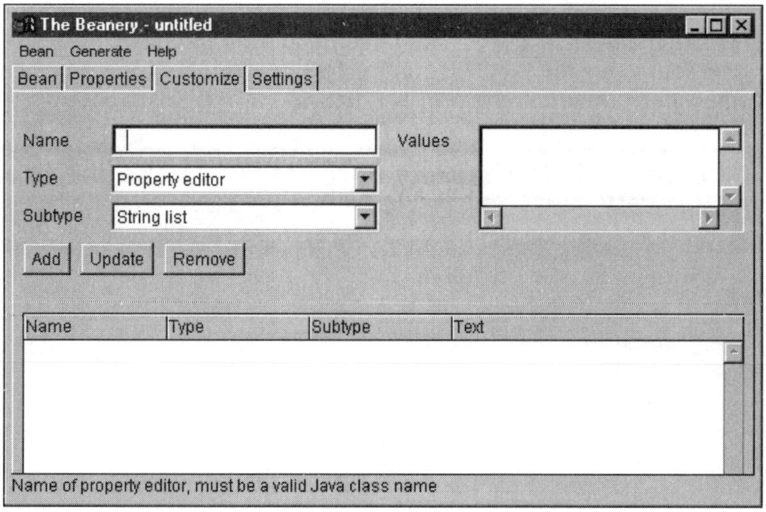

Figure C-10:
The
Customize
page of the
Beanery.

✔ **Settings:** On this page you fill in your name, company, and any copy-right information you feel compelled to provide. (These values are used to add comments to the generated code). Take a look at Figure C-11 for an example of how this page might be completed.

Some of the values on this page are inserted into the Java source code the Beanery produces; the others are used to tell the Beanery where to place the source code it generates.

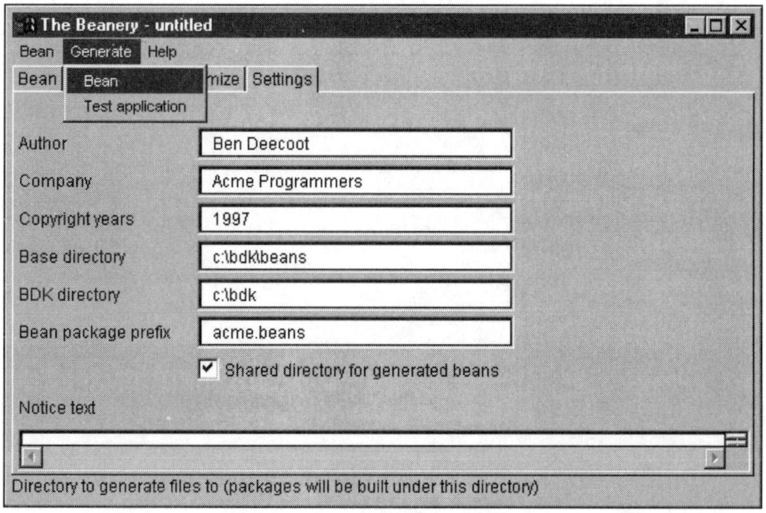

Figure C-11:
The
Settings
page of the
Beanery.

When you finish filling out all of the Beanery's pages, all you have to do to create the bean is select Generate⇨Bean from the menu. Listing C-6 shows the source file for the `PintoBean` class that the Beanery generated based on the values shown in the previous listings.

Listing C-6   The Beanery-Generated `PintoBean.java` **File**

```
/*
    Package: acme.beans
    Bean   : PintoBean

    Author : Ben Deecoot

    Copyright (c) Acme Programmers, 1997
        - all rights reserved
*/

package acme.beans;

import java.awt.*;

public class PintoBean extends java.awt.Canvas implements
          java.io.Serializable {
    // Attributes
    private Integer age;
    private String address;

    private java.beans.PropertyChangeSupport csBound = new
          java.beans.PropertyChangeSupport (this);

    //* Constructor */
    public PintoBean (){
        setSize (50, 50);
    }

    //* Paint */
    public void paint (java.awt.Graphics g){
        g.setColor (getBackground ());
        g.fillRect (0, 0, getSize ().width, getSize
            ().height);
    }

    //* getPreferredSize */
    public java.awt.Dimension getPreferredSize (){
        return (new java.awt.Dimension (50, 50));
    }
```

```java
//* getMinimumSize */
public java.awt.Dimension getMinimumSize (){
    return (new java.awt.Dimension (50, 50));
 }


/**
* @see #setAge
*/
public synchronized Integer getAge (){
    return (age);
 }


/**
* @see #getAge
*/
public void setAge (Integer value){
    age = value;
 }


/**
* @see #setAddress
*/
public synchronized String getAddress (){
    return (address);
 }


/**
* @see #getAddress
*/
public void setAddress (String value){
    String old = address;
    address = value;
    csBound.firePropertyChange ( address , old, value);
    repaint ();
 }


/**
* Listener for outside objects to attach to

* @see #removePropertyChangeListener
* @param l the PropertyChangeListener
*/
```

(continued)

Listing C-6 *(continued)*

```
public void addPropertyChangeListener
        (java.beans.PropertyChangeListener l){
    csBound.addPropertyChangeListener (l);
}


/**
 * Let outside object release listener

 * @see #addPropertyChangeListener
 * @param l the PropertyChangeListener
 */
public void removePropertyChangeListener
        (java.beans.PropertyChangeListener l){
    csBound.removePropertyChangeListener (l);
}
```

If you look closely at the code in Listing C-6, you can see the values that were input into each page of the Beanery tool: the name of the class and the parent class, property names, the fact that one of the properties was designated as bound, and so on. This quick-and-dirty implementation of a bean is designed to give you a head start on your bean development effort. (In most cases you want to add to the implementation and modify it with your own Java code.)

Like the code in Listing C-6, the class definition in Listing C-7 is a rough implementation (in this case, of a `BeanInfo` class) that you flesh out with details.

Listing C-7   The `PintoBeanBeanInfo.java` **Source File**

```
/*
    Package: acme.beans
    Bean   : PintoBean

    Author : Ben Deecoot

    Copyright (c) Acme Programmers, 1997
        - all rights reserved
*/

package acme.beans;
```

```
public class PintoBeanBeanInfo extends
        java.beans.SimpleBeanInfo{
    public java.beans.PropertyDescriptor[]
            getPropertyDescriptors (){
        java.beans.PropertyDescriptor pd[] = null;

        try {
            java.beans.BeanInfo bi =
                java.beans.Introspector.getBeanInfo
                (java.awt.Canvas.class);
            java.beans.PropertyDescriptor pdParent[] =
                bi.getPropertyDescriptors ();
            int index = pdParent.length;

            pd = new java.beans.PropertyDescriptor[index +
                2];
            System.arraycopy (pdParent, 0, pd, 0, index);

            pd[index + 0] = new
            java.beans.PropertyDescriptor ("age",
                PintoBean.class);
            pd[index + 1] = new
            java.beans.PropertyDescriptor ("address",
                PintoBean.class);

            pd[index + 0].setDisplayName ("Age");
            pd[index + 0].setShortDescription ("Age of the
                pinto bean");
            pd[index + 1].setDisplayName ("Address");
            pd[index + 1].setShortDescription ("Address of
                the pinto");
        }
        catch (java.beans.IntrospectionException e){
            System.out.println ("Introspection error");
        }

        return (pd);
    }
}
```

Index

Visual Java Development Environment
Special Upgrade Offer

Dear Java Developer:

If you're doing Java, we think that you should be doing it with Mojo . . . Mojo's had some great press lately. Like a Lan Times review that said "Mojo could become the standard bearer among Java Development Environments for some time to come." That's a feather in our cap. But in our book, the reviewer who really counts is you! That's why there's a Mojo 2.0 *eval* included with this book.

If you like what you see, consider a special upgrade offer to the full version of Mojo. When you order Mojo, you will receive over 500 pages of documentation (with lots of tutorials and sample apps), access to club Mojo (for direct technical support, new components, and other fun stuff) and the latest and greatest features.

Mojo comes in two flavors to suit your development requirements. Mojo Client is for rapid development of the most robust applets and applications you can imagine. Mojo Enterprise supports database connectivity through JDBC and ODBC and comes with a multitude of data aware components.

Best of all, Mojo is available to you at a special upgrade price: $99 for Mojo Client and $495 for Mojo Enterprise. Compare that to the $195 and $895 price from our web site. To order your copy, call 770-352-0100 ext.180 and mention this special offer or visit us at www.penumbrasoftware.com. We look forward to helping you get your Mojo going!

Happy programming,

Mittel

Michael Mittel
VP of Marketing

To Order Mojo 2.5:

http://www.penumbrasoftware.com
email: sales@penumbrasoftware.com
fax: 770-352-0123
phone: 770-352-0100 ext. 180

Or mail this form to:

Penumbra Software, Inc.
4015 Holcomb Bridge Road
suite 350
Norcross, GA 30092

Java™ Development Kit Version 1.1.1 and BDK Version 1.0 Combined Binary Code License

This binary code license ("License") contains rights and restrictions associated with use of the accompanying software and documentation ("Software"). Read the License carefully before installing the Software. By installing the Software you agree to the terms and conditions of this License.

1. Limited License Grant. Sun grants to you ("Licensee") a non-exclusive, non-transferable limited license to use the Software without fee for evaluation of the Software and for development of JavaTM compatible applets and applications. Licensee may make one archival copy of the Software. Except for the foregoing, Licensee may not re-distribute the Software in whole or in part, either separately or included with a product. Refer to the Java Runtime Environment Version 1.1 binary code license (http://www.javasoft.com/products/JDK/1.1/index.html) for the availability of runtime code which may be distributed with Java compatible applets and applications.

2. Redistribution of Demonstration Files. Sun grants Licensee the right to use, modify and redistribute the Beans example and demonstration code, including the Bean Box ("Demos"), in both source and binary code form provided that (i) Licensee does not utilize the Demos in a manner which is disparaging to Sun; and (ii) Licensee indemnifies and holds Sun harmless from all claims relating to any such use or distribution of the Demos. Such distribution is limited to the source and binary code of the Demos and specifically excludes any rights to modify or distribute any graphical images contained in the Demos.

3. Java Platform Interface. Licensee may not modify the Java Platform Interface ("JPI", identified as classes contained within the "java" package or any subpackages of the "java" package), by creating additional classes within the JPI or otherwise causing the addition to or modification of the classes in the JPI. In the event that Licensee creates any Java-related API and distributes such API to others for applet or application development, Licensee must promptly publish an accurate specification for such API for free use by all developers of Java-based software.

4. Restrictions. Software is confidential copyrighted information of Sun and title to all copies is retained by Sun and/or its licensors. Licensee shall not modify, decompile, disassemble, decrypt, extract, or otherwise reverse engineer Software. Software may not be leased, assigned, or sublicensed, in whole or in part. Software is not designed or intended for use in on-line control of aircraft, air traffic, aircraft navigation or aircraft communications; or in the design, construction, operation or maintenance of any nuclear facility. Licensee warrants that it will not use or redistribute the Software for such purposes.

5. Trademarks and Logos. This License does not authorize Licensee to use any Sun name, trademark or logo. Licensee acknowledges that Sun owns the Java trademark and all Java-related trademarks, logos and icons including the Coffee Cup and Duke ("Java Marks") and agrees to: (i) to comply with the Java Trademark Guidelines at http://java.com/trademarks.html; (ii) not do anything harmful to or inconsistent with Sun's rights in the Java Marks; and (iii) assist Sun in protecting those rights, including assigning to Sun any rights acquired by Licensee in any Java Mark.

6. Disclaimer of Warranty. Software is provided "AS IS," without a warranty of any kind. ALL EXPRESS OR IMPLIED REPRESENTATIONS AND WARRANTIES, INCLUDING ANY IMPLIED WARRANTY OF MERCHANTABILITY, FITNESS FOR A PARTICULAR PURPOSE OR NON-INFRINGEMENT, ARE HEREBY EXCLUDED.

7. Limitation of Liability. SUN AND ITS LICENSORS SHALL NOT BE LIABLE FOR ANY DAMAGES SUFFERED BY LICENSEE OR ANY THIRD PARTY AS A RESULT OF USING OR DISTRIBUTING SOFTWARE. IN NO EVENT WILL SUN OR ITS LICENSORS BE LIABLE FOR ANY LOST REVENUE, PROFIT OR DATA, OR FOR DIRECT, INDIRECT, SPECIAL, CONSEQUENTIAL, INCIDENTAL OR PUNITIVE DAMAGES, HOWEVER CAUSED AND REGARDLESS OF THE THEORY OF LIABILITY, ARISING OUT OF THE USE OF OR INABILITY TO USE SOFTWARE, EVEN IF SUN HAS BEEN ADVISED OF THE POSSIBILITY OF SUCH DAMAGES.

8. Termination. Licensee may terminate this License at any time by destroying all copies of Software. This License will terminate immediately without notice from Sun if Licensee fails to comply with any provision of this License. Upon such termination, Licensee must destroy all copies of Software.

9. Export Regulations. Software, including technical data, is subject to U.S. export control laws, including the U.S. Export Administration Act and its associated regulations, and may be subject to export or import regulations in other countries. Licensee agrees to comply strictly with all such regulations and acknowledges that it has the responsibility to obtain licenses to export, re-export, or import Software. Software may not be downloaded, or otherwise exported or re-exported (i) into, or to a national or resident of, Cuba, Iraq, Iran, North Korea, Libya, Sudan, Syria or any country to which the U.S. has embargoed goods; or (ii) to anyone on the U.S. Treasury Department's list of Specially Designated Nations or the U.S. Commerce Department's Table of Denial Orders.

10. Restricted Rights. Use, duplication or disclosure by the United States government is subject to the restrictions as set forth in the Rights in Technical Data and Computer Software Clauses in DFARS 252.227-7013(c) (1) (ii) and FAR 52.227-19(c) (2) as applicable.

11. Governing Law. Any action related to this License will be governed by California law and controlling U.S. federal law. No choice of law rules of any jurisdiction will apply.

12. Severability. If any of the above provisions are held to be in violation of applicable law, void, or unenforceable in any jurisdiction, then such provisions are herewith waived to the extent necessary for the License to be otherwise enforceable in such jurisdiction. However, if in Sun's opinion deletion of any provisions of the License by operation of this paragraph unreasonably compromises the rights or increase the liabilities of Sun or its licensors, Sun reserves the right to terminate the License and refund the fee paid by Licensee, if any, as Licensee's sole and exclusive remedy.

IDG BOOKS WORLDWIDE, INC.

END-USER LICENSE AGREEMENT

Read This. **You should carefully read these terms and conditions before opening the software packet(s) included with this book ("Book"). This is a license agreement ("Agreement") between you and IDG Books Worldwide, Inc. ("IDGB"). By opening the accompanying software packet(s), you acknowledge that you have read and accept the following terms and conditions. If you do not agree and do not want to be bound by such terms and conditions, promptly return the Book and the unopened software packet(s) to the place you obtained them for a full refund.**

1. **License Grant.** IDGB grants to you (either an individual or entity) a nonexclusive license to use one copy of the enclosed software program(s) (collectively, the "Software") solely for your own personal or business purposes on a single computer (whether a standard computer or a workstation component of a multiuser network). The Software is in use on a computer when it is loaded into temporary memory (i.e., RAM) or installed into permanent memory (e.g., hard disk, CD-ROM, or other storage device). IDGB reserves all rights not expressly granted herein.

2. **Ownership.** IDGB is the owner of all right, title, and interest, including copyright, in and to the compilation of the Software recorded on the disk(s)/CD-ROM. Copyright to the individual programs on the disk(s)/CD-ROM is owned by the author or other authorized copyright owner of each program. Ownership of the Software and all proprietary rights relating thereto remain with IDGB and its licensors.

3. **Restrictions on Use and Transfer.**

   (a) You may only (i) make one copy of the Software for backup or archival purposes, or (ii) transfer the Software to a single hard disk, provided that you keep the original for backup or archival purposes. You may not (i) rent or lease the Software, (ii) copy or reproduce the Software through a LAN or other network system or through any computer subscriber system or bulletin-board system, or (iii) modify, adapt, or create derivative works based on the Software.

   (b) You may not reverse engineer, decompile, or disassemble the Software. You may transfer the Software and user documentation on a permanent basis, provided that the transferee agrees to accept the terms and conditions of this Agreement and you retain no copies. If the Software is an update or has been updated, any transfer must include the most recent update and all prior versions.

4. **Restrictions on Use of Individual Programs**. You must follow the individual requirements and restrictions detailed for each individual program in Appendix A of this Book. These limitations are contained in the individual license agreements recorded on the disk(s)/CD-ROM. These restrictions may include a requirement that after using the program for the period of time specified in its text, the user must pay a registration fee or discontinue use. By opening the Software packet(s), you will be agreeing to abide by the licenses and restrictions for these individual programs. None of the material on this disk(s) or listed in this Book may ever be distributed, in original or modified form, for commercial purposes.

5. **Limited Warranty**.

   (a) IDGB warrants that the Software and disk(s)/CD-ROM are free from defects in materials and workmanship under normal use for a period of sixty (60) days from the date of purchase of this Book. If IDGB receives notification within the warranty period of defects in materials or workmanship, IDGB will replace the defective disk(s)/CD-ROM.

   (b) IDGB AND THE AUTHOR OF THE BOOK DISCLAIM ALL OTHER WARRANTIES, EXPRESS OR IMPLIED, INCLUDING WITHOUT LIMITATION IMPLIED WARRANTIES OF MERCHANTABILITY AND FITNESS FOR A PARTICULAR PURPOSE, WITH RESPECT TO THE SOFTWARE, THE PROGRAMS, THE SOURCE CODE CONTAINED THEREIN, AND/OR THE TECHNIQUES DESCRIBED IN THIS BOOK. IDGB DOES NOT WARRANT THAT THE FUNC-TIONS CONTAINED IN THE SOFTWARE WILL MEET YOUR REQUIREMENTS OR THAT THE OPERATION OF THE SOFTWARE WILL BE ERROR FREE.

   (c) This limited warranty gives you specific legal rights, and you may have other rights which vary from jurisdiction to jurisdiction.

6. **Remedies**.

   (a) IDGB's entire liability and your exclusive remedy for defects in materials and workmanship shall be limited to replacement of the Software, which may be returned to IDGB with a copy of your receipt at the following address: Disk Fulfillment Department, Attn: JavaBeans For Dummies, IDG Books Worldwide, Inc., 7260 Shadeland Station, Ste. 100, Indianapolis, IN 46256, or call 1-800-762-2974. Please allow 3–4 weeks for delivery. This Limited Warranty is void if failure of the Software has resulted from accident, abuse, or misapplication. Any replacement Software will be warranted for the remainder of the original warranty period or thirty (30) days, whichever is longer.

(b) In no event shall IDGB or the author be liable for any damages whatsoever (including without limitation damages for loss of business profits, business interruption, loss of business information, or any other pecuniary loss) arising from the use of or inability to use the Book or the Software, even if IDGB has been advised of the possibility of such damages.

(c) Because some jurisdictions do not allow the exclusion or limitation of liability for consequential or incidental damages, the above limitation or exclusion may not apply to you.

7. **U.S. Government Restricted Rights.** Use, duplication, or disclosure of the Software by the U.S. Government is subject to restrictions stated in paragraph (c) (1) (ii) of the Rights in Technical Data and Computer Software clause of DFARS 252.227-7013, and in subparagraphs (a) through (d) of the Commercial Computer — Restricted Rights clause at FAR 52.227-19, and in similar clauses in the NASA FAR supplement, when applicable.

8. **General.** This Agreement constitutes the entire understanding of the parties and revokes and supersedes all prior agreements, oral or written, between them and may not be modified or amended except in a writing signed by both parties hereto which specifically refers to this Agreement. This Agreement shall take precedence over any other documents that may be in conflict herewith. If any one or more provisions contained in this Agreement are held by any court or tribunal to be invalid, illegal, or otherwise unenforceable, each and every other provision shall remain in full force and effect.

Installing the JavaBeans For Dummies CD-ROM Software

●●●

The *JavaBeans For Dummies* CD-ROM contains a whole batch of tools intended to help jump-start your JavaBeans development efforts. The first two items listed contain the bare-bones Java and JavaBeans APIs you need to create JavaBeans components; all the rest are Java development tools that make JavaBeans development easier and better-tasting.

- ✔ The Java Development Kit, version 1.1
- ✔ The Beans Development Kit, version 1.0
- ✔ AppletAuthor (recently renamed *BeanMachine*)
- ✔ Jamba
- ✔ Java WorkShop
- ✔ JPadPro
- ✔ Kawa
- ✔ Mojo

For descriptions of the items, along with detailed installation instructions for each, please see Appendix A, "About the CD."

Use of the Java Developers Kit and the JavaBeans Development Kit is subject to the Binary Code License terms and conditions located after the index in the back of this back. Read the license carefully. By opening this package, you are agreeing to be bound by the terms and conditions of this license from Sun Microsystems, Inc.

IDG BOOKS WORLDWIDE REGISTRATION CARD

Title of this book: **JavaBeans™ For Dummies®**

My overall rating of this book: ❑ Very good [1] ❑ Good [2] ❑ Satisfactory [3] ❑ Fair [4] ❑ Poor [5]

How I first heard about this book:

❑ Found in bookstore; name: [6] _____

❑ Advertisement: [8]

❑ Word of mouth; heard about book from friend, co-worker, etc.: [10]

❑ Book review: [7]

❑ Catalog: [9]

❑ Other: [11]

What I liked most about this book:

_____

_____

_____

What I would change, add, delete, etc., in future editions of this book:

_____

_____

_____

Other comments:

_____

Number of computer books I purchase in a year: ❑ 1 [12] ❑ 2-5 [13] ❑ 6-10 [14] ❑ More than 10 [15]

I would characterize my computer skills as: ❑ Beginner [16] ❑ Intermediate [17] ❑ Advanced [18] ❑ Professional [19]

I use ❑ DOS [20] ❑ Windows [21] ❑ OS/2 [22] ❑ Unix [23] ❑ Macintosh [24] ❑ Other: [25]_____

(please specify)

I would be interested in new books on the following subjects:

(please check all that apply, and use the spaces provided to identify specific software)

❑ Word processing: [26] _____

❑ Data bases: [28] _____

❑ File Utilities: [30] _____

❑ Networking: [32] _____

❑ Other: [34] _____

❑ Spreadsheets: [27] _____

❑ Desktop publishing: [29] _____

❑ Money management: [31] _____

❑ Programming languages: [33] _____

I use a PC at (please check all that apply): ❑ home [35] ❑ work [36] ❑ school [37] ❑ other: [38] _____

The disks I prefer to use are ❑ 5.25 [39] ❑ 3.5 [40] ❑ other: [41]_____

I have a CD ROM: ❑ yes [42] ❑ no [43]

I plan to buy or upgrade computer hardware this year: ❑ yes [44] ❑ no [45]

I plan to buy or upgrade computer software this year: ❑ yes [46] ❑ no [47]

Name: _____ Business title: [48] _____ Type of Business: [49] _____

Address (❑ home [50] ❑ work [51]/Company name: _____)

Street/Suite# _____

City [52]/State [53]/Zipcode [54]: _____ Country [55] _____

❑ **I liked this book!** You may quote me by name in future
IDG Books Worldwide promotional materials.

My daytime phone number is _____

IDG BOOKS

THE WORLD OF
COMPUTER
KNOWLEDGE